About the Author

A former actor, standup comic, and Buddhist monk, Michael McAlister leads retreats and weekly meditation gatherings for the Infinite Smile Sangha and shares his teaching on InfiniteSmile.org. Currently he teaches psychology and lives in Pleasant Hill, California with his wife and his daughter.

For Alycia

my friend, my wife, my teacher
my love

Table of Contents

A Note to the Reader

Let it be known to each of you reading these words that neither my story nor my version of spiritual teaching offers anything that hasn't already been offered many times before. At its core, there is absolutely nothing original about this work. I'm merely passing a baton, of sorts—one that was generously offered to me by circumstance, deep peace, great teachers, and more than a little commitment. The only thing that I've written in these pages are pointers and suggestions that have been helpful in my journey as a student and especially now as a teacher. This isn't false modesty. Ask anyone who knows me; I'm not always as modest as I should be. Rather, I'm simply trying to be transparent and offer an honest evaluation and explanation of credit that is not and will never be mine to take.

With that critical disclaimer out of the way, *Awake in This Life* has a simple message. It is about seeing through old habits and letting go of old psychological reference points so that we might consciously and continually live from a place of grace and ease, no matter what our circumstance might be. Ultimately, the work of awakening in this life is about metaphorically going up the Mountain of Spirit, reaching the summit, and sharing the view from the summit with others as we come back home into the real world. Every bit of this book is inspired by meetings, teachings, and dialogues I've had with my students in the Infinite Smile Sangha, as well as conversations I've had with spiritual teachers in the mountains of Nepal, the forests of Thailand, and along California's coast in Marin County. So it wouldn't be much of a stretch to suggest that my words are actually theirs. To this end, I owe each of these helpful men and women who relentlessly pushed me to consciously, and continually, uncover in this life what we might call "the fullness of Emptiness" an expression of gratitude that goes beyond any word or deed. I owe them nothing short of everything. Deep bows to each of them.

Awake in This Life has grown out of a desire to support those among us who don't want to wait until our next life in order to awaken to what both the ancient and contemporary mystics and sages often refer to as "the Truth beyond name and form." This book is written as a functional map, or guide, or at least a series of guideposts, for those trying to integrate a relevant and meaningful spirituality into their busy lives.

I keep noticing how people are so often frustrated by an awful dilemma: Do I stay with a tradition that no longer reflects what I believe to be true, or do I negate spirituality altogether? This book shows readers how to bridge this gap. I'm also hopeful that this book supports and inspires conversations that help facilitate a maturation of the way we regard spirituality so that we are neither confined to magical or mythic traditions nor confined to scientific fundamentalism. Just because anthropomorphic versions of God don't hold much serious weight in today's religious dialogues doesn't mean that atheism is right on all counts. God isn't dead any more than you or I are, but adhering to old ways of talking about Him and honoring Him can diminish our potential as a species and can lead to disasters. Our way out of this mess is to develop a way of uncovering and supporting an approach to spirituality that is relevant for today's practitioners, yet doesn't throw out the wisdom offered to us so generously from the past.

Awake in This Life attempts to help all of us, regardless of our traditions, explore the notions of God, or Spirit, or Being, or whatever name we choose in reference to the Infinite. It is not an attempt to advocate one path to Spirit over another. This book is an offering that keeps its sights on where the path is leading us, not on the path itself. In order to help this journey along as effectively as possible, I have taken liberty with some of my examples to construct composite sketches of people and situations, changing names to protect privacy, and leaving out some of the details that might either bore you or detract from the essence of what's being illustrated.

Along these lines, there is one key point to this book that you might do well to remember: this book is not simply about a way to uncover an unsurpassed, penetrating, and perfect Enlightenment so that we can stay there in a blissful state of freedom for eternity. That approach only points toward half the journey. This book is written for those interested in going a step further, to a place where they can find themselves Awake in this very moment while they consciously work to bring their realization of freedom with them, into the world, wherever they go, for all of us.

Communicating on this level isn't always easy. Confusion is bound to arise initially but will, I hope, give way to clarity as sentences lead to paragraphs, and paragraphs to chapters. To be sure, different words and phrases will be used to communicate the same key points. For example, I will often use the phrase "small self" which one of my teachers used skillfully as I began my journey. This small self will also be referred to as the "ego," the "mind," the "subjective self," as well as the "circumstantial self," the "contraction," the "personal," as well as "form," the "manifest," "ignorance," "delusion," "time-bound existence," and other terms. Basically, these labels all point to that in us which feels separate from the Universe and which takes action from a place limited by perpetual defense and fear.

The other phrase that this same teacher used effectively as a pointer was "Big Self." This Big Self will alternately be referred to as "egolessness," "No Mind," the "Infinite," the "Ultimate Life," the "Expanse," as well as "Emptiness," the "Unmanifest," the "impersonal self," "timelessness," as well as the "All," "Spirit," "Being," "Awareness," the "Deep Singularity," the "Absolute," and sometimes even "God." For the most part, I try not to use the word "God" since it automatically tends to conjure up personal images of an anthropomorphized deity. Besides, this word always carries lots of baggage with it and so usually it gets in the way of what's being said. But, periodically, God fits in nicely with the writing, so please excuse its use if you don't like it.

Similarly, I try not to abuse the word "Enlightenment," which, like God carries a lot of weight with it. I try to use the words "Awakening" or "Enlightenment" only in order to point to boundlessness breaking through what binds us, but feel free to substitute the words that work for you. If you ever get too confused by the words, try your best to look past them and open your whole body to what is being said. While there are no guarantees of their effect, I assure you that the words themselves will never be able to carry the weight either of their message or that to which they are pointing.

Also, please recognize that there will be lots of repetition in these pages. In fact, every bit of what I'm trying to communicate can be summed up like this: *Let go to what is real in this moment, and then fully participate in the world from this openness.* That's it. You'll read it, or some facsimile of it, plenty of times. I had to hear it thousands of times in thousands of different ways before it ever gained any traction in my experience. (Again, to all of my teachers, thanks for your patience.)

I hope readers will also notice that even though my spiritual training is Buddhist, I've tried to make this book something that any person can use to support whatever spiritual practice he or she might have. All traditions can use this approach to the Infinite as a method of deepening an appreciation of what their version of the Sacred represents. This is important since, again, *Awake in This Life* is just a simple map drawn to help lead us away from a limited view of God as well as the fundamentalist practices that always fail to honor Him, and into an ever-expanding recognition of all that God is. This map, then, directs us to a deeply inclusive recognition that everyone is at least partially right as he or she hikes up the Mountain of Spirit. This means that no one has exclusive rights to the whole Truth. Merging these partial pieces and atomized versions of Truth takes time and patience on all of our parts, but listening deeply and watching carefully helps each of us uncover that which is forever beyond fragmentation—that which is always and forever whole. As I often say to those I work with in the Infinite Smile Sangha, wisdom traditions are simply different paths up the same Mountain. Let us talk about that Mountain, and the view that it offers, rather than argue about the various paths used to climb it.

In order to make this process a little easier, I've organized the book into three parts: the climb, where we begin to identify obstacles and challenges; the summit, where we witness the unity of all things; and coming home, where we consciously bring what we've uncovered on the summit back into the world for everyone's benefit. My Buddhist friends will recognize this approach as a rather crude reformulation of the teachings. Rest assured, it's intentional. Not to take anything away from the Buddha, but I'm sure that he appreciates contemporary twists on the things he taught. Connoisseurs of more recent spiritual writings will find evidence of their influence throughout the text. Philosophers, teachers, and contemporary sages like Nisargadatta Maharaj, Sri Ramana Maharshi, Eckhart Tolle, Norman Fischer, Reb Anderson, Gangaji, Adyashanti, Jack Kornfield, Pema Chodron, and Ken Wilber have all had their hands involved in the unchaining of my heart and mind as well as in the writing of this work. I have shamelessly thrown their articulations and punctuations into this work. Deep bows to all of them, and I thank them for the blessing of allowing me to stand on their shoulders.

Part One of the book examines the origins of greed, hate, and delusion. I look, as others have looked, to our sense of being bound by our separation as the source of all of our suffering. As we climb the Mountain of Spirit, we begin to see how a life lived from this sense of separation will quite normally act to defend against any and all threats to its sense of control. I will go into this matter in some detail and show how our tendency to act from this place of terminal threat explains much about our behaviors, and points to the very source of our suffering.

Part Two explores the ways that our minds and bodies can support our conscious expansion beyond the whole drama into a deep union with all things. Knowing this union allows us to get to the summit of the Mountain of Spirit where we begin to develop skills that enable us to be free of whatever circumstance might veil Truth from our experience. This freedom helps us to uncover the opening within each of our life situations that then allows us to act as vehicles of Awakening.

Part Three suggests ways for us to integrate the separation discussed in Part One with the unification discussed in Part Two. Bringing both aspects of our experiences back down the Mountain in order to share them is the ultimate work of integrating Enlightenment in to the world. As we become more deeply informed by the Infinite, a continual knitting together of expansive Awareness with all that is contracted within us begins to keep us close to what's real and true in life. Looking with honest, inwardly focused eyes at our deepest intention and then vowing to live intimately and compassionately with all beings will generate all that is necessary to shift from circumstantial living to Ultimate Living. At the moment we start living from an Ultimate orientation, we suddenly find that in every situation we have a choice: do we retract into the familiar, or open to the divine chaos that can never be known? As our practice matures, the decisions we make change everything. Literally. And we have come home.

I've tried to keep the writing light on the recommendation of some of my most worthy critics. Comments like, "make it funnier," and "this is way to heavy," have been thrown at me since I started work on this project. Know that I've done my best, but also know that deep spiritual work almost always kills your sense of humor.

Just kidding.

Bows.

Introduction

From the time I was about nine years old until I entered my last year in college, I hated God. I would often find myself railing internally and sometimes even externally against the small-mindedness of those who adhered to a patriarchal and largely superstitious approach to Him. The wars fought in His name, whether large or small, collective or personal, seemed like nothing other than horrific human folly built on a corrosive, fear-based addiction to "faith." In some ways things haven't changed. Brutality still presents itself in the name of faith, and humanity still tends to center itself on rather primitive notions of God. My anger surrounding the issues of religion, however, has softened substantially over the years. This doesn't mean that I've necessarily "found God"; it's just that after lots of travel, stillness, and study with some great teachers, the whole divine mess makes a little more sense to me now, and as a result, there is more peace in my heart and mind.

Uncovering this peace gave rise to the book you now have in your hands. In my journey, I was introduced to a path that continues to inspire me. This path reveals that there is a way for each of us to approach our spiritual lives that neither negates nor excludes any religious tradition. There is a path for each of us that supports a deepening appreciation of the Infinite while still allowing for us to live engaged lives—where we get the kids to school on time and enjoy those things and those people who truly matter to us. All of us have exactly the tools we need to awaken to this spiritual Path, to become enlightened by it, and to be radically free from the things that hold us back from becoming all that we are. The only requirement is that we must want it enough to examine our lives honestly with patience, purpose, and care. This book attempts to show us how to take on this challenge.

Before we go on this journey, however, you should be aware of how I got to where I am. My spiritual life started early. I enjoyed the kids and teachers at my Sunday School. My family attended a rather progressive church in suburban San Francisco, where guitars were played, various approaches to God were openly discussed, and love for each person was central to the community. I'm guessing that Christ would have liked what was happening there. Unfortunately, the minister left. I heard all sorts of rumors, but the one that stuck with me was that the old guard of the church felt that he was a little to loose in his interpretations of Christ's teachings.

As I remember it, we changed churches soon thereafter, and my experience at our new place of worship left me confused and angry. One of these new ministers, for example, told a bunch of us after a service that the Jewish and Muslim friends I had in my second-grade class were going to hell since they didn't accept Jesus Christ as their personal savior. I thought this was ridiculous since there were grown-ups in this new church who had accepted Christ as their personal savior, who, I knew, after seeing their behavior at sporting events and cocktail parties, didn't deserve to get in to heaven before my "non-believing" friends. This and other hypocrisies didn't help to open my heart or mind to the kind of God that I was used to honoring. Then, in the years to come, seeing the televised images of Jim Bakker being led away from court in handcuffs and Jimmy Swaggart whimpering through a confession of indiscretion to his flock only encouraged me to withdraw further behind a wall of my own making. Insulated from religion and its trappings, I felt safe, impenetrable, and closed off to the effects of their harmful extremes. Ah, the feeling that one's truth is The Truth—This must be the road to hell, I thought.

Extremism in general worked wonders in alienating me from any and all wisdom traditions. My loving suburban San Francisco parents, with their progressive mindsets largely agreed with me, yet they still wanted me to have some sort of spiritual grounding. To this day I'm amazed at how remarkably tolerant they were of my early seeking of alternatives. I remember telling them as a nine year old that I wanted to become a Jew since it "had a star as a symbol instead of a cross, which was used to torture people." (Besides, Mark Spitz was Jewish, and I saw him as a god.) My parents never once discouraged me. They simply smiled and suggested that maybe we should all "keep exploring the questions" that were coming up. Lucky me. They could have suggested that I go to the nice therapist with the sandbox in her office, or worse yet they could have taken me to the minister at our church either for some pastoral guidance, or as one of our more conservative neighbors suggested, for an exorcism.

I'm grateful that they continued to support me as I struggled with the deep questions about life, death, and God that I had percolating within me.

As soon as the teenage years arrived, I grew out of the whole questioning phase and began the simpler path of outright rejection. The more books I read as a teen, the more that God, and the exclusionary worship of Him, became something that any person of education, thoughtfulness, and care must reject on principle, I thought. Since the concept of Him and the human tendency to hold on to this concept was at the core of so much pain and injustice, God must be avoided. I remember thinking that Nietzsche had it right when he told the world in the early 20th century, "God is dead." Any celebration of His eternity and the salvation that His messengers offered us was simply a fear reflex, not unlike whistling if we were to walk past a graveyard. We were all going to die, I would say to any one of my friends who would listen, so why not just maximize our pleasure in the process? Be selfish, and enjoy the ride. Ah, hedonism—This must be the road to heaven, I thought.

The only problem was that the more pleasure I sought, the more pain I eventually felt. While attending the University of California, I continually succumbed to the temptations offered by pretty girls and flowing beer, yet no matter how much of any kind of indulgence I enjoyed, the pleasure of it was only fleeting and the payback of my excess weighed heavily on me. No matter how many skirts I chased or pints I drank, it was never enough. Hedonism, I decided after four years on an existential trampoline of bliss and pain, only leads us into a deeply personal version of the same spiritual war that all other faiths fought collectively. I was lost.

But at this point of doubt, something shifted in me as I questioned my blind pursuit of pleasure. Even in my darkest moments, I knew there was more to life than the cliché, "Life is hard and then you die." It made sense to me intellectually, and yet like every other version of truth, living hard until death seemed so incomplete. Increasingly, as my questioning intensified, there were moments in my day-to-day experience that were transcendent, beautiful, loving, all-encompassing forays into something beyond anything I'd ever experienced. Sometimes these moments occurred as I walked across the Berkeley campus on my way to class. At other times

I'd be holding hands with my girlfriend, afraid to tell her that life was bursting in me in some indescribable way that made all of us One Infinity.

At one point during the summer before my last year at Cal, I was coaching a group of six year old swimmers at one of our biggest meets of the season, when during their freestyle relay, I began to feel as if my body no longer had any boundary. I still functioned as a coach, enthusiastically offering cheers of encouragement to my precious little swimmers as they chopped haphazardly through the water, but I was conscious of what felt like a total lack of separation. In the midst of it all, neither my body nor mind existed as anything other than an extension of the moment at hand. I was the pool, the deck, the excited parents, the little swimmers, the sun, the sky, the zinc oxide on my nose. All of it.

What struck me over time was that none of these increasingly common blasts of universal tenderness and peace were anything like the all-too familiar alcohol-induced numbing of my mind and body. Instead, I can best describe these events as hyperconscious extensions of "me" beyond, and yet paradoxically closer, than my own skin. It was unsettling, yet so very beautiful. What was all of this, I wondered? Was I losing my grip on reality? Was this some schizophrenic break getting ready to tear into my life? Or was this the miraculous and mysterious Truth about which the ancients had spoken? Ultimate Reality, perhaps? Or maybe I had a tumor, or some other terrible neurological ailment. Whatever the case, I wondered whether there was a way to stay near this place forever. How could I serve whatever this vast Opening was? Ah, to follow this path—It must be impossible, I thought.

After graduating from college I moved to New York where I toiled as a waiter and bartender by night, and as an actor perpetually out on auditions for bad theatrical and commercial projects during the day. During this time, my intimacy with the experiences of "Opening," as I called them, diminished. Within a short time, my life in New York was in dire straits: my girlfriend at the time was leaving me, my rent was due, and I had no money. Waiting on tables and slinging cocktails for the rich and famous only reminded me that I wasn't where I wanted to be. I felt so alienated from everything I'd come to regard as sacred, and worst of all, I had what felt like a hole in my heart that ached for a reprieve from all of the pain and frustration I felt.

It all came to a head when I came home to my cold East Village apartment one Christmas Eve. I didn't have enough money to pay for January's rent, let alone afford the trip home to San Francisco for the holidays. My parents were in the midst of both a divorce and a bankruptcy, so couldn't pay to get me home either. In lieu of a celebratory tree, I had purchased a small wreath to set in the corner of my East 5th Street studio. Around it I had placed a few wrapped presents sent by my three younger brothers that had come in a care package days earlier.

I sat down and opened the presents. There was a book of Gary Larson's Far Side cartoons, a coffee mug with "No. 1 Fireman" written across the side, and a flashlight without batteries. My mom had included a plaid duvet cover, but I didn't have a duvet—only wool blankets. I laid down on my stomach and listened to the quiet of the space around me, and I started to cry.

I missed my brothers, my friends, my parents, and most of all, my life as I'd known it before. Now there seemed to be so few smiles. My father's recent business failure had torn apart what was left of my parents' relationship. Their divorce and increasing indebtedness were decimating everything I'd always considered stable. When I thought about it, the home I'd always known didn't exist any longer. So there really was nothing left to call home—no place to which I could return. For the first time in my life, I felt absolutely and truly alone and in an emotional place of total disconnect from everything. I felt raw and unapproachable, angry and unstable, filled with pain brought on by a profound and endless alienation. Then, at the moment that it all felt most heavy, something broke wide open in me with a tremendous force. My words can't describe or even point to what the experience was like. I just remember feeling like I was melting into the floor of my apartment, into the gifts from home, into the wreath, into the strain of my situation, into the hurt and glory of all experience of all beings all at once. This event went way beyond the blessed "a-ha" moment of non-division I'd experienced on the pool deck. This was deeper. It was as if I'd died somehow. I was still in this body, in this time and space, but the separate sense of "I" had really gone away.

Like all experiences, this one was temporary. I stayed there on my floor for several hours, until I finally got hungry and had some ramen noodles. After a while, the intensity of the shimmer I was sensing all around me started to diminish. But in this internal explosion was a reminder that lingered for months. The pressure-cooker of all that pain had given birth to what any of us might call "a sacred journey" that, over the years, helped me contextualize the temporary death of my "I-sense." I was still in the deep, dark, emotional pain of a life that wasn't going according to plan, but I consciously vowed to open myself to the whole mystery of it all. Where this mystery and its intentional unfolding continues to lead me is described in the pages of this book.

Living from this openness, we simply work, live, and love with our whole being. In continuing this very life of ours, we also can help all of humanity if we're careful not to think, once again, that we've got a monopoly on Truth. Even the articulation of teachings in these pages is only partial, yet it points to a fullness that each of us already has. As much as I'm hopeful that this book can support a deepening of lives led, I'm even more hopeful that the time-honored teaching that I'm sharing can ripple out to everyone that you might ever touch in this precious life, at some precious moment. Like right now.

Bows to all that is sacred and holy within and without you.
Michael McAlister
Pleasant Hill, CA
January, 2008

Part One

—

The Climb

The Universe has a way of reminding us that no matter how hard we try, we can't control everything. Regardless of our efforts, however heroic, things eventually fall apart. As unwelcome as these reminders of ultimate entropy might be, we can't prevent them. Over a long enough timeline we find that all things are temporary. Things get lost, bodies break down, relationships end, circumstances shift, and all of us eventually must succumb to death. The law is simple: all things change.

Good news comes with this law of the Universe, however, once we see that things like despair, depression, pain and fear are also impermanent. Just as darkness eventually takes light away, so does light break the hold of darkness in our lives. When we begin truly to realize and accept these rhythms of give and take, we are instantly invited to take on a deeply personal quest so that we might find peace and stability in the face of life's uncertainties. At least this is what all the world's mystics, both ancient and contemporary, have been telling us. Despite all the chaos brought on by the temporary nature of everything, they say, there is a peace that each of us can uncover that supports conscious living. Realizing this, however, means that we have to agree to meet the challenge of climbing the Mountain of Spirit fearlessly.

Once we decide we are ready for the ascent, we recognize quickly that the adventure at hand is unlike any we have ever attempted before. It is demanding of our time and patience, and it continually challenges us to question all that we've always thought to be true. What's more, the climb is not linear. It starts off leading us in two directions simultaneously. We find ourselves moving outward into the thin air of spiritual altitude, and, at the same time, we are moving inward, exploring the depths of our sense of self. We find that the higher we climb, the more our steps seem to take us in several directions at once, thus rendering our familiar tools like intellect, wit, and instinct useless since we are not simply moving forward, trying to gain some type of intellectual understanding. Rather, the climb allows for our consciousness to expand in all directions. As we purposefully let go of more and more of the things to which we usually cling, we spontaneously find that we are increasingly aware of every single attachment in our experience, all at once.

Climbing the Mountain of Spirit helps us each become students of both our experience and ourselves, constantly uncovering what makes us happy and sad, what generates pain and suffering, as well as what brings us peace and joy. With continued effort, we start seeing that we are connected with all things, and that the deepest levels of being point out that we are never separate from anything. The higher we get, the more we realize our interconnectedness and interdependence with the Cosmos. As we climb even higher, we see that most of our discomfort is self-created since it comes from the mistaken belief that we are separate from the Cosmos. This belief in separation, or the sense, as the Zen teacher Yasutani Roshi says, that "I am in here, and everything else is out there," perpetually generates greed for anything that can protect this internal sense of a distinct and separate "I" and aversion to anything that threatens its sense of security. Living from separation may appear to be normal, but the higher spiritual seekers climb, the less they are satisfied with what has always appeared normal. Seekers at even higher spiritual altitudes want to be free of all that generates the patterns of resistance, fear, anger, pain, and negativity. The more openly we observe all of these normal appearances, the more we can recognize the inherent and perpetual struggle that the experience of separation carries with it. "Why carry on living this way?" climbers will ask.

Why, indeed? Climbers realize that the vast majority of their pain and suffering is something that they create themselves. As odd as this sounds, spiritual mountaineers see how the very thing in us which always feels separate from everything else—what psychologists would call the ego—works constantly to attach and identify with various ideas, feelings, roles, and situations in order to "normalize" our circumstances, thereby limiting our altitude. Metaphorically, the ego needs the air generated by separation in order to survive. This means that normal living, for most of us, is about constant, low-grade, and sometimes high-pitched battles between our egos and whatever might oppose them. When any ego successfully defends itself against an attack, it celebrates its success by immediately preparing for the next assault.

This ascent can get difficult. At every turn in the path we have to look into the depths of our experience fearlessly without avoiding whatever the view shows us. Climbing with integrity and intention means we must be ready to offer nothing less than total honesty and radically open observation for whatever shows itself at each of our steps. Doing so helps us see that in order to move up the Mountain of Spirit, we must live lives that continually come from an open place of attention rather than a closed place of judgment. This is the essence of our climb. As the spiritual teacher Krishnamurti says, "Observation without evaluation is the highest form of intelligence." Using this kind, open, non-judgmental intelligence of ours frees us from the traps set up along the path by our minds, thus allowing for us to climb and eventually to reach the summit of the Mountain of Spirit.

Unconciousness I

To myself I am only a child playing on the beach, while vast oceans
of truth lie undiscovered before me.
— *Isaac Newton*

The Four Noble Truths: Suffering; the origin of suffering;
the cessation of suffering; and the Noble Eightfold Path,
which leads to the cessation of suffering.
— *Dhammapada*

Most of us have a deep and resonant longing to live lives of balance, yet we tend to get blown around continually by the winds of circumstance. Some of these winds are positive and fulfilling, some are not. Either way, these circumstances tend to push us off center and keep us from living lives that are informed by peace. At least, this was my situation when I first entered a meditation hall. I was about to graduate from college and was living a life filled with anything but peace. My day-to-day experience was totally out of balance, and I had no idea how to fix it. More than anything else, I just wanted a break from all of the stress that I was feeling. What should I do about getting a real job? What should I do about the unhealthy patterns that keep showing up in each of my relationships? What should I do about all the pain I'm feeling as I watch my parents divorce? These and other questions puzzled me. What was going on within me was in torment, and this torment seemed to be brought on by situations outside of me that I couldn't control. I felt like I was being torn apart, and I craved some kind of internal and external stability.

After sharing my dilemma with a friend, he suggested that I go out to Green Gulch Farm in Marin so that I could simply "sit still with all of it for a while," as he said, and then listen to a lecture on Zen Buddhism. I took his advice and drove to the beach from Berkeley early one sunny Sunday morning. Spring was alive as I walked onto the temple's grounds. Birds sang in the trees, frogs croaked in the pond, deer quietly grazed on the hillside, and flowers bloomed everywhere. The scene was a powerful reminder of the beauty and peace that my life seemed to lack. After wishing to myself that I could hold onto what I was witnessing, I walked into the meditation hall and took a seat on one of the sitting cushions, next to an old man in a black robe. I must have looked like a beginner since he stared at me as I awkwardly crossed my legs. Without saying a word, he offered two additional cushions to support my knees.

After I got settled, he leaned over and whispered, "Just sit still and be quiet after the bell rings. That's it. That's all you need to know. If your mind is chattering, count your breaths until it quiets down."

The moment he finished speaking, a bell rang, signaling the start of the meditation period. I closed my eyes and listened to a deafening silence. Upon realizing that my mind was trying to fill the quiet with its own chatter, I counted my breaths, just like my neighbor had told me. It didn't do much good. Whether I counted my breaths or not, my mind danced around constantly, distracting me from any meaningful focus. Maybe this Zen stuff was simply beyond me.

Once the meditation period was over, a little bald man, dressed in flowing black robe with a brown sash, sat in full lotus at the front of the hall. The lecture that the Zen master gave that day ironically dealt with what he called our "unconscious, habitual dualism that divides everything between the 'in here' sense of self and the 'out there' sense of everything else." As he went on, I felt like he was reading my mind even though I couldn't really understand what he was saying. It was like poetry of some kind with his words and phrasing continually hitting me on deeper and deeper levels. I remember being both taken and confused by his assertion that the division I was feeling was "precisely what generates all of our suffering, and yet nearly all of our activity in life is informed by this felt sense of separation." Maybe I'd get it later, I thought. Whatever the case, I knew I'd be back.

As time on my meditation cushion and spent around this particular teacher increased, I became aware of some interesting insights. My teacher suggested that if we simply look at the ways in which we categorize and compare ourselves, both with and against, everything else, we can get an idea as to how imbedded this process of separation is. For example, I am a human being, and that over there is a fish tank. Or, I am a believer, and that person is a non-believer. I am kind as well as intelligent, that person is really obnoxious and stupid, and I wish he'd stop being such a jackass.

This sense of separation, and the process through which it develops, is totally natural but it gets in the way of any meaningful peace that we might be able to feel. Instead of uncovering that which makes us feel at one and in turn at peace with everything, we spend our time defining what makes us distinct. Those of us who are parents know how our favorite two-year-olds do this all the time. They tirelessly work to prove that they are indeed distinct and special and deserve to be heard. And yet even as they grow out of this stage, they won't leave their sense of being distinct and special behind. In fact, they bring this sense of being separate, distinct and special along with them as they, and the rest of us, continue to develop stronger and stronger senses of identity. From this activity of becoming a separate and special somebody we begin to interact with the world as an entity that we call the "me," or the "self," or the "I," or the "ego." We use these words interchangeably as a way to point out our most basic sense of being a separate entity in the world. To be clear, this impulse to be something separate and special is not necessarily a bad thing. In fact, it gives life color and variance. But in the context of climbing the Mountain of Spirit, our tendency to think of this sense of separation as the full story of our reality is precisely what distorts our view as we attempt to get to the top.

Most likely each of us can remember an experience that helped this process of separation along. For me, it was getting laughter out of people at a very young age. It just didn't take that much effort, it seemed, to crack people up—especially if I made funny noises. Of course, I was reminded rather forcefully at times that timing was worthy of careful consideration.

"Michael," my father would say, pounding his fist on the dinner table, making his knife and spoon rattle and bounce, "that behavior is way out of bounds."

My three younger brothers would do their best not to snicker at his outbursts, and on most occasions, I could tell by the twinkle in my father's eye that he found my behavior at least mildly entertaining. Regardless of his scolding, over time I began to incorporate into my identity the idea that my "good sense of humor" could help me keep threats at bay. Once again, this isn't necessarily a bad thing, but when any of us clings to qualities that make us feel special, we are in essence identifying with what separates us from the deep singularity of the Universe.

Living from this place of division and separation causes constant insecurity, because we're vulnerable either to those "other" things or people we fear might overtake us, or to those "other" things or people we think might offer us protection from threats. In other words, when we live from a sense of separation we will act, in varying degrees, either defensively or aggressively. Whether our defensiveness or aggression is subtle or overt, this perpetual fight-or-flight position is psychologically exhausting and eventually runs us down emotionally, leading us down the path of suffering. Fight or flight may help us maintain the depths of the gene pool, but it won't allow for either peace to be felt or balance to be incorporated in the ways that we live.

We see that from our "normal" position of separation, our day-to-day lives can feel extremely unstable, and the ego (in here) will compensate for this perceived instability by pursuing the things (out there) that it believes will stabilize experience and somehow support perpetual peace and restfulness. How many times have any of us felt like we'd be able to find peace in our lives if only we had some more money to spend, or better furniture, or a Ph.D., or better relationships with significant people in our lives? Any one of these examples might be helpful to our sense of self-worth and stability in the short run, but in the long run each of these potential acquisitions can act as a distraction from facing what appears unstable and lacking within us. Will any of it ever be enough?

Unfortunately, if we don't face what is going on within us, we will tend to find ourselves in unwinnable contests of unconscious grasping and avoidance patterns. These patterns prevent us from ever finding the connections we desire. The higher we climb in our journey the more we gain new, more open, perspectives on our assumptions. The more perspective we gain, the greater our sense that there is hope for us, as individuals and as groups, not only to break this cycle of "normal" dissatisfaction and aggression but to rewire our neurological habits of selfishness that so often push us here in the first place. This rewiring helps us to act from places of clarity, and in doing so, we become engaged and helpful to all those whose lives we touch.

Separation

It has not deserted its creation for a place apart; it is always present to those with strength to touch it.
—Plotinus

In the beginner's mind there are many possibilities, but in the expert's mind there are few.
—Shunryu Suzuki

Although living a life sourced from a sense of separation consistently leads to suffering, separation itself is not bad. In fact, feeling separate from everything is pretty natural. But our attachment to both our sense of separation and to the activities that perpetuate it results in what many traditions call "delusion." While, here again, there is nothing inherently wrong with delusion, or what we could just as easily refer to as unconsciousness, it usually gets us into trouble. And in a spiritual sense, it is the major impediment to an opening to the enlightened perspective. Put another way, unconsciousness is what keeps us from ascending the Path up the Mountain. Our journey is thwarted since the ego sees itself as separate from everything else, and it survives by building a fortress around all that could potentially support its ability to manage everything about our lives. It does this by clinging to the things that it sees as useful for maintaining its sense of control and by avoiding the things that challenge its authority. A common example of this is our tendency to look for certitude in everything. People so often feel uncomfortable in the chaotic uncertainty of life that they grasp at certainties such as religion, political dogmas, clubs and communal organizations in order to make them feel safe, cared for, and understood. The delusion that our grasping will defend us from the Universe is exactly what inhibits an awakened expression of life.

Put another way, the natural perception of separation on the relative level—for example, the perception that the dog and the cat are separate creatures, or that the chocolate ice cream I'm eating is separate from the vanilla ice cream that my wife is enjoying—doesn't cause suffering. Instead, the problem arises when we cling to the erroneous view that the dog and the cat, as well as the chocolate and vanilla ice cream, are essentially separate and not also profoundly interconnected. This interconnectedness shows up the minute we start to look carefully at anything. In our examples, we can see that chocolate and vanilla, as well as the dog and cat, are all subject to the laws of nature. They share the need for air and water if they are to exist. What's more, they depend on our labeling in order to occupy any type of categorization. We'll explore this in greater detail as our climb continues, but we would do well to consider how this very same logic applies to the human experience. The ego begins to fortify its position when it perceives that it is fundamentally apart from others as well as the rest of the Universe, to the exclusion of a deep and unavoidable connection to everything. As a consequence of this delusion, we constantly either go after or avoid the circumstances that show up in our lives, and this unrelenting, psychological push-and-pull eventually leads to suffering.

It's important to remember, at this point of our climb, that attachment and avoidance are fundamentally the same psychological movement, since both try to dodge the circumstances that present themselves to us. Studying these circumstances as well as our corresponding leanings into or away from these mental mechanisms is a critical step in unlocking the enlightened perspective. The simple awareness of each experience, regardless of how the ego judges it, comes from a spaciousness that is unattached and beyond clinging and aversion. This spacious awareness is the place where wisdom meets compassion. It's where we begin meeting whatever arises in our conscious experience, without trying to do anything other than observe it. It is from this highest form of intelligence that we are offered a chance to see how we might live lives of deep balance.

If any of this sounds confusing, know that you are not alone. I had a horrible time with all of it when I began my practice. As Buddhist teachings, known as Dharma, came my way, my ego kept me moving constantly. I couldn't stop. Even when I was physically still while sitting on my meditation cushion, my mind raced. I spent so much time trying to "get" what the books and teachers described, so much effort trying to discover shortcuts to living a life of conscious balance, that I missed what all the books and teachers were saying. I finally got so frustrated with all of my movement toward this idea and away from that practice that I just stopped. Literally. I sat in the meditation hall, tears rolling down my cheeks, wondering what I was doing wrong, and then I just stopped doing anything. I just sat still. At that moment of surrendered stillness, my mind truly quieted down. Then glimpses of what everybody kept pointing out started to arise. This is why, as I lead groups of people interested in this kind of work, I make so much out of the practice of simply sitting still, shutting up, and watching our experience. Whether or not we find ourselves confused by all of the words and concepts doesn't matter. All one needs in order to begin his or her climb is to practice watching experiences as they come up—without grabbing or avoiding them, either mentally or physically.

Along these lines, one of my students approached me after a Dharma talk and said, "I've been able to observe and witness my experience like you keep telling us, and it's really useful." She then asked, why we don't "teach this to our kids in school?"

It's a great question, since this kind of open awareness changes lives by creating a welcome space for the kind of internal expansiveness necessary for transformation. I think teaching it to children in school is a great idea, but barring some miraculous revamp in school curriculum, we can still do our part in making sure that all of our kids get the chance to develop a keen sense of their internal lives. One way to help this along is for us to ask any person of any age how they are feeling. This can help facilitate a growth in this expanse beyond the chattering mind that always wants to "get it." On the other hand, asking someone what they are thinking merely energizes the chattering mind whose noise we're trying to get beyond. Of course the mind is not a bad thing, but it is exactly what keeps us feeling separate from all things. Checking in with our bodily experience, on the other hand, will always assist us as we climb since we cannot answer questions about how we are truly feeling without openly observing what is going on in our bodies, and it is the open observation of our experience, rather than the mind's evaluation of it, that gets us to the summit of the Mountain of Spirit.

So for those of us interested in getting to the summit and then returning home, we must be willing to free ourselves from our identification with our ego and all the attachments associated with its activity. When we drop our identification with what feels separate, we are walking a path that leads us toward Enlightenment. When we drop our need to judge and evaluate, we begin to uncover and support a realization of what has always been at the core of who we are. When we simply stop trying to "get it" and we become still, we are primed for a realization that allows us to lead what we might call an "Ultimate Life" that goes far beyond the normal, conventional circumstances we typically experience. This Ultimate Life is a life that is consciously connected with, rather than separate from, all things—a life lived from, with, and as Spirit, Being, Essence, or whatever else we might call it.

By contrast, life's "conventional circumstances" are the normal, everyday experiences we so often call the "real world." We could just as easily call this realm our "day-to-day reality" or our "normal life." Regardless of the name, it's the solid and substantial world we experience and sense from our individual perspective. While conventional circumstances are most certainly real, they are also the place where our mind begins to help us always feel separate, and this place of separation is always incomplete in its attempts at offering us peace.

The view from the summit gives each of us the chance to recognize and access the part of us that is aware, alert, connected, and therefore stable and at rest in every situation. Once we've climbed high enough to uncover this perspective, we're offered an opportunity to act from an infinite spaciousness rather than from our habitually contracted state. As we open into greater awareness and spaciousness, our activity begins to express itself as compassion and caring. In this space, we begin to embody the radiance of the enlightened perspective in our everyday world. We literally become a continual, undivided expression of wisdom and compassion.

Some of you may have been lucky enough to meet someone who lives from this place. Seeing this embodied radiance can be breathtaking. Many of us who have been fortunate enough to meet authentic masters walk away from the experience mysteriously moved. This is exactly what happened to me when I first met the most influential of my teachers as I began to climb the Mountain. I couldn't put it into words at the time, but just being in his presence changed something in me. Whatever defenses I had built up to prevent the circumstances of life from tearing me apart, this guy took from me. In his presence, I felt suddenly alone, exposed, and unable to function the way I'd always functioned. Initially this was incredibly unsettling since I was rarely at a loss for words. But I saw this as a good quality for a spiritual teacher to have, since it would keep me from leaning on my old habits. Over time, I found many more people along my path who were able to meet the world, and all of us that are in it, from this deeply conscious place. These people are the ones who know Spirit radiates through all of us equally, and their recognition of this and their intimacy with what this recognition means is what allows them to teach with integrity. Finding someone who can live in the world but not be confined by his or her circumstance helps us immeasurably along our journey since they offer us a divine invitation to join them in shedding our sense of separation.

Just Words

At this point, it might be helpful to go over a few words in order to stay clear. For instance, when I speak of wisdom, I'm referring to the knowing that flourishes beyond the separate sense of self—we could call it Knowing with a capital "K." Wisdom is beyond the judgments and evaluations of the mind, or, we could say, the ego. Wisdom continually realizes the simultaneous, supportive coexistence of our Ultimate Life with our conventional circumstance. It's the result of any person's shift in perspective from the habit-driven contraction of unconsciousness to the vast opening of Spirit. From this new perspective, we begin to simply intuit a consciousness that "Knows" the totality of the All.

Wisdom is the Knowing of our total unification and interconnection with everything in the Universe. An occurrence of this is not an intellectual understanding but rather experiential in nature, and it arises whenever we begin to wisely recognize, or Know, the ego and its continual performance in our experience. Just watching it do its thing without judging it is wisdom. Nurturing this wisdom, as a spiritual sensibility, limitlessly fuels our journey toward becoming awake in this life.

When I speak of compassion, I'm referring to the activity that is supported and sourced from wisdom—activity free of egoic clinging. It is the same as a feeling of love without any greed. It's simple, caring, natural, and at the same time, the most breathtakingly beautiful expression of tenderness we can experience. When any of us acts with compassion, we're allowing Infinity to express itself through us *as* us, which is a great way of describing the path we might take in order to lead an enlightened, or Ultimate, life.

As an example of compassion, imagine walking in a crosswalk and finding that an elderly man is beginning to fall as he tries to cross the street. Few of us would decide to let the old man hit the ground. Most people would reach out to support him without ever taking into account the their potential trespasses against anything or anyone. We would just attempt to catch the man spontaneously without any evaluation or contemplation, without consideration of gain or consequence. This unconditioned helpfulness beyond the grasp of ego also fuels our journey of becoming awake in this life.

Being awake in this life means that we live from an enlightened orientation. The term Enlightenment may be the most challenging concept of all since its definition can change depending on one's tradition. For our purposes, Enlightenment shows up as a conscious meeting of two things at once. When the continuous and total acceptance of whatever is happening to us at any given moment supports deeply conscious activity, we meet the world as an enlightened being. So Enlightenment is the simultaneous recognition of a profound interconnected unity among all things, with the natural impulse to share this Knowing with everyone and *for* everyone. As this sharing occurs consciously, the whole of humanity is offered an evolutionary spark that can light a collective fire of Awakening for all beings in this very lifetime.

On an individual level, this fire of Enlightenment involves a mind that does not identify with thoughts or feelings and is never limited by either the past or the future. This doesn't mean that an enlightened master has no concept of past or future. Rather, it means that the enlightened aren't caught by their relationship to either the past or the future. This allows them to be upright yet flexible in any situation. Also, an enlightened being will always surrender to the fact that there is no substantial difference between you and me. This means that the awakened among us, in other words, continually see that there is no difference between themselves and others. Furthermore, their enlightened perspective shows them unmistakably that there is only ever God, or Spirit, or as we say in Zen, Emptiness. Everything is seen and experienced as an infinite variety of Spirit, which shows up in a dramatic series of conventional circumstances that we call life. When this realization becomes our new frame of reference, Spirit consciously informs the world through our activity. From here, wisdom becomes intimately connected with compassion, which results in an Enlightenment that can show itself through every one of us, as every one of us. Encounters with individuals who live from this spaciousness are rare. But have confidence in the fact that the more attention we pay to our spiritual life, the more often meetings with this kind of embodied grace will show up.

The Builder of Boundaries

From the point of view of quantum mechanics, separation doesn't really exist. At least that's what scientists keep telling us. I don't pretend to understand very much when it comes to quantum physics, but its implications point us in an interesting direction when it comes to discussions about the experience of being a "self." For example, the only real difference between your "self" and the things around you is organization and energy. The last meal that you ate, for instance, is made up of the same, carbon-based physical matter that you will find in your own body. The molecules might be organized differently, and the flow and expression of energy are certainly different. But that's about it.

To unpack this a little bit more, consider that on the scale of the very small, all things are simply the subatomic spin of the same Universe. Of course, structures, including subatomic structures, may be differentiated. Although I've never tasted them, quarks evidently vary in flavor. And I know that cows are not Cadillacs, and tennis balls are not bananas. But regardless of form, on the level of our most basic constituents, all things are made up of the same basic stuff. In addition, the flow of energetic impulses may vary significantly. My car functions differently than my liver, and on most days my computer functions differently than my dog. Looking closely enough, however, we find that despite their obvious differences, all of these things abide by the same physical and chemical rules of the Universe.

On the scale of the very big, the Universe contains everything and expresses itself as everything. In other words, nothing is ever separate from either the Universe's structure or energy. The mathematics of our galaxy's spiral is the same math that is at play in the waves at the beach and the double helix of our DNA. Every bit of every experience is always, simply and elegantly, One Song (Uni-Verse).

With this song playing, it's not much of a leap for any of us to see that nothing can really be separated from anything else. It's all just the Cosmos playing itself out with conventional boundaries, offering us the diversity that we see expressed in every moment of every day. And yet every bit of this diversity is still interconnected with everything else in the Universe. Since everything is connected, any separation we might perceive ultimately can't be real. Since separation isn't real, boundaries are illusiory. So who is it that makes and interprets these boundaries that we perceive and encounter in the real world?

Could it be our individual and collective minds that are doing the interpretation and implementation of all boundaries for us? In a word, yes. The mind is conditioned to build boundaries. As a boundary-builder, the mind will do its best to keep things organized and separated, since if there are no boundaries, it is out of a job. We rarely live from the perspective of seeing through the boundaries made by our minds. Instead, we habitually attach to them. Like monkeys swinging from tree limbs, our minds grasp whatever experience our minds tell us will maximize our pleasure, and we avoid whichever experience our minds tell us will threaten the continuance of this pleasure. Instead of getting out of the jungle altogether and recognizing ourselves as functional expressions of the Infinite, we struggle to hang onto the vines made by our minds. And this keeps us ensconced in a world of delusion.

Many of us have experienced crashing through the boundaries of our minds at some point even if we weren't fully aware of it. Recall the last time your heart was opened by something as basic as a commercial on TV. You weren't expecting it, but just seeing the tender images blended perfectly with the music pushed you out of the recognition that you are watching a pitch designed to separate you from your cash. Instead of feeling manipulated to tears, you relish the fact that you can have an emotional connection with a situation expressed by your fellow man. To be sure, the manipulation was intentional, and the job of any ad is to get you to buy a particular product. But the experience also points to a much bigger signpost on the path up the Mountain. That is, despite the normal sense that we are separate from everything, we are hungry for the felt sense of deep unification that the flow of the Universe offers us all the time.

Despite the odds against successfully altering the course of our mental flow, the mind, or we could say the ego, willfully fights for more boundaries, more separation, and more permanence. The ego does this by making sure that threats to its position of power are eliminated. At once it takes on the role of builder, fixer, and helper, as well as saboteur, destroyer, and assassin, all in the service of keeping itself in charge of its experience. In other words, if the ego senses it is losing control, it will either make things or break things, depending on what's needed for its survival. It may make a new relationship or break one, depending on what it thinks it needs to stay in charge. Maybe it will buy a new car or home in order to make some pleasure, or it will avoid therapy sessions if it perceives therapy could break its ability to manage its pleasure.

By contrast, a self-sense that is consciously informed by the Infinite isn't affected by any boundaries and doesn't get caught by any of these perceived psychological threats. Rather, it is beyond the experience of separation and therefore free of fear. We can call this the "Big Self" since it is consciously informed by the deep unity of Spirit and simply witnesses this whole charade of the busy ego, or what we might just as easily call the "small self." In all cases, the Big Self simply observes dispassionately as the small self either goes after or avoids the flow of circumstances in life. And while the Big Self isn't separate from the small self, it is never subject to getting beaten down by the constant flow of the Universe's currents. Nor is it ever caught by the cycles of pleasure and pain experienced by the small self. The Big Self goes beyond and yet permeates the entire unreal performance of greed, avoidance, separation, boundary and judgment offered by the ego.

At any point that we might consciously watch the ego play out any of its dramas, the Big Self arises as the watcher. It neither judges nor resists anything that shows up, it simply is open to whatever is there much like a mirror is open to what it reflects. Just as a parent might watch his or her eight year old in a school play, the Big Self lovingly observes that entity within us that flubs its lines and bumps into the scenery and does so without criticism or contempt. Recognizing this expansive quality and realizing that it is always available is a critical step on our journey.

Right now, in fact, there is nothing stopping you from recognizing the relationship that your small self is having with these words you are reading. Is there acceptance or resistance; appreciation or indifference? What are you feeling right now? Regardless of whether your feelings are positive, negative, or indifferent, the ability to witness them is the effortlessly still and open activity of the Big Self—something that we all share, all the time. Practice this throughout your day, and you will uncover a space within you and without you that is beyond decay and death, beyond greed and fear. This Big Self can watch death and decay, as well as greed and fear, arise in our experience, and yet it will never get caught by any feeling, since its sole purpose is to remain as an observing presence. Spiritually, this observing presence, as I'm describing it, is referred to in traditions as that which has never been born. Once again, we can also call this God, Spirit, Emptiness, Oversoul or the Unmanifest. Pick your own label. Just know that the Big Self points to what is precisely beyond these words. It is total stillness, and this ever-present stillness is what gives birth to positively everything that moves—including the contracted self. Since this still Big Self never moves, it is not subject to the movement of time. Since it is not subject to the limitations of time, we can say it is eternal.

The Shift

Many seasoned spiritual seekers mistakenly believe that in order to experience living as a Big Self, they need to destroy the ego, or small self. But this idea is one of the greatest misunderstandings that new practitioners make as they ascend the Mountain of Spirit. Getting rid of the ego is a massive impediment to any authentic awakening, since attempting to do so exemplifies the unconsciousness from which practitioners wish to awaken in the first place. When we first become interested in the spiritual quest, we usually think that enlightened sages have no egos and have evolved into Infinitely Big Selves without human impulses. But it's a naïve mistake for us to think that the enlightened among us have no physical or emotional desires, no wants, no passion, no humor, or any other qualities we might attribute to the small self. This simply isn't true. Yet our egos would conveniently have us believe this in order to idealize Enlightenment and thus effectively discourage us from trying to awaken from our habitual slumber.

To be clear, Enlightenment will not prevent you or anyone else from getting hungry or thirsty. It won't keep anyone from dying. It won't bestow powers of healing upon you, nor will you be able to show off miracles to your friends. And it certainly won't eliminate your desires— such as the desire for your next breath. Nor will an authentic awakening keep you from avoiding a foul ball that is hit in your direction. Nor will Enlightenment mean that you will no longer have any sexual desires. Having no desires isn't Enlightenment. Having no ego isn't Enlightenment either, but rather a form of mental illness we might call psychosis.

With all of this said, what the Enlightened people who live among us do have, that most of us fail to realize, is a different relationship with every thing and every one that they meet. The difference is that a new relationship with all things and all people informs the desire and avoidance patterns associated with the boundaries built by the ego. The Enlightened among us simply aren't held by any of the ego's trappings, nor are they enslaved by its perpetual activity of attachment. The Enlightened among us who have realized their True Nature have bodies and minds that are simply and radiantly informed by something more expansive—a Big Self that allows them perpetually to use their bodies and minds as conscious expressions of Spirit in action. The Sufi saying, "to be in the world but not of it," sums this concept up beautifully. Twentieth century sages such as Gandhi, Mother Teresa and Ramana Maharshi are classic examples of people who consistently and purposefully generated articulations of Truth from places beyond their unconscious egoic needs for praise, pleasure, and gain. With very rare exception, the core of their words and deeds were free of being caught, either by themselves or by the world. Because of their expressions of deep freedom and compassion, they inspired millions, forever changing the way humankind sees itself.

This ability to respond as a Big Self to the world comes from recognizing the delusion brought about by our habitual identification with all that is contracted inside and outside of us. To be fair to the ego, we must never fail to see that no matter how meddlesome it might be, it is still a divine expression of the Infinite, just like everything else. As we expand our awareness of the ego and its contracted behaviors, we begin to see that shifting our relationship with it is critical. This shift automatically begins when we simply, and continually, observe its activity without getting caught by it. Doing so effectively diminishes its position of control.

This formula is nothing new. The Buddha, Jesus, and the rest of history's spiritual heavy hitters have all done some version of observing the small and contracted self from an eternally huge and expansive vantage point. And none of them had to kill their little, contracted egos in the process. It's entirely fair to say that all of history's enlightened sages had egos; indeed, they had big egos in the most profound sense of what we mean by "Big." The Enlightened always have more to work with because their everyday mind is informed not only by a personal sense of Spirit, or what we might call "soul," but also by the impersonal, spacious, reality of Spirit at the same time. This simultaneous embodiment of a personal sense and an expansive impersonal sense shows up in an Ultimate Life as a Big Self. This conscious unification between the personal and the impersonal is what helps any one of us show up in the world with a deep, immovable strength and an undivided sense of purpose.

All of the greatest teachers of Awakening have lived in this undivided way. They have been able to use the functionality of the ego as an everyday tool, without being "tooled" by the ego or anything else that is contracted. With each step and breath, the Enlightened among us are literally free of ego because they are consciously connected with something much bigger. They are informed by the infinitely expansive and unchanging Awareness that is beyond both the confines of time and the judgmental nature of mind. And because of this, their lives have the ability to open our hearts and minds to an amazing mystery.

Identification

Once you label me, you negate me.
—Søren Kirkegaard

The true value of a human being can be found in the degree
to which he has attained liberation from the self.
—Albert Einstein

One of the most interesting and powerful ways that attachment shows up in our interior landscape is through the process of identification. As we've discussed, the ego stays secure when it latches onto things that it perceives will offer it protection. The ego continually works to incorporate these things into its sense of both what it is and what it is not, and then building an identity out of these perceptions.

For example, consider any opinion that we might have. This opinion comes from our mind's bound sense of what it judges to be right or wrong, good or bad. The ego is only at home if it has something to either go after or something to avoid, so holding onto an opinion gives the ego a place to stay—a place that gives it an identity. If we take this a step further, we can see that when we attach to anything, be it a person, an ideology, a framework, a type of food, or a style of fashion, the seeds of identification are automatically sown. In other words, the more we cling to any viewpoint, preference, or position, the more threatened we become that we might lose it. The more threatened we become, the more defensive we get. The more defensive and protective we get, the more pain we eventually feel when we lose whatever we're fighting to keep. The more pain we feel, the more desperate we are to find relief. The more desperate we are to get out of our pain, the more aggressively we will do one of two things: reach for things that we think will make us feel better, or resist the things we think will make our circumstance worse. And so this cycle of suffering continues, endlessly turning from the moment we attach or identify with anything.

The Mask

When the ego's activity of identification begins to be exposed to a more expansive awareness within us, it begins to resist what it perceives as a loss of all it has worked so hard to achieve over the years. The more we pay attention to exactly what is going on, the more we begin to see that our identity, or personality, is simply a mask that we have learned to maintain in order to participate safely in the world. The word *persona*, in fact, is Greek for mask. Once we begin to gain some sense of how exactly we wear this persona, we begin to see that nearly all of our life we have been covering up and protecting ourselves against psychological threats by enhancing our mask's appearance and fitting it over us ever more securely. But as the altitude of our spiritual climb increases, we will find that we can more carefully study ego's actions and reactions. Once this shift in perspective occurs and the fire of our Awareness begins to increase in its intensity, the ego starts to sweat; not just because things get hot, but because the mask that it has been working on for so long starts to melt.

As this happens, the ego becomes more and more ingenious in its efforts to maintain the structural integrity of its mask. The ego will work to maintain the fit, position, and durability of its mask by identifying with anything that it sees as a useful tool. Perhaps it might be an idea, a group of like-minded people, or an object or belief structure it can imbue with meaning. Any thing might work to stave off what the ego sees as threatening to its sense of control. Whatever its choice, it will initiate a process of identification so it can metaphorically keep its mask in place, but as soon as its object of identification has outlived its usefulness, the ego will drop it and then identify with something else.

This process of "grab, use, and drop" is simply egoic exploitation. Since there is an unlimited amount of stuff with which one can identify and the mask always needs upgrading, the ego can always maintain some sense of job security. Consider anything in your life that you may feel strongly about: a political party or movement, a style of clothing, a type of stroller for your baby, a religion, a soccer team, or a social or family role that you might play. Each of these examples is a potential tool of identification that the ego can use to fortify its mask. The more fortification, the more the ego feels secure in its sense that it can keep the Infinite on the outside from busting in, and the Infinite on the inside from busting out. But as tastes, styles, and roles shift, the ego must adapt by finding yet more things with which to identify in order to keep its boundary sound.

This doesn't mean that our spiritual journey will leave us without a personality or sense of self. Our climb simply helps us understand how truly unimportant our wearing of any mask is. But the ego needs to guard against this realization if it wants to survive. In fact, one of the most important parts of the ego's job description is that it must act as a sentry or guard over the domain of the very boundaries that cause suffering. What would be left for ego if the only thing that really exists is an utter and total lack of boundary? A lack of separation? An absence of "in here" versus "out there"? The ego's fundamental work, its *raison d'etre*, is to establish and then keep fortifying all boundaries and guard against all threats to itself. As long as this contracted self, this ego, can categorize, criticize, and conquer, it remains in charge of our experience. And its mask remains firmly in place, blocking all threats through identification.

A common method of maintaining the mask shows up whenever the ego starts pulling our attention into the past or it pushes our attention into the future. This anchored position in time is what keeps us out of the present and in turn keeps us from opening to what is timeless and real in each of us. Uncovering what is timeless and real is helped along when we simply rest fully in the present without attaching to anything. Here is where the Infinite meets itself by breaking through whatever boundaries the ego has established. Yet the ego will never give up trying to sabotage this process by rooting itself safely in time. How often, for instance, do we have any mental experience that is not oriented toward something that has already happened? How often, for that matter, do we have any mental experience that is not oriented toward something that hasn't happened yet? In fact, the only activity the ego can engage in, other than to past and future, is an act of judgment. Explore this for yourself at any point by carefully noticing your thoughts. Any thought you might be able to recognize has its roots in one of three areas: past, future, or some type of evaluation. The only place where the past, the future, and judgments are totally irrelevant is in the space between our memories, plans, and judgments—a place we know as the present moment, or what we might also call "the Now". The spaciousness of the Now is exactly the point where ego's services relating to time and judgment aren't needed.

I see this process in action quite frequently. So often well-meaning people who proclaim their deepest longing to awaken, suddenly decide to change course the minute their egos recognize what's going on. Often, at the beginning of someone's practice, things are quite pleasurable. There may be a few rough meditations to start off, but soon things begin to settle down and then, often suddenly, along comes the bliss. Deep quietude begins to envelop their practice and they feel as if they've been invited to a party that they never felt worthy of attending. Enlightenment, it seems, is at hand, since stillness is now informing large percentages of their day. The only time they have problems with maintaining their seemingly infinite calm is in the presence of their mothers-in-law, or with their teenagers who have started dating someone with multiple piercings, or with their spouses who, after all these years, still can't get anywhere on time. In all other situations, however, peace reigns supreme.

But as these diligent souls continue to practice being still, certain things shift. Conflict with those closest to them may begin to settle down, but something even more difficult then shows up and this radically disturbs their practice. There is a profound realization that in order to go further up the Path, they must do more than just accept the distractions of others. They see that now they must start accepting themselves. Their egos, which were initially fully behind this process, now begin to revolt. These initially enthusiastic egos see that meditation practice is not just about feeling good; rather, it is about facing all aspects of life and staring, with full attention, into the mirror that reflects the mask that veils the Big Self. Over time, staring into this divine mirror renders our mask obsolete and exposes the raw truth of who we are; yet, the more we do this, the more the ego is relieved of its power. The ego sees this job loss as nothing short of its own death, and it will fight with everything it has in order to prevent the unsurpassed, penetrating, and perfect Enlightenment that it used to seek.

Another way that the ego can prevent Enlightenment is to hide behind various roles that it can play. Let's say, for example, that in life we are a parent, or a son, a lover, wife, teacher, or even a victim. Whatever the role might be, the ego can use it in order to filter any experience through its attachment to that role that it has built over time. In other words, the ego uses the layering, so to speak, of whatever role serves it best to further fortify its mask. This added structure prevents the Infinity we truly are from recognizing itself through any experience of the present moment. This is all precisely because the ego is still clinging to its own constructs and resists the Now.

Some years back I was in a relationship with a woman who considered herself to be spiritual. I thought this was fitting since I was coming to the same recognition in myself. Our seeking together made us, in my mind, somewhat of a "spiritual team," and being on a team could only speed up the process of finding the spiritual peace that we were seeking. Or so I thought.

It took some time before I sensed that something was wrong with our efforts. Both of us seemed to be reaching for the same goal, but our personalities were comfortable with different forms of spiritual identification. I liked the simplicity of Zen and wrapped myself in its practices, while she liked the magical nature of certain New Age practices and dove in to a community that didn't square with the way I felt my climb could best progress.

"Why can't you allow yourself to join in expressing Gaia's rhythm, seeking the wisdom she gives us through all parts of her earth body?" she once asked.

"Why can't you just sit still, be quiet, and stop looking for anything other than just this moment?" I replied.

My response didn't go over well. To her credit, she was doing the right thing for herself by sticking to what was comfortable for her, and looking back on it, I was doing the same. Getting out of this particular relationship was difficult since I liked the idea of connecting to someone with whom I could share a team identity, but ultimately our split offered a critical lesson. Our separation, and its grief, showed me that being "spiritual," looking for answers offered by either Gaia's wisdom or Zen's simplicity, is nothing other than a role to which our egos can cling—and a subtle one at that. My identity as a Zen student was an attachment.

So, too, was her identity as a student of Gaia's rhythm. Despite our best intentions to find Enlightenment the "correct way," we each explored the Path through eyes clouded by our attachments.

Each of our egos interpreted its spiritual practice from a limited perspective that was colored, enhanced, and then brought into focus by the roles our egos most liked. Whenever this happens, egos weave material with which they can then cloak themselves as they manage our walk along any spiritual path. In essence, the ego can protect itself from the Infinite offering of the present moment as long as it has convinced us that we are seekers. As seekers, we see Enlightenment as always being outside of our experience, which is exactly why we are seeking it. Since we are attached to the role of seeker, we consistently end up looking for an Enlightened revelation in exactly the wrong place: outside of ourselves, outside this very moment, and outside each of the experiences that are always arising.

This point is very important: as long as Enlightenment, or spiritual Awakening, is seen as outside of us, we will be forever blind to its grace. The cruel trick for those of us climbing the Mountain is that as long as we seek, the ego is in charge, and we are thus totally oblivious to the Divine Estate beyond the habitual limits of time, judgment, and identification. The longer we seek, the tighter and more ossified the ego's grip can get. With this hardening of the ego's grasp, we merely become more and more blind to what's real and true.

This blindness allows the desperate and skillful ego to assume the role of perpetual interpreter of all things, acting as if it knows what is true and what is false. Our ego thinks that it understands Enlightenment and the teachings that point toward it as well as those that point away from it. These enlightened egos can be seductive, since they often offer what the unsuspecting might consider to be wise interpretations of what the Buddha, Christ, the Mother, and countless other sages have said about the Path to Awakening. They even try to wear the sage's robes metaphorically since they identify so strongly with their teaching.

But even while the ego's interpretations may at times be inspiring and compelling, the conscious Awareness beyond all egoic attachment can't inform these interpretations with any authenticity because the ego is still doing its best to keep the Infinite out of its way. This is why, in spiritual work, we should bring a healthy sense of skepticism along with us. Even at their best, teachers with egos who think they are Awake offer only limited perspectives that are bound by the mind. But this type of guide cannot offer the conscious brilliance that informs teaching from the Absolute. This isn't only a problem for teachers, though. Watch for this even in your own experience as you climb, since many egos on the Path will eventually try to wear the Buddha's robe, working to become self-anointed agents of a falsely enlightened understanding.

Examples of this form of abuse can be seen in every tradition. Those who have been at the spiritual game the longest might be very knowledgeable of sacred texts. They may have mastered certain states of consciousness. But these successes often work to add strength to the egoic masks that need to be dropped in order for an authentic Awakening to flourish. The closer any of us comes to Awakening into the Big Self, regardless of time spent on the Path, the more the ego will get in the way of Enlightenment's fruition. As long as there are any threats to the ego's own survival, it has job security. And as long as it can keep its job by staying in the driver's seat of anyone's experience, it lives. Ironically, it stays in the driver's seat by making sure that it can constantly tend to all of the dangers on the road, both behind and in front of us.

Two Truths

Many teaching traditions speak of two kinds of truth: Absolute Truth, or what has been called the "Ultimate realm"; and the everyday truth, or what has been called the "circumstantial realm." Our day-to-day lives are filled with lots of ordinary circumstances. We get up, brush our teeth, change some diapers, get the paper, shower, feed the dog, and kiss those we love good-bye before we set off to work. Yet at the same time, our day-to-day lives are also filled with unquantifiable aspects of what we might call "Being" or "Spirit." This expansive aspect of our day-to-day living is totally beyond any human trapping of any kind, and yet Spirit is always already everywhere whether our minds recognize it or not.

But a conscious and continual recognition of Spirit doesn't necessarily come easily. We can always expect the ego to resist any incorporation of the Ultimate into its circumstances since the Ultimate is something it can't control, just like the clouds can't control the radiance of the sun. The clouds can temporarily diffuse the sun's light and some of its warmth, but they, like all circumstances, will eventually yield to what shines. So in the circumstantial sense we might say that it is cloudy, or that it is even raining, but in the Ultimate or expansive sense, we recognize that the sun is still shining.

Although both the rain and the sunshine are both "true," we tend to work hard to avoid the rain. In our life circumstance, our minds may be distracted by storms of resistance, indulgence, pain, pleasure, horror, excitement, desire, glory, or fear, among other things, but there is also a vast spacious radiance within us that transcends all of our personal feelings and perceptions. Like the sun, this simple spiritual grace never stops radiating light, no matter what storms are brought by our situation. It is always beyond any mind bound by circumstance.

Living as this light takes lots of practice, and can take a while to open through us. And sometimes we don't even see when the pointers are showing us the Path. After some years under the watchful eyes of my Zen teachers, I read an account of a teacher in another tradition who told his students that the presence we have in each of us that witnesses the mind is forever free of mind. This freedom from mind, he went on to say, is the realization of Truth. I remember being blown away by this, and I wondered why after all of the time in meditation, listening to Dharma talks, and conversing with fellow students, not one teacher had ever suggested this approach to me. When I asked one of my teachers about it, she smiled and then said, "Michael, while the words have been different, we've been saying this to you for some time."

As we uncover the Ultimate within our experience, we begin to practice leaving behind the things that we recognize as no longer useful on our climb, and we do this by giving our total attention to everything that arises in our moment-to-moment awareness. This awareness always points us in the right direction up the Mountain. For instance, when we pay close attention to whatever mental chatter we hear in our consciousness, which we can do at any time during the day or night, we begin to realize that we are not the chatter but that which is actually hearing the chatter. We start to ask ourselves just what is that part of us that is aware of this chatter? What is it that is aware of past and future? What is it that is aware of these thoughts, and these feelings? What is it that is aware of absolutely everything that arises in our consciousness?

The answers to these questions open us to the recognition that our thoughts and feelings are always there in our conventional circumstance, and yet they don't define the whole of who we truly are since there is always something there, watching the whole thing. No matter what we are paying attention to, there is a remainder of attention itself. Suddenly, all attachment to past and future, as well as everything with which we've ever identified, begins to be seen as little more than tiny ripples in a sea of freedom. In fact, we begin to see that the ego's attachments to all of our rippling thoughts and feelings supply it with all it needs in order to build an identity. The simple awareness of this unfolding drama, and the inner presence that can effortlessly watch our circumstances, is exactly what points us in the direction that all of history's sages have been pointing to for so long. Choosing this path offers us a radically different perspective—one that is sourced from and a conscious expression of Spirit.

The Stage of Mind

One practice that can help us become more conscious is to look at our typical, circumstantial condition by comparing it to a theatrical experience. Imagine that the stage in a theater is our "mind." On this stage of mind is a brilliant actor called the "ego." On this stage, the ego acts out a drama called the "life experience," or what we've referred to as our "circumstance," and it always does its best never to take a break because the actor can only be in control of circumstances if it is on stage delivering its lines convincingly. What's more, these lines come from a brilliant filing system that the ego has written and worked tirelessly over its lifetime to organize, so that no matter what circumstance arises, it can quickly access and cross-reference any script it might need in order for the production to stay relevant to whatever situation might arise. The ego is not only in charge of this theater of mind, but is also the protagonist of each tragedy and comedy. Moreover, it is the supporting cast as well as the director, the writer, the lighting and set designer, and the stage manager.

The drama that the ego produces can be long or short, deeply resonant or only superficially noticed. Whatever the case may be, it's important to realize that to the ego, every bit of every drama counts.

In fact, it acts from the conviction that any missed cue or forgotten line in any part of its performance means that it might be discovered as a phantom player acting out a scene that doesn't reflect anything other than its own partial version of a vast, incomprehensible reality. The ego knows that if it is ever seen in this way, it will be deemed as insubstantial and incomplete. So, to keep up the façade, at every moment it does everything it can to convince its audience that its production is not only believable, but the whole truth and nothing but the truth.

Continually producing these theatrical experiences might sound exhausting, but the ego has recognized that it can self-generate a boundless supply of energy from its attachments. In other words, as long as the ego can plug itself into to both the past and the future and identify with its judgments, the performance will be convincing. Stories anchored in our past, for example, give the ego an endless supply of templates for scripts relating to what it might like to either gain or avoid. Similarly, the future offers the ego the chance to project an unlimited array of potential outcomes onto the life experience. These unlimited potentials also impel the ego to act out forms of greed or aversion, which inevitably produce anxiety, stress, fear, and sometimes paralyzing panic. They all create great drama and allow the ego to evaluate and grasp all the things that will assist it in generating a great theatrical experience.

A woman from a sitting group that I was leading some years back asked me, "How then do I use this practice to deal with my daughters' college admission process?" She seemed consumed by the circumstances surrounding this series of tasks. She went into great detail, telling me what needed to be done before her daughter could apply to her first-choice school, and I could tell by the tone in her voice that she felt the stakes were high. The mother appeared so caught by the circumstances that she and her daughter were facing, yet the more she and I talked, the more it became clear that the mother and daughter differed in their views as to what school should be chosen. And this was generating some suffering for everyone involved.

"What do you find yourself attaching to?" I asked the mother.

"I don't want my daughter to make the same mistakes that I did when I was her age," she said. "I had no encouragement and as a result, I sold myself short. So I guess that means that I'm clinging to a future outcome for my daughter."

While this was only part of the story, it was huge for her to realize this. Her ego was busy at both ends of the stage, so to speak, trying to keep a reoccurrence of her past from happening by attaching to a future outcome for her daughter. Great scripts, great drama. As the mother began to see this, the stage play began to carry less weight for her. It took time and considerable attention on her part, but both mother and daughter were able to have more meaningful dialog once neither one of them was limited by attachments to the other's past and future as well as her own. As it turned out, the girl chose a school that her mother never would have picked. Currently, the daughter is pursuing her doctorate, and her mother is quite proud.

Of course, not all stories turn out so nicely. As we all know, life circumstances are often messy and confusing. Regardless of this, as we climb higher on the Mountain of Spirit and we begin to enter the stream of Awakening, we become aware of the ever-present audience that watches the events unfold on stage and couldn't care less whether things are messy or neat. It just watches. This audience of our ego's show can be equated with what Buddhists call our True Nature, or our Original Face, or our Big Self. This audience is a relaxed, non-judgmental, and open presence that reveals itself as an unattached, and therefore enlightened, perspective. Instead of being caught by, and believing in, the ego's portrayal of circumstance, the audience just watches the drama unfold just like a mirror reflects images put before it. This watching produces a shift from a small self orientation to a Big Self, witnessing awareness. Any of us can experience this shift if we can fearlessly be present enough in our lives to watch all of the unfolding drama without trying to adjust or modify any of it.

Perhaps there is no other situation better suited to support this shift than an extended meditation retreat. My first experience with a seven-day Zen retreat, or *sesshin*, was more than a little unnerving. I was crammed in a little dorm-style room with two other guys, both of whom snored loudly; the gentleman to my left in the meditation hall was a mouth-breather who always sounded like he was eating a banana with his mouth open; and there was a woman across the zendo who would sob whenever we were served rice during meals. This crying lady would then gag on whatever food she had in her mouth between sobs. This generated tension among those of us trying to focus on our food. Of course, this retreat was in silence, so I didn't want to say anything to anyone about the distractions, least of all the people offering them.

Instead, all I could really do was watch what was going on within me as their activity was expressed. At first, the experience was maddening. I would ask myself why they all couldn't just respect what all of us who were following the rules and being silent were doing? Couldn't the guy next to me keep his mouth closed and breathe through his nose? Couldn't the sobbing lady just toughen up a little? It's only rice, for Buddha's sake. Is there a medical name for this kind of attachment? Couldn't everyone keep their rattling slumber, their slurping, and their overly-dramatic impulses to themselves so that I might enjoy a little peace and quiet on my cushion?

After three days of this, something shifted. The snoring kept on, the mouth kept salivating and smacking with each breath, and the rice still brought forth sobs and gagging. None of it ever abated, but my relationship to all of it changed. The moment that I let go of any notion of modifying or changing my situation, the shift occurred. As long as I accepted the fullness of each distraction as nothing more than something to watch on the Stage of Mind, and as long as I didn't try to change any part of it, the shift from actor to audience, from small self to Big Self, was expressed abundantly. Looking back on it, I consider these people some of the greatest teachers I've had along the Path. My resistance to their behaviors was a simple expression of my unconsciousness. Having each of them to help me see this gave me and everyone else in the meditation hall a chance to climb a little higher up the Mountain.

Grasping 2

If a man owns land, the land owns him.
—Ralph Waldo Emerson

One does not err by perceiving, one errs by clinging; but knowing
clinging itself as mind, it frees itself.
—Zen saying

As our climb up the Mountain of Spirit progresses, some things begin to stand out. First of all, we recognize how our small self works to keep its distance from the broader sense of the Infinite that we call the Big Self so that it can maintain a sense of control. Secondly, the higher we climb, the more we learn that simply watching our small self in action helps us to become aware of its mechanisms of attachment. These mechanisms show themselves as craving and resistance, both of which are simply two faces of the same coin we call grasping.

Buddhist teaching tells us that if we aren't conscious and accepting of the vast, interdependent, temporary, and totally infinite nature of everything in our lives, then our small selves will naturally grasp at things that arise in our experiences. This happens because our small selves always feel threatened by the chaos that shows up in life, so they grasp at anything they believe will help steady them and defend their positions of perceived power. Despite the fact that these acts of attachment appear to be pretty normal, they are what generate our suffering. This is because as we exhaust ourselves grasping onto a great unreality that holds the material world as the only truth there is, when in fact there is infinitely more to the story. Yes, we have relationships to possessions, ideas, and loved ones that we may cherish dearly. None of these things are much of a problem in and of themselves. But our egos grasp at these things in the attempt to make them permanent, and this always fails. Nothing is ever permanent, so any attempt to establish permanence will be forcibly undone eventually. This means there is no such thing as ultimate security. Too bad for the small self, whose job it is to grasp for things that will make it feel like it can establish ultimate security. Attachment is the small self's sole purpose for being, and attachment causes our suffering. This means that unless we consciously awaken out of these unwholesome habitual patterns, each of us is doomed to repeat all of our old cycles of unfulfilling action and reaction that we've experienced in our lives.

A teacher of mine once gave a talk about this subject right about the time I began meditating regularly with a group. I remember one Sunday morning sitting still for forty minutes in a packed meditation hall. The distractions were enormous but I did my best to stick it out. It was very cold, and the talk that this diminutive woman was giving made little sense to me.

"All of our pain and suffering, arises out of our attachment to things," she said. Her talk kept repeating this phrase with slight variations. "Your clinging to comfort is what fuels your pain," she said. "If you are avoiding a situation," she went on, "you are simply grasping for something other than that situation." For more than an hour, she kept hammering this point home. "So watch your grasping, especially as it takes its form in craving and resistance," she said. "Watching your craving and resistance frees you of it." This seemed to be her prescription to all of us.

At the time, I was busy setting a foundation for an entire life of attaching to goals and clinging to outcomes, so her words didn't resonate with me at all. I remember thinking that nonattachment might not be so hard if we were able to live in a monastery. Real life, on the other hand, was all about attaching to goals and clinging to whatever might help realize them. Plus, this woman's ideas of not grasping seemed like an excuse for avoiding what was going on in the world, and I didn't want any part of a tradition that didn't focus its energies, actions, and teachings on making the world a better place. Blissing out on one's cushion seemed to invite more injustice and pain. I didn't see how any of us could change the world without clinging to, and fighting for, the things that would make it better.

I felt my mind begin to justify my resistance to what I'd experienced that day during the meditation as well as to what she was saying. Why did I need any person to tell me to "let go" when I was trying so hard to hang on? Besides, what about those distractions during meditation? In addition to this teacher's confusing and, what seemed to me, uninspiring words, the sitting period before her talk was filled with distracting challenges like the cries of children, what sounded like a cat in heat near one of the exits, and a gigantic man sitting behind me who kept directing his sneezing fits at the back of my neck. Perhaps worst of all, the woman sitting to my left was absolutely beautiful and smelled like lightly perfumed, French-milled soap. For much of the sitting, I expended a fair amount of energy fantasizing about how I might ask her out. Where might we go on our date? Is she vegan? Can she dance? Does she have a sense of humor? Is she even single?

At first I seriously doubted that I'd found anything of value on this day in Marin, but as usual, on my drive back to Berkeley, I heard the Zen master's talk rattling in my head. In fact, for weeks I kept thinking about how my whole life was little more than greed and aversion. By her definition, I was grasping at nearly everything in my life. Could this explain why I always felt that despite my successes, something always seemed to be missing? Maybe the Zen master was on to something that I just couldn't comprehend. Maybe she was right, and my small self was fighting to defend its position. Regardless, I was hooked.

A deep longing to walk an authentic spiritual path was born in me around that time. Taking those first few steps allowed for several surprising and wonderful things to show up, perhaps none more important than recognizing that the Zen master was right that "all of our pain and suffering, arises out of our egoic attachment to things." Such power expressed so simply. Of course it took years of study and stillness for me to even begin to recognize what she meant. But despite the hard work, I kept at it. Every time I thought about giving up the climb, something miraculously showed up to entice a few more steps out of me. Sometimes it was something I read that inspired me; other times it was words of encouragement from friends I'd met along the Path; still other times it was direction offered by one or another of what became an amazing stable of teachers. I can't really explain it, but the higher the climb got, the more the summit seemed to come as a secondary wish to the primacy of climbing. Maybe I'd get to the top, maybe I wouldn't. Either craving or resisting the summit would keep Awakening inaccessible, or so they told me. So over time I just began to continually practice receiving the open invitation to live each moment as consciously as possible.

Craving

> *Every form of addiction is bad, no matter whether the narcotic be*
> *alcohol, morphine or idealism.*
> —*Carl Jung*

> *The newer people, of this modern age, are more eager to amass*
> *than to realize.*
> —*Rabindranath Tagore*

Our unconscious habits develop from our inability to experience and accept things for what they truly are. We might, for instance, make ourselves coffee when we wake up each morning, but if this activity is merely a habit, we are unplugged from the miracle of the whole experience. Do we notice the weather outside in the morning? How about what it feels like inside our home? Are we aware of the sounds at play around us? The sound of the coffee dripping into the pot? The songs of the birds outside our window? Are we aware of the silence between the sounds? Can we truly notice the smell of what we're pouring into our cup? Can we openly consider how the whole experience came to us in this moment? Do we feel gratitude for those who picked the beans? Gratitude for the sun and the rain that allowed them to grow? Can we taste all of this as we sip our hot morning drink? Are we truly thankful for this brand new day, guaranteed to be filled with mystery and possibility? Maybe we are. Then again, maybe we aren't. Maybe we'd rather slog down the coffee in order to stave off the deep urge to get back into bed.

Regardless, if we plug into the mystery and powerful nature of this inherently chaotic Universe, the ego's sense of control gets overwhelmed. This is because the Universe's activity is impossible for the ego to manage, just like it's impossible for a child to get the world to obey its commands.

Of course, just like the child, the ego can pretend all it wants, but when we climb the Mountain of Spirit, something in us starts to see the folly of ego. Once this happens, the ego's managerial position is radically diminished.

In order to prevent its loss of stature, the ego creates systems and structures of habit and repetition that it believes will prevent it from being overwhelmed. As we discussed in the last chapter, one of the ego's perpetual charges is to fill our lives with pleasure and keep out all of the pain, even though the ego's attachment to this task is exactly what generates pain in the first place. This inadvertent fueling of suffering happens because whenever we experience pleasure, at some point we sense that it will be a temporary event. From here, the ego immediately begins grasping at whatever it thinks will ensure that the pleasure continues. The problem is that pleasure can't perpetually continue, no matter how much any ego might want this to be true. All things change over time, and suffering will always eventually arise out of any opposition to this natural aspect of life.

Take, for example, our experiences with good food and drink. No matter how we try to keep the pleasure of good food and drink going, it eventually ends. We get too full, or too drunk, or both. If we deny the physical limits of our bodies in order to keep the pleasure going, and we keep eating and drinking, nature has a way of violently reversing our indulgence. On the other hand, if we recognize the temporary nature of our meal, if we fully realize that we ultimately have to let it go, we have a chance to get beyond our craving and rest in a spaciousness that is always and forever fulfilled. Becoming intimate with our dining experience allows each bite of our food and each sip of our wine to be enlivened with an open sense of wonder and awe. Some restaurants help this realization along by serving us slowly and in stages, allowing us to take in the experience of our food and drink with our whole being. Some families approach meals in the same way at home: with care, and a mindful intention that allows the meal to support not only our physical body's needs, but also our spiritual connection to the miracle of food and the blessing bestowed upon all of us when we share it with others.

The same kind of non-grasping that we can apply to our eating can just as easily be applied to our meditation practice. It's always nice, for example to have one of those meditation sessions that really puts us at peace. But do we attempt to hang onto the feeling? For that matter, do we try to avoid the more difficult periods of stillness where we can't seem to escape, say, a bad memory, or pain in the body? Whether we are having an experience of all-encompassing bliss, or we are mired in negative feelings while we sit, the ego will crave for less of the negativity and for more of the bliss. This is natural enough, but in the craving of the bliss the seeds of suffering are sown, since the bliss can't be maintained perpetually. Bliss, like all other feelings, is temporary.

"Moving toward what you like," another one of my teachers used to tell me, "or moving away from what you dislike are the same move." This particular priest had a way about her that put everyone at ease. I loved her for this. In the face of so much seriousness around the Zen community, she offered smiles that could light up the night.

"Comfort and discomfort are temporary states," she would always say. "They, like everything else, will fade away. So get right in there with all of it, as best you can, again and again, with total relaxation. Do this continually and know that in that still space that notices your state, the potential for deep realization will offer itself to each of us."

While I liked the sound of her words, I always felt like telling her that sometimes things hurt and you want to avoid them. But I kept quiet and followed her advice to see if just sucking it up would lead to what I hoped would be an actual experience of what she described. In time I saw that she, and all those before her who had said the same thing, were right. Honestly recognizing that both bliss and discomfort are temporary states frees us from fearing the loss of anything.

"Get over it," she'd say with a laugh. "Whatever it might be. Get over it, and get real. Don't deny it, just let it go, again and again. You can't keep anything anyway. Again, whatever it is will eventually be gone. So take responsibility for the way you relate to this fact, process it, deal with it, and then when you're ready, let the whole thing go. Nothing lasts! This is one of the great Laws of the Universe; one of the great Truths of Buddha's teaching. In trying to find a creative way to break this Law, we realize that the Universe always wins. Always. Fighting this law is the reason why we suffer."

As harsh as her words sounded, it was an incredible offering. After more and more hours on the meditation cushion, it also seemed that pleasure and pain were tied together. Whatever pleasure I felt, I wanted to keep, and yet I knew that I had to "get over" the fact that the Universe was going to take it from me. This recognition brought disappointment and pain. It was as though right underneath the pleasure, pain was lurking. But then when I looked at the pain with all of the awareness I could muster, I kept seeing that the Universe was going to take all of my discomfort away, too. There came a time when I decided to ask the teacher about this one directly.

"So pleasure and pain are connected, aren't they?" I asked

"Pleasure and pain are born together out of the same Infinity," she beamed. "They coexist and are co-connected, like everything else. They're like conjoined twins of experience."

It was a disturbing image but it made sense. I then asked, "Okay, then once I see this truth, what's next?"

"You mean what's the next thing to grasp?" she asked with a devilish grin.

She had caught me. I didn't even see it coming. I could actually feel a craving within me. I felt as if I was on to something, and I desperately wanted to know more. Then again, I was conditioned to crave. I'd been doing it since I was a little kid. Craving helped get me my first real date in high school, just like it got me through college. *Does it ever stop?* I wondered to myself. *Do I even want it to stop?*

"Just practice noticing your grasp," she said with tenderness. "This is what will allow you to open to what is beyond suffering. Knowing that which is beyond suffering supports steadiness and peace in your life."

"So what about craving Enlightenment?" I asked. "Isn't that why all of us are here at the Zen Center?"

"Maybe," she nodded. "But know that the craving itself isn't bad or good. Nor is craving something you are trying to get rid of." She paused and smiled again—she could tell I was frustrated. "We should simply be aware of our craving in whatever form it takes, be it mild or intense. That's what we practice. And this practice is exactly what loosens the ties that bind us."

"Fine. Then what about someone addicted to something?" I asked, recognizing that a fire had been lit inside of me. "Are you suggesting that they not try to quit their habit?"

I had only experienced addiction on the level of a six-month long smoking habit several years earlier, but quitting was a miserable exercise in self-control. I didn't know much about the Dharma that this priest was offering me, but I knew enough about my experience to be convinced that just watching my misery wouldn't have made the misery of kicking the habit any more bearable.

"When our craving becomes unbalanced to the point where it cannot be observed in our experience, it becomes pathological," she said. "This is what we refer to as addiction."

She then took a deep breath and closed her eyes, as if she had decided to meditate in the middle of our discussion. After a few seconds, her eyes opened.

"Whenever we refuse to face our circumstances," she continued, "we begin to rely on our cravings and addictions to insulate us from feeling what's really going on. We may cling to drugs, alcohol, sex, shopping, codependent behaviors, eating, mastering a particular topic, music, spiritual practices, or any other behavior or conviction that we habitually turn to in order to keep us from the uncertainty that the Universe is actually giving us at each moment. In this space of perpetual grasping, we live lives that revolve around addiction. If we look carefully enough, we can see that each addiction begins and then ends in a place of pain. Every single time."

"Yeah, but just watching your pain doesn't stop it. I can't imagine telling someone deeply addicted to something to get near the pain, watch it, and you'll be fine."

"You're right," she laughed. "And if you told me that when I was trying to quit smoking all those years ago I might have gotten off of my Harley and punched you."

The thought of her on a motorcycle distracted me for a moment.

"No doubt," she continued, "some addictions deserve extra attention and should get extra care. But after dealing with the most obvious levels of addiction, our meditation practice can help us uncover our avoidances at the subtle levels. Watching our pain won't keep it from us, but it will change the way we meet it. Watching our pain changes our relationship to it by keeping us from getting caught by it."

"Okay," I said, still trying to shake the image of this lady as a biker, "but I've seen it happen that well meaning people around this temple seem to become addicted to, or caught by, their practice of Buddhism."

I knew I was beginning to stand on shaky ground here since she was one of the senior priests, but rather than glaring at me as if I'd cast an insult, her smile broadened and her head nodded slowly.

"People often grasp the forms, scriptures, and rituals," she said, "in my view becoming one-sided in their approach to the Buddha's teaching."

This seemed interesting. Rather than defend what I saw as her life's work, she openly questioned it with me.

"And in the process of their grasping, practitioners will lose two things," she said.

I just stared back at her, listening intently.

"Practitioners of any faith," she continued, "who are addicted to their tradition first lose their balance along the Path and then fall. Things get ugly for them, and they feel even more lost than when they started with their practice. It can be a real mess. Second, people who are addicted to their tradition lose the opportunity for Enlightenment. They become religious; closed down by the mind's interpretation of texts; addicted to ritual, instead of letting forms and ceremonies show us how the mundane is also sacred. They get caught in a cycle of becoming good Buddhists instead of becoming actual Buddhas; or becoming good Christians, instead of becoming Christs."

Her words seemed to put everything into an elegant context: the barbs of our craving can't snag us as long as we're fully aware them. Still, I knew I shouldn't cling to any of what she said. We chatted a bit more. We even talked about the San Francisco Giants' post-season chances that fall. Bowing to her as I left, I felt so fortunate. Just to be able to have this kind of conversation was nice enough, but as I walked back to the meditation hall, the temple grounds seemed to speak the colorful language of autumn. Everything about this moment seemed over-the-top gorgeous. Of course, I did my best to watch how much I craved for more days like this in the future. I entered the zendo and got back on my cushion with tremendous hope. *Be fearless in the non-grasping*, I thought. The priest hadn't been afraid of my questions, and I could tell that she recognized some of the hypocrisy that I'd noticed. It didn't scare her—it seemed like nothing did. She didn't grasp at anything. Maybe that was her greatest gift—to be so devoid of grasping, so totally fearless, so totally comfortable with the way things are.

The Most Basic Negotiation

Unfortunately, none of us can truly give of ourselves as long as the ego is attached to any of our activity. This is because any activity sourced from the ego will always play itself out as a giving for the sake of getting something in return. The moment this happens, unity gives way to separation as a result of our craving for something other than what we already have. In other words, rather than giving freely from a place of deeply surrendered recognition that all things are a simple interconnected Oneness, ego turns the situation into a basic negotiation.

For example, the ego thinks to itself, "I'll give you this so I will gain your favor." Or, "I'll donate this so that I can avoid feeling guilty." While neither of these two statements will normally be expressed overtly, they are often a subtle reality that prevents the expression of true giving, of true compassion, since the ego is looking to get something in return for its offering—either more praise or less guilt. At their core, these actions are about getting rather than giving. Because of this, well-intentioned giving is often only partial in its expression.

We do stuff like this all the time and convince ourselves that we are behaving in what we consider to be compassionate ways. Yet, authentic compassion arises only if there is no expectation, no wanting, and no craving of any "gain" in relation to giving. As a rule of thumb, notice if there is any craving for yourself in any situation where you find the opportunity to give. If any personal gain informs any of your giving, your ego co-opts what could be a purely compassionate expression and transforms it into something that veils the Infinite from your experience.

This issue came up in a discussion I had with one of my meditation students. In our exchange I was made aware of how strongly this particular lady felt about getting thank you notes. It was around the holidays, and she brought up the issue of manners and how important it is for kids to learn them. I happen to agree that manners, and written expressions of gratitude, are important ways for us to show we care about other people and their efforts of kindness. But I was most interested in the lady's personal sense of being slighted after not getting what she wanted after her acts of generosity.

"So when you didn't get the thank you note from your grandson, you felt let down?" I asked.

"Of course," she said. "I felt let down by my daughter for not teaching him to write notes like I'd taught her to do when she was young. And when I don't get the slightest recognition for a gift, it makes me not want to give as much in the future."

I could tell this was important to her. The script, in other words, that her ego was delivering so eloquently on her Stage of Mind came from a deep place.

"So where is the grasping in all of this for you?" I asked.

She paused, looked at the floor for a moment, and then took a very deep breath. Her lower lip quivered slightly, then she said, "I want to feel love reflected back to me when I give it—I guess I'm attached to that feeling. I always seem to want more of it. Or maybe I want to avoid feeling unloved. I don't know."

I sat silently looking at her.

"I guess," she said slowly, "that's pretty much my small self running amok, isn't it?" She smiled. "When I look at it now, it seems that expectation is always in there when I offer gifts. I always want to get something back. And that's not giving, is it?"

"Sure it is. It's just that it's partial giving rather than complete giving," I said.

"It's negotiation," she said, eyes wide.

"You think?" I asked her, knowing that she was uncovering a great insight.

"Yes, and negotiation is like a cooperative way of grasping," she paused. Then, after a moment she nodded saying, "My small self seems to need them to show their love for me in a certain way."

Her gaze then met mine. She said, "Can't get more egotistical than that."

We sat in silence together for a few more minutes. Before she got up, we bowed to each other. Whether she knew it or not, she had just climbed much higher up the Mountain.

Near Enemies

The more we become aware of ego's activity, the less important its drama becomes. Climbing higher, we are reminded continually that the ego is rooted in self-concern rather than generosity. Seeing this for what it is allows for us to make increasingly selfless choices. In making deeply selfless decisions we take power from the ego, and then notice that the less power the ego has, the less that the drama being played out on the Stage of Mind matters. Rather than identifying with the actors on the Stage, we begin to notice that our essence is actually the audience of the charade. From here the Big Self, or the Witness, begins to unfold as an unattached awareness of our experience, and here we can then become more acutely aware of ego's very subtle attempts at controlling what might otherwise be genuine spiritual realization.

For example, instead of experiencing an authentic loving kindness for another person, ego can skillfully disguise this wholesome event as an attachment, and attachments are the "enemy" of Awakening. This egoic deception shows up all the time in romantic relationships when feelings of what we might know to be unconditional, boundless, and freely felt love yield to conditional feelings of clinging, jealousy, fear, and at times even hatred. Like we've discussed, this conditional love is simply a negotiation of limits between egos: a *quid pro quo*, where one ego only gives of itself if another ego gives it what will secure its position of control. Any time we sense this negotiation arise, the ego is inhibiting what might otherwise be an opportunity for Awakening. Whenever feelings are actually rooted in an egoic desire, they can become disguised versions of what we might ordinarily see as pure and wholesome. The Buddhist tradition calls these disguised expressions "near enemies." The near enemy of true love, for instance, is conditional love. The near enemy of true compassion is pity, the near enemy of sympathetic joy is comparison, and the near enemy of equanimity is indifference. Becoming aware of near enemies can be a challenge, since, for so many of us, we operate in this space of subtlety without knowing it.

As an example, ego separates us from our boundless nature when, instead of experiencing an unadulterated sense of compassion for a person, we instead feel the near enemy of pity for them. Consider a friend who has gone through a tragedy. It is normal to feel pity for them. You are sorry for their loss, but at the same time, there is something that is glad that this loss was something that you didn't have to endure. Your friend's experience of tragedy is sensed as being separate from your not-so-tragic experience, which allows for *you* to feel sorry for *them*. In the space between you and them, the ego still manages to stay in charge, allowing for pity to arise. Put another way, pity can only exist if we attach to the sense that someone else is having a bad experience while we are not. Ego has us believing that we are separate, in general, from others, and that we are separate, specifically, from other people's pain. So when we feel separate from another's experience of pain, ego can get us to a place of feeling pity.

But when an Awakening spawns a boundless connection to all beings, another's pain is no longer experienced as being separate from our own. When we realize our connectivity to everyone, we see that instead of pity arising, compassion springs forth effortlessly from all of our activity. We become opened to the world not only through others' pain, but through their happiness as well. Walking this talk means that we see ourselves in every aspect of everyone else. Another being's pain is our own. We see their situation as one that is ultimately inseparable from our own, so our responses to their circumstances become filled with a much broader, selfless interest than if we were acting to simply alleviate their personal sense of pain.

"Until he extends his circle of compassion," writes Albert Schweitzer, "to include all living things, man will not himself find peace." If we truly recognize our connection to everything beyond an intellectual understanding, we can't help but live the peace we seek. We begin to feel and openly meet every bit of the world. In fact, the higher we climb, the more we can feel. The more we can feel, the more we can empathize with all other beings. The more we can empathize, the more we can see how all beings are simply doing the best they can to get their needs met. This simple observation unifies all of life, and frees up an undivided sense of our place within its flow. Our dealings with those who cross us or those who cross others we care about can be met with greater openness and sensitivity. While they may indeed hurt more than when we lived solely from ego-based separation, we no longer cling to this hurt. This non-clinging frees up our responses to any perceived injustice in ways that are sourced from love rather than fear.

Just as Awakening shows us that we share in each others' pain, it also shows us that others' experience of happiness is ultimately shared as well. However, the ego often does an amazing job of getting in the way of this whole process once it starts to compare and contrast itself with others. All too often, our egos see another's joy as something that it needs for itself; something for which to compete; something to earn, and then covet; something to own. When this happens, there is no room for Enlightenment to unfold, and we radically diminish our ability to live with any kind of true or lasting contentment. When we live lives of comparison we are always trying to keep up, or keep away, from others, which makes the peace of a shared, sympathetic joy impossible. We rush and push for the next object, achievement, or success that might make us feel that much more complete. Instead of recognizing our inherent completion, as we are in this moment, we stay busy keeping score against those with whom we share the life and death experience.

I have a childhood friend whose father always impressed me. He drove the coolest cars, designed and built the most amazing house, and was the most accomplished athlete of any other dad I knew. He was well-traveled, charismatic, brilliant, and infectiously fun to be around. And yet he always seemed so preoccupied with adding more to his life. I remember hearing for the first time the phrase, "keeping up with the Joneses," and thinking to myself that this guy was the King of All Joneses; the High Scorer of Suburban One-Upmanship. His purchases and way of life allowed him to be the standard bearer for our local leisure class, until suddenly, some years later, it all came crashing down. His marriage fell apart, and shortly thereafter he lost his business. All that he had built had disappeared, his score showing itself to be zero.

I ran into him at a café, shortly after he started to collect the pieces of his life and reshape them into something more stable.

"The amazing thing," he said, "is that I'm okay." He then paused, sipped his coffee. "I mean I can't buy the things that I used to, and I'm single for the first time in nearly thirty years, but I can't believe that I feel okay about the whole thing."

I confess that in my egocentric twenty-something nature, I was confused. How do you feel okay about having it all and then losing it all?

I didn't want to put it like that because this was the last guy I wanted to offend. He still had that flash in his grin and despite his circumstances, I was enchanted by his presence just as I had been as a kid. But how does anyone feel "okay" about a situation like his?

"I know that must sound weird," he answered as if reading my mind, "but I'm free of the whole silly game. So now there's no need for scorekeeping."

What a great place that must be. I was amazed at the peace on his face, and even more amazed at the conversations that he and I started having on regular intervals. This former MVP of Conspicuous Consumption became one of my first spiritual guides. Sometimes a few days apart, sometimes months apart, he and I would meet in various spots in the East Bay to discuss life and philosophy as we read contemporary and ancient spiritual texts together. And to this day, the relationship he and I have continues, with our scores each remaining at zero.

And yet this "scorelessness" in no way means that we should avoid caring about anything and start to unplug ourselves from life's vibrancy. In an "unplugged" relationship to life we find yet another, perhaps pathological, category of egoic clinging. Rather than finding balance and equanimity in the midst of life's offerings, the ego can get us into a place of withdrawal and indifference. This lack of caring is in fact ego's clever way of reacting to its basic fear of losing its position of power. The scoreless nature of Enlightenment necessitates the deeply intimate participation in all of life's offerings, no matter what they might be. Rather than encouraging a withdrawal, Enlightenment necessitates participation. In fact, withdrawal defines the subtle motion that keeps Enlightenment from being realized. Ego, in other words, can stay in charge as long as it can claim indifference to anything from which it withdraws.

I experienced a version of this withdrawal first hand at a monastery in Asia. "I'm here to leave the whole world behind," I remember one earnest, middle-aged monk telling me. "I want to realize Enlightenment, and then rest in that space for the benefit of all beings," he added in a wonderfully rich accent with smiles in his eyes. His wish sounded good enough, and his story was an interesting one. He was a father of two and used to be a bartender at an upscale restaurant in Singapore. He went on to tell me that he could no longer remain happy with the distractions of parenthood, sex, drugs, and alcohol. I was a little taken aback at his choice to leave so much of his life behind and asked if he, at least, missed his kids.

"Every minute, and I want not to care anymore," he replied. After a moment he gave a little sigh then told me that he "needed to get rid of all attachments in order to get to real peace."

Living in a monastery is one of the many ways we might look for Enlightenment, but regardless of our location or environment we won't find any equanimity, or evenness of mind, if we simply withdraw from our lives. Avoidance is the same move as greed; it just moves in the opposite direction. Enlightenment therefore only comes to those people who can uncover the stillness that is always and already present in the midst of their busy lives. This is accomplished only when we stop avoiding whatever our current experience might be.

Practicing this can be a challenge, since we're used to avoiding things in life. What's more, as we begin to see how the ego subtly gets involved in helping us avoid the fact that we are deeply connected with all things, we often can get overwhelmed. To make this simple, remember that the near enemies—conditional love, pity, comparison, and indifference—are decent enough impulses, but ones that are still diminished by the ego's need to either gain or avoid. Freeing ourselves from these traps requires us to stay, once again, in the audience of the Stage of Mind rather than getting caught by the ego's drama. We can feel this catch whenever we sense a division arise in our consciousness; where we can feel the dualism of "in here" as opposed to "out there," "me" as opposed to "all of us," which only reaffirms the ego's attachment to separation. The ego must maintain this wedge between itself and everything else, or it will be seen as irrelevant. Maintaining this wedge is important because if everything is seen as One, there is no need to defend the illusion of separation. This doesn't mean that we Awaken whenever we become so deeply absorbed in an experience that we lose our sense of personhood. If this were the case, then the unconsciousness associated with drunkenness might lead to much more than embarrassment and bad headaches. Instead, Enlightenment is realized when, and only when, we participate totally, in all of our situations, from a place of conscious Unity with all things, where there is never any division. The moment this is realized, ego is out of work, and the delusion ends.

Becoming aware of ego's moves, no matter how stealthy and subtle they might be, allows us to begin the experience of deep purification as we incorporate an observing, witnessing orientation into each and every aspect of our day-to-day lives. Love is no longer conditional. Instead, it is experienced as a continual, egoless, spiritual surrender into Infinity. Pity is no longer central to our reaction to others' pain. Instead, compassion arises as a felt sense of deep, tender connection with all beings in the universally shared experience of birth and death. As this opening in us continues to unfold, any person's joy begins to fuel our own since, in this Ultimate sense, it is our own. And so is everything else. All things are not separate from us. They are us, and the steadiness that comes from this realization allows for a profoundly powerful manifestation of equanimity to occupy our consciousness in this very life. From this peaceful presence, we can begin to trust in the Infinite's ability to show up continually as the loving and joyous stillness that lies underneath all experience.

Body, Mind and Soul

The body, mind, and soul are also seen as separate entities by the ego, even though they, like everything else, are actually aspects of the same Infinity. Body is our personally felt physical vessel of the infinity of Spirit in this world of form. Mind is our personally felt conceptual vessel of Spirit in this world of form. Soul is our personally felt sense of Spirit in this world of form. So body, mind, and soul are all actually personal attachments within the deeper context of a single, impersonal Spirit, in the same way that human faces are all essentially slight variations on a single, impersonal face. So a more complete picture might be to suggest that all things are simultaneously distinct and at the same time part of the deep singularity of the All.

Recognizing this simultaneous separation and union usually leads us straight into the heart of one of the great contemplative Big Questions: "Who am I?" There isn't a standard way of answering this question that has ever satisfied human curiosity. But through this kind of questioning we can uncover who, or even better, what we are not. The desires of the body and the thoughts of the mind, as well as the experiences of the soul, are part of "I's" experience, but they are not really "I." The real "I" is a radiant interplay of all these separate things that are ultimately never separate from the infinity of Spirit. Your body, for instance, may feel pain, or your mind may wrestle with thoughts of alienation, or your soul may intuit a great disconnect, but these perceptions are not "I," they are simply perceptions felt by a thing we call "I."

"So what is the real 'I' then?" I once asked a Hindu teacher who was sitting on the steps of a temple in Bhaktapur, Nepal. I was told this particular person was a "real" master by one of the locals, so I figured I would ask him a tough question to get things rolling.

He turned toward me, leaned in close and said, "The real 'I' is located where your question comes from."

I had no idea what he meant. It must have showed, since he pointed his finger at my face and chuckled, revealing to me and the rest of the world a mouth with only a few teeth. I couldn't help but smile back, but I was frustrated. I had always been able to do pretty well when it came to figuring stuff out and getting some type of intellectual understanding of things. But this whole Dharma thing, this spiritual quest, was kicking me pretty hard. I just couldn't grasp it.

The Hindu on the steps had nothing else to say to me on that day. But I learned from our exchange that not grasping meant not getting in the way of the questioning. This is the whole point of the work. The core of the teaching can't be grasped with the mind or anything else, and the realization of this points us in the direction of a profound truth that any of us can uncover regardless of our IQ score. Think of these questions: If you can observe any disturbance or any bliss in the body, the mind, or the soul, then what is doing the observing? What is it that observes the perceptions of body, mind, and soul in the first place? Quick answers from sharp intellects don't really have much relevance here since they are simply interpretations of what the mind is thinking. The thinking, in other words, can be observed. What is observing the thinking that you are experiencing right now?

Be encouraged if you can't uncover an answer. Not knowing, according to Buddhist tradition, sets us up perfectly for Enlightenment since it cultivates our capacity to surrender into a place of alert curiosity. By patiently and fearlessly sitting still with this wonder, we are invariably shown what we truly are. Having said this, we should be careful of a common trap that ego uses to keep us from developing this unattached relationship to Enlightenment. Simply put, we need to be very careful not to confuse Enlightenment with whatever grand perceptions we gain as we sit in stillness. Often we mistake peak experiences perceived by the body and mind as Spirit itself. The deep felt sense of grace, for example, that often accompanies a profound experiential opening to Truth is often amazingly blissful. So it is common for the ego to identify its profound experience with Enlightenment, when in fact the experience itself is still confined to one's individual experience. This point is critical: Enlightenment must not be confused with a state of bliss. Enlightenment occurs when our attachments to the experiences of both the body and mind fall away entirely and Realization itself breaks down all boundaries of any subject and object. This recognition continually supports an impersonal Knowing that everything is all One. Only when we see that any experience of spiritual recognition is only pointing us toward Enlightenment but is not itself Enlightenment will there be an opening to the awakened context about which the mystics have written. William Blake, for example, points this out beautifully when he says, "We are led to believe a lie, when we see with and not through the eye." Confusing our perceptions of any experience with the experience itself, in other words, keeps us bound by that in us which is always and forever limited.

This isn't to say that the bliss any of us might feel during meditation, or after a yoga class, or in the arms of our beloved isn't a spiritual event. Of course it is. In fact, there isn't anything that is not a spiritual event. But any spiritual euphoria or peak experiences that we might have are merely our personal senses of bliss rather than an Awakening to Truth itself. This is because our senses are centered and oriented in personal experience. In fact, our senses are typically just an expression of our most basic egocentricity. On the other hand, authentic spiritual practice systematically exposes the egocentric contraction to the openness of the unquantifiable Infinity that is always and already the essence of everything. The witnessing of our senses, in other words, is exactly prior to the senses and is therefore forever beyond their influence. Unfortunately for the ego, Awakening to this insight cannot be understood as a personal experience since "understanding it," or "grasping it," awkwardly attempts to force the Infinite into the boundary of our own mind.

Fortunately for me, another one of my Zen teachers was rather ruthless about this point. Years ago, I had been having a rather remarkable time during one seven-day silent meditation retreat: vivid imagery, intense emotions, and bliss beyond anything I could ever put to words. I've tried to write it all down of course, but each time the words only worked to diminish its essence. If only a poet were with me at the time so that I could communicate the whole of it. Then again, that would only have given me something to cling to.

Anyway, after one particularly explosive event during an early morning meditation, I met with the teacher. As I bowed to him, the sense that I was bowing to myself and the rest of the Universe arose with a brilliant clarity. There was no more me to be found. Just bowing. At least this is the best way I can describe what happened. It was strange, and yet it was as real as the curls of the smoking incense that burned in the little room where he sat. After some discussion with him, it was clear that I had experienced a *kensho*. This is the Japanese name for the awakening experience for which we are not supposed to strive. As much as I thought I should have jumped off of my cushion and celebrated, it was as if it didn't really matter. The phrase "no big deal" actually came out of my mouth.

"No big deal is right," the teacher said. "Except that it may change your life substantially, as long as you don't do one thing."

"What's that?" I asked, with my attention focused fully on whatever was about to come out of him.

"As long as you don't cling to this experience, you won't defile where it's pointing you."

The teacher made a crucial point here: just because I had an experience suggesting that my ego was transcended, didn't mean that my ego had been, in any way, permanently transcended. The work is not about simply glimpsing an opening beyond the ego. It's about the continual practice of uncovering what the glimpse shows us. It's about resting as the space that is before and after the ego's grasp.

This took lots more attention than I expected. I thought for a moment, that I was done, that I'd achieved something, that I'd gained a foothold, an understanding of Enlightenment. But I soon realized that I was wrong. More talks with the teacher only got me more confused by what I'd experienced.

"You can't put an experience of Awakening in a box and take it with you," he said some months later. "That only lets your mind try to interpret what it can never grasp."

Just as our conceptual minds work to diminish the fullness of Awakening, this same thing, I learned, also happens a great deal in relationship to physical practices. For instance, any exercise, or committed body or healing practice, can set us up for incredibly rich and helpful exposure to deeply personal experiences along the Path. Because of this, I wholeheartedly endorse integrating the body and mind into spiritual practice no matter which tradition you might follow. Having some kind of physical practice in our lives helps us align our living experience in a holistic way that sutures together the body with the mind. However, the traditions that emphasize denial of either the body or the mind in order to Awaken won't take us very far. The body and mind go together in this work. In fact, without a conscious connection to body as well as mind, Awakening will always be partial. Just as we should not confuse actual Awakening with the mental experiences we have in meditation, neither should we confuse actual Awakening with feelings of euphoria brought on by any physical practice. An authentic Awakening goes past, and yet also brings along, the experiences of body and mind. Any practice that falls short of this transcendence and inclusion will trap us in the very place from which we are seeking freedom.

So how is this freedom of Awakening ever uncovered if it can't be grasped? As we walk the Path, our work is to maintain a free-functioning position of non-grasping in relationship to everything, including the experiences that point to Awakening. When we refrain from grasping, we also refrain from defiling the things we want the most. For example, when we witness the beauty of floral blooms rather than grasping them, they have the chance to offer us, and others, their beauty. When we witness the joy of a child rather than trying to manage it, we have the opportunity to offer and receive love. The same appreciation applies as we Awaken to Truth. By not defiling the Truth as it smashes through everything we've ever built to protect us from its power, we Awaken to it. In other words, the minute we turn the signs that point us toward Truth into Truth, we miss a precious chance to Awaken. The sign is neither the road, nor is it the goal. It is just a sign pointing us in the direction of precisely what is beyond the road. Confusing the sign with either the direction or the road itself will always clip the wings of Awakening, and keep us from uncovering the infinitely spacious vehicle of embodied Enlightenment that we have always been.

Awakening to Truth means that we must fearlessly allow for the boundlessness of Infinity to arise continually, not just for us, but as everything. Once we do this, we begin to see that everything is Spirit. We notice the holiness of all things: that we are spiritual beings having human experiences, rather than human beings having spiritual experiences. In order to stay close to this opening, we cultivate practices that help us to meet our lives creatively as more than just inflated expressions of our egoic understanding and its corresponding attachment to the experiential glories of the mind and the body. But this opening can only be done by disarming from deep within ourselves. When we relax and drop our resistance patterns that guard against Infinity and its chaotic and divinely disastrous Love, an awakening ignites within all of us. The world changes to reflect this opening, bit by bit, as each step of this journey unfolds.

Resistance

*If a man wishes to be sure of the road he treads on, he must
close his eyes and walk in the dark.*
—St. John of the Cross

*What is it like when force becomes the standard of conduct?
The great attack the small, the strong plunder the weak, the many oppress
the few, the cunning deceive the simple, the noble disdain the humble.
The rich mock the poor, the young take from the old, and the states of the
empire ruin each other.*
—Ma Tzu

When we don't want something that shows up in our lives, we
typically do our best to resist it. This resistance can mean that we refuse
to accept things that arise in our experience, or that we manipulate them,
or that we fight against them, or that we even work to destroy any of the
causes and conditions that might lead to anything we find undesirable. As
we continue our climb, we begin to see that all of our resistance centers
itself around a contracted, egoic intention of pushing away what is
presenting itself and grasping at what is not presenting itself in order to
either force or avoid a particular outcome. As with any form of grasping,
this causes suffering.

Yet we have all the tools we need to break this cycle. Every one
of us, for instance, can feel our resistance to what's going on in our
immediate circumstance if we just tune into it. Sometimes, resistance is a
feeling that arises slowly in our awareness, as might an opinion about some
issue that someone has expressed. Sometimes, it shows up with amazing

speed, as might an evaluation of someone's preference of a particular political view or candidate. The intensity of our resistance can vary, too. Sometimes it's a vague sense of unease, while at other times it is brutal and fierce. Any situation where we might feel resistance arise, however, is a gift in that it shows us in a powerful way exactly what we are unconsciously trying to grasp. Once we can recognize our resistance, we can then bring the powerful energy of our observing presence, or Witness, right into the circumstance. Becoming aware of the Witness offers us the chance to be curious about whatever feelings are making themselves known in our experience. With a calm curiosity, we begin to identify not with the contracted feelings of our personal resistance, but rather with the flowing and conscious wonder of simple, impersonal, and boundless Awareness. It is exactly in this way that resistance, and any other feelings of negativity, can be surrendered. Once this surrender occurs, there is peace.

One simple way to practice this recognition of resistance is to simply observe any distraction while you are meditating. Maybe your neighbor is making noise; maybe the family pet wants your attention; maybe your knees hurt. Any distraction will do. First, recognize the situation at hand. For our purposes, we'll look at one of my early obstacles to practice, the "itchy nose scenario." Notice the extent of the itchiness. Notice where exactly the itch is. Notice the fullness of the entire experience. After this full embrace of the itch, recognize the resistance you might have to it. Notice the impulse to do something about it. Notice just how much you want to reach up and alleviate the itch. Notice especially how you might begin to feel about not doing anything about the itch at all. Notice your resistance to the stillness, to this teaching, to everything that asks you to not indulge your habitual tendency to scratch your nose. Explore with deep curiosity everything that is coming up in relation to your itchy nose. Then let this curiosity guide you to release all that is resisting the itchiness. Notice, with patience and wonder, how the energy of the itch eventually diminishes with each breath. Notice how the itch fades from the forefront of your experience into the background. Notice the release of the itch entirely, how it disappears, as you recognize, resist, and eventually release the itchiness of your nose. While this example is a relatively easy point of practice, over time we find that the technique can be applied to any arising annoyance.

Anger and Dogma

One of the most common ways that we feel resistance is anger. Anger is an intense and specific form of resistance to something that is presenting itself in a given moment. Hatred, on the other hand, is an even more deeply attached, and therefore intense, form of anger that is directed very specifically at something or someone. The root of both anger and hatred, as well as other resistance patterns such as anxiety and indifference, is fear. We will be dealing with the subject of fear much more extensively in the next chapter, but for now it is important to see that fear arises whenever the ego senses that it will be forced to do something it doesn't want to do. There is nothing more threatening to the limited ego than the unlimited Infinite. As we've discussed, ego sees Infinity as always chaotic and unmanageable, something that it just can't handle. So as the ego recognizes the actual and potential chaos in any situation, fear arises. Fear then can turn quickly into a resistance pattern. The more intense the fear, the greater will be the ego's attachment to resistance.

There are several places in our daily lives where resistance patterns such as anger, hatred, anxiety, and indifference have the opportunity to play themselves out in short order. Perhaps there is no more fertile place of resistance than the arena of politics. Not surprisingly, politics can generate massive resistance because opinions can be very threatening, especially when some egos have the power to act on their opinions while other egos feel powerless. Rather than being about compromise, political situations are usually about attachment. The deeply egoic attitude of "I'm right, you're wrong" can color so much political discourse, yet it is nothing other than attachment in action. Attachment blinds us to the potential for any kind of appropriate response. Just take any of the issues associated with human rights: racial or ethnic discrimination, gender issues, child labor, gay marriage, or any other that you may find interesting. Regardless of our political sensibilities, communication rooted in defending an attached position will only ever perpetuate the cycle of craving and resistance. This isn't to say that we shouldn't resist those attached to denying human beings their dignity. Studying our own attachments, however, allows us to bring deeper consciousness to our political voices so that any "resistance" is informed by the openness and caring supported by fearlessness, rather than the closure and anger brought on by fear. In this place of non-resistance, we see that what we do or say may, or may not, make much of a difference, but we engage ourselves anyway. From non-resistance, we find that our protests aren't diminished. Rather they can compassionately contribute to waking others up. From non-resistance, we see that we do not have to "put on the cloak of nonviolence," as Gandhi says, in order "to cover impotence." From non-resistance, we expose ourselves, and others, to the behavioral irony of angrily and divisively supporting policies that oppose divisiveness.

As another example of resistance, in today's global religious culture, we find major attachments to division and resistance not only between groups of people but perhaps, more importantly, between people and their sense of God. Most churches do not operate from a place of interconnection with the Divine, but they rather have a tradition of relating to both God and each other from a hierarchical place of separation. Most traditions tend to view God as something apart from what we experience each moment as ourselves. We pray to God rather than living as a conscious expression of Him. And yet, for many, to recognize ourselves as expressions of all that is holy is considered blasphemy. In truth, seeing ourselves as separate from God in any way indicates that our ego, either singularly or collectively, is at work. Churches, mosques, temples, and all the other traditional organizations that fixate, codify, and dogmatize their ideology will only impede an Awakening, since their work centers itself around the convictions and attachments of the ego. These convictions lead to absolute certitude, and certitude eventually leads to violence. As such, if a government or religion decides to identify itself with a system of institutional separation it will only generate more clinging and, in turn, more resistance, more anger, and more suffering, for more people. And yet, this is exactly the situation that the world seems to be in: people are forced to commit themselves to a stunted spirituality or to nothing in particular. In either case, we feel less connected to each other and ourselves, while our spiritual landscape becomes more and more barren.

It surprises me in my discussions with people how their spiritual lives seem to reflect a felt sense of this frustration. The places they worshipped as youngsters seem irrelevant to the way they live in today's world. And yet they yearn for some type of shared spiritual connection.

"What should the Pope care if my gay cousin is allowed to marry?" one of my students recently asked. "And why is it that because I'm a woman, I can't be a priest in the church where I was raised? For that matter, why can't priests marry? Does God make distinctions like this, or do men make them in order to stay in control?"

Her points were powerful. Where was the inclusiveness? This applies to all traditions, Buddhism as well. Any faith that tries to separate Spirit's inherently inclusive quality from its practitioners will deny them an authentic Awakening to the Truth beyond name and form. This is because these organizations still cling to spiritual expressions that are limited by egoic attachment rather than opened by conscious expressions of the Infinite. Unless we awaken to this perpetual disconnect as well as its causes, we may be in for a rough time in the years ahead. The stakes are exceptionally high. This is perhaps the most important reason to walk an authentic spiritual path, one that opens us to Spirit, as opposed to one that separates us from it. Doing so allows for our relationship to Spirit to mature, thus breaking the hold that has made this relationship so irrelevant for so many, for so long.

The teachings of Christ, Mohammed, the Buddha, and all the other great sages, it should be noted, are not the problem. The problem arises when countless spiritual and religious practices and doctrines, as well as many contemporary psychological perspectives, advocate separation between person and Infinite and therefore work to support the position of the ego as being an end in itself. But ego and its relationship to everything, including its own interpretation of Spirit, is the major impediment to Enlightenment. Despite this challenge, we can take the next step when we open our being to that which transcends our most basic delusion of separation and our most basic patterns of resistance. If we can study our tendencies to hold fast to personal ideas, opinions, and faiths that best represent a fixed "us" positioned against a fixed "them," we might be able to offer something to each other that deepens whatever faith or non-faith we currently practice. From the perspective of the Divine, there is both difference and sameness, yet there is no resistance to either. Regardless of our politics or our religion, we can act from this place of internal unity that brings together our difference and sameness. An external unity can't help but follow.

To bring this back to practice, we can enter into stillness with the recognition that we are all divine manifestations of the Infinite and that none of us is separate from anything else. As our spiritual center of gravity shifts to meet this profound Knowing that is beyond clinging and resistance, we discover that kindness, rather than fear, anger or dogma, has the opportunity to flow as effortlessly as the all-encompassing compassion and grace from which everything originates. However, if we do not endeavor to walk the tightrope between these conventional and Ultimate truths of life through the daily practice of stillness, we will remain trapped by our delusions and a sense of separation. Until we can experience, Know, and center our activity from a spacious heart and mind, all relationships will only be egoic negotiations that, again, keep us from the radiant and ever-present awareness of Spirit that is both the source and destination of positively everything.

Losing Our Religion

Religions have the potential of offering us a much closer relationship with our spiritual nature, yet, more often than not, the doctrines used in most traditions act to reinforce separation between believers and non-believers. This doctrinal wedge is also exactly what separates any seeker from Spirit. Attaching to any sense of separation significantly diminishes our chances at living an Ultimate Life. Put simply, separation nourishes fear, and fear nourishes grasping, and grasping gives birth to fundamentalism. And fundamentalism, in all of its forms, offers every fearful ego a place, albeit a temporary one, to hide. For any of us who feel strongly about our spiritual practices or the practices of others, we should be careful not to get caught by the fires of fundamentalist passion, since, by definition, fundamentalism is merely grasping by another name. Instead, we should try to witness our experience of fear as it happens, and then participate in its intensification and its waning from a position of open curiosity and peace. Simply noticing our attachments to the things that we are afraid of losing helps us, and our various wisdom traditions, to evolve. If we continue to allow ourselves and our respective faiths to be governed by fear, we will continue to act as pawns in unnecessary spiritual wars, and religion will only continue to exacerbate personal and collective suffering.

Unfortunately, religions tend to root themselves in attachment. Even Buddhist teaching can generate grasping. This is because any institutional structure is made by, and built for, egos. This is more than a little ironic since the mystical teachings of Christianity, Islam, Judaism, Hinduism, and Buddhism, speak so much about egolessness and compassion. But for a teaching to develop a following, it must offer something onto which followers can grasp. Since attachment is what gets in the way of establishing an enlightened perspective in anyone or any group, we shouldn't ever count on religious doctrine to truly transform us.

On the other hand, we can definitely count on religious doctrine to help our egos make sense out of the chaos of our circumstances. Religions give simple translations to what the ego sees as the infinitely complex and threatening language of the Universe. Religions provide salvation, safety, luck, and even promises of immortality. This is exactly the kind of assurance that the ego wants, and it is also something that the ego will fight to protect. The important point to remember is that for any serious person climbing the Mountain of Spirit, transformation is the goal. Simple translation isn't. Translation will only allow for the small self to feel a temporary sense of security. Transformation gets us past the threats altogether and helps us realign ourselves as beings who embody an enlightened view and live an Ultimate Life.

Seekers of true transformation will do well to remember that religions grasp at their self-authored versions of truth in order to survive. They are, once again, merely institutions built upon collective egoic clinging. As such they will always have the potential to generate suffering over time. The Upanishads, the Old and New Testaments, the Koran, the Lotus Sutra, all have the potential to help us awaken, but our individual and collective attachments to the words, ideas, and perspectives expressed in these texts always inhibit our opening to Spirit. What's more, our religious convictions simultaneously feed on and fuel an entire cultural pattern of interpretation. Once this codification happens, there is little room for flexibility, and this lack of flexibility is the manifestation of division, fixation, extremism, and the associated fears that arise within and among these various versions of grasping. This leads us into war. Even if our religion is science, or the market, or nature, we are susceptible to the call offered by our attachment to our particular version of faith the minute we cling to it. And in that moment of clinging to what we believe to be right, we give birth to war. It may be small. It may be huge. But it's war.

So why do we cling? Because, once again, ego wants to be able to manage our lives with as few complications as possible. Religions essentially offer the ego candy when they promise future salvation if the ego merely commits to believing in its particular version of Truth. When this happens, a tradition's version of Truth offers absolute safety for a separate self that feels threatened by absolutely everything. Getting on the other side of this prison masquerading as salvation will change the entire world by opening us up to a profound freedom. Ironically, it is the very freedom toward which the founders of the world's great wisdom traditions pointed. But neither Christ, nor the Buddha, nor Mohammed, nor any other founding sage of the world's religions has offered any critique of the doctrines that they inspired. Instead, we have to follow their example by leading conscious lives informed by the wisdom and compassion brought on by stillness. Egos will think this assertion naïve, yet it is entirely possible for an individual, no matter how entrenched or attached, to unlearn his conscious and unconscious attachments to all of the mind patterns that get in the way of a deep liberation from fear and suffering. Continuing this climb, however, takes courage and work. And while it might not necessarily be easy, the process can be undertaken by anyone wishing for, and committed to, Awakening.

Fundamentalism

Fundamentalism arises when any religious organization, or any person, attaches so intensely to some version of truth that it must be defended. In this space, the ego continually seeks security by playing out its drama of "attack and defend." This drama offers all sorts of teachers and practitioners an opportunity to commit to various forms of separation where an attitude of "we're right and they're wrong" not only rules, but begets more attachment. This space can sow seeds of terrible violence all in the name of the collective egoic version of what it deems sacred.

Fundamentalism, in any of us, destroys that which it seeks to protect. It's as if a hand, enticed by the elegant simplicity of a flower and wanting to possess its beauty, grasps its bloom and crushes what it wants most. Living from a place of true intimacy, where flowers could be experienced rather than possessed, would mean that ego would have to allow itself out of its own cage of security. Yet to do this the ego must surrender to that which it cannot control.

This Awakened surrender is rare since the ego is always busy seeking control. Even when this opening happens for any of us, Spirit often gets interpreted and then boxed in by ego. This interpretation always forces the boundlessness of Spirit into a newly created exclusivity, and this is exactly what Spirit is not. Rather than surrender to the total and complete inclusive nature of Spirit, ego labels its packaged version of Spirit as "the only thing worth believing." Here is where an opportunity for kindness and compassion for the All gets cast aside as weakness by a deeply threatened ego, and this is the psychological space where destructive attachments perpetually emerge.

In order to break free of the bindings that fear and fundamentalism offer, we need to study our own fundamentalist tendencies. When we continually look within to see where we "get fundamental" ourselves, we are employing the consciousness that will free us from it. But we need courage to ask ourselves difficult questions. Does hatred arise within us? That's fundamentalism. Is the world black and white to us? That's fundamentalism. Does a feeling of defensiveness arise about certain topics? That's fundamentalism. Is there any blaming of others for anything? That's fundamentalism. This doesn't mean that any of us should give in to things our common sense sees as wrong. Rather, it means that our responses to every situation should be sourced from openness rather than spiritual closure. This openness will do all of us some good since it is exactly what will keep us from throwing gasoline on any fundamentalist flames, especially our own.

The Big House

It is important to remember that the events of insight are neither the measure nor the point of meditation. Rather than the flashiness of the Zen awakening experience called *satori*, our Path to Enlightenment is only about incorporating disciplined and conscious stillness in our day-to-day life. It's a simple recipe for each of us: stop grasping, and engage the relaxation of our individual consciousness into the expansiveness of Universal Awareness—and, in doing so, move into our Big House.

As our practice begins to mature and our psychological and spiritual reorientation begins to express itself more deeply, we can generally see our experience develop along three stages. First, we watch the mind work to make the whole spiritual endeavor recognizable and manageable. Second, we experience resistance when uncomfortable stuff begins arising in our awareness. Third, we experience an unquantifiable glory descending upon and coming through us as we begin to move past the first two stages. These qualities—of recognition, resistance, and release—all may show up at different times, in different orders, or even all at once, but they all show up at some time as our practice deepens. The fact that they don't necessarily follow any particular order, and that their intensity can vary, makes things confusing unless we have a good guide. But it's also important to know that none of these processes is ever skipped as we move toward Awakening. There is no better shortcut other than simultaneously having a meditation practice, a teacher, and a group of like-minded spiritual friends.

In the stage of recognition, we tend to start our search by flirting with spirituality and its various practices. We get our feet wet, so to speak, but the mind doesn't want us to jump in because that would require it to surrender too much of its sense of control. There are many practitioners with whom I've worked who stay at this level for quite some time. And why not? The small self can easily look superficially at whatever it is doing spiritually and turn it into something fun and interesting for both the body and the mind. Recognition is a stage rooted in deep familiarity and comfort for the small self since it may be reminiscent of its early collegiate experiences. Experimentation, conquest, intellectual stimulation, and inebriation are all qualities marking the high tide of the small self experience. Here, the ego is in charge. But more importantly, the ego is comfortable, and it loves for things to be comfortable and not too demanding of its energy. In spiritual terms, the ego often likes the soft and gentle approach of what a teacher of mine called "grandmother Zen." This is because the comfort of the grandmotherly embrace allows the mind to stay in charge of both everyday life and a spiritual practice. A grandmotherly approach to practice might sound something like, "Best not push yourself too much with this sitting practice. Maybe sleeping in this morning is the best thing that you could do for yourself." And so the ego stays in charge, recognizing that it can manage the spiritual quest. Ironically, this activity is little more than the ego seeing from its limited view and deeming it enlightened. This is a mistake.

Our minds work intensely at this stage to become enlightened, even though the mind is precisely what gets in the way of any truly liberating realization. As much as we might like to think of ourselves as being deeply rooted in a profound practice during this stage of recognition, our work here is usually quite shallow. It may be sincere, but its egoic orientation limits its depth. So this level of practice won't be able to offer an end to anyone's suffering. In fact, this level of practice usually makes our suffering worse.

The shallowness imposed by the ego eventually generates the source of resistance that defines the second stage of practice. As we've spent some time noting, ego's job is, among other things, to resist what lies beyond itself. The feeling of resistance arises when the Infinite bangs on the door of our limited home. At this point, we can either choose to open the door to the Truth in spite of what awaits us, or we can run from the whole noisy affair and generate even more pain, deeper unconsciousness, and more intense patterns of resistance.

It's a tough situation made tougher by the partial recognition of the Infinite. I've seen practitioners close to me get really discouraged at this point in their spiritual maturation because they have left the first stage of recognition and yet wherever they turn, there is neither Awakening nor complete delusion. They know enough to be dangerous to their own well-being, and their egos try desperately to get comfortable again. But they can't find comfort. When we are in a place of resistance where we've outgrown the old and familiar egoic clothes and can't yet fill the clothes we see hanging in the closets of the Big Home, we get torn apart. At this stage we are desperate, naked, and in a panic, which makes the challenges of a stillness practice even more overwhelming. Lots of practitioners, especially those who don't have teachers and groups with whom to work, will decide at this point to give up on becoming Awake in this life. Still others press on.

Those who decide to keep up the practice of stillness, even when it hurts, move on to the third stage of release. When we no longer need to recognize or resist, we find that we are in a place of released spaciousness where massive shifts can occur. Sometimes, our stillness practice offers us glimpses of heaven when we are able to celebrate the mystery of it all, while at other times it lets hell in the door. Getting past the need to feel comfortable with either the view from the Summit or the arduous ascent allows for us to uncover a deep acceptance of whatever life may bring. When we no longer need to feel a certain way, resistance starts to dissipate. Once resistance falls away, we can release into the deep union of all things, whether our egos like them or not. Practice shows us that stillness brings an offering of peaceful resonance to every circumstance that might ever arise. This uncontracted Awareness is a bold reminder of what we are beneath all of our ideas, opinions, identities, roles, and feelings. We are the formless Infinity that includes and yet is beyond all form. Knowing this, we are no longer bound by our grasping.

But the realization of this third stage of release only means that we've glimpsed the Truth of who and what we actually are. Whether we have the discipline to remain close enough to our Big Home in order to eventually embody its offering is another deal entirely. Can we get past the stage of recognition, with all of its superficial trappings? Can we get through the stage of resistance, with its ever-increasing intensity? Can we surrender in a way that doesn't deny or go after the things that arise in this life? Can we just sit still and be quiet, and release it all?

In stillness, we are the embodiment of surrender. We've let go of all the things that are personal and find ourselves relaxing in the midst of all that is impersonal. Stillness, and its impersonal nature, doesn't move. It is the source of all movement. Silence, and its impersonal nature, doesn't make a sound. It is the source from which all noise emanates. Stillness is never separate from anything, just like Spirit is never separate from anything. It is a radiant clarity that can't be seen, since it is what gives birth to sight. It can't be heard because it is the source of hearing. It can't be sensed as a thing at all. But by surrendering to all things in each moment, we begin to know stillness deep within our bodies as the activity of our Ultimate Life, breaking through the cracks of our limited circumstance. In this instance, we are offered an open door into our new, Big Home.

Fear

3

Fear is the main source of superstition, and one of the main sources
of cruelty. To conquer fear is the beginning of wisdom.
—*Bertrand Russell*

The most terrifying thing is to accept oneself completely.
—*Carl Jung*

Fear is ego's fuel. This is because ego's role in our life experience is to defend itself against all perceived attacks. As long as the ego sees itself as separate from everything, it will continually fear the potential of an attack. The ego also senses that every potential attack could annihilate it. As we've discussed, it defends against these scary situations in two ways: by seeking the things that make it feel secure, and by avoiding things that threaten it with death.

Yet oddly enough, the higher we climb the Mountain of Spirit, the more we start to see how the ego actually works to remain threatened so that it can keep its job. No matter what type of psychological work we take on in order to undo our pain, there is ultimately nothing that will make the ego feel secure in any permanent way since the ego must feel threatened in order to have something to do. If it ever begins to develop a sense of security, it will sabotage this experience in order to remain in control. Because of this paradox, the ego finds itself perpetually on the move, in search of a lasting peace that it will never find since its movement toward the things that make it feel safe and away from the things that threaten it is the primary impediment to lasting peace.

As much as the ego might claim that it can't stand this situation of constant threat, it is right at home in this perpetual and exhaustive search for the peace it will never find. It may not be comfortable, but the constant fear associated with survival is at least deeply familiar to the always threatened ego, and this familiarity is something that it can cling to and so feel secure. But, like everything else, its sense of managerial safety is forever only temporary. So, it constantly searches for things to prolong the intensity of its grasp. This dysfunctional search depletes us and also provides each of our circumstances with a structural foundation mixed and set with mortar made from an unlimited supply of fear.

If we think about it for a moment, anything we fear centers around avoiding the future loss of something we value. Perhaps it is the loss of our life or another's, the loss of a livelihood, the loss of health, the loss of reputation, or even the loss of our mind. As long any threat of loss exists, the ego can remain in control of our consciousness by endlessly generating fear and then seeking to overcome it. To be sure, loss can be frightening. But an enlightened perspective supports the growth of a different relationship with loss. Instead of habitually trying to preserve the permanence of everything, the enlightened among us accept the fact that absolutely no part of our real world experience will last. From the perspective of the Big Self, we see and accept that all things are impermanent, even though our egos would have us preserve, protect, and defend the status quo. Once this insight gets authentically integrated into our experience, neither seeking, nor death, nor gain, nor loss becomes a particularly important part of daily living.

So while our small self will always be concerned with bettering its circumstances, the Big Self is totally at peace with exactly what is available. Your small self might see Enlightenment as the main focus of its existence, while the Big Self can't see what all the fuss is about. Your small self might fear losing control, while your Big Self sees that there is nothing to control in the first place. Your small self might see itself and others as being a good or bad Buddhists, while your Big Self sees only Buddhas. Your small self might do everything it can to prevent the loss of what it covets, while your Big Self sees that there is absolutely nothing to lose and never anything to oppose.

Relaxing deeply into this realization of non-opposition, we begin to find the courage to stand intimately with everything that is Unknown. In this upright meeting with all that we do not know rests our greatest potential gift. Not knowing is the mind's way of surrendering to whatever is offering itself in the present moment, which, ironically for the ego, is exactly what Buddhist teaching says will put each of us on the Path to Enlightenment. Intimacy with the Unknown is what forces the ego to give up its perceived sense of control and managerial purpose. Once the Stage of Mind is flooded with the light of Big Self Awareness, the small self is exposed as being just an actor rather than as the whole of reality. Seeing this, we are invited to Awaken to the infinitely expansive heart of all existence.

As much as the ego fears losing its attachments, what the ego really fears, more than anything else, is an authentic meeting with anything that forces it off Stage and brings the Audience, our witnessing awareness, in direct contact with itself. If this happens, the ego's relevance diminishes and our relationship to all things transforms radically. In this openness beyond the constraints of the ego we are no longer caught by anything, and nothing catches us. Not even fear.

Seeking

> *What we are looking for . . . is what is looking.*
> —*Wei Wu Wei*

> *The more you know the less you understand.*
> —*Tao Te Ching*

The small self is always seeking outside itself for stability. Once it finds something that it feels will protect it for a while, it will attach to it. But the small self won't rest for very long since it must continually seek outside itself for new attachments in order to replace those that are no longer useful. Even if the small self finds something that it believes will offer it permanent salvation, it will only stop seeking briefly before it either finds flaws in its acquisition or it finds something it thinks will better suit its needs.

Positively everything is fleeting, and this puts pressure on the small self to be prepared to go to war at any time in order to protect its interests. And yet all things, including the threats to ego as well as the solutions to its dilemmas, no matter what they are, will eventually fall apart. This universal law of entropy simultaneously exhausts the small self and yet keeps it in the driver's seat. This allows the ego to begin seeking anew the moment anything fails to offer total security. This cycle of seeking generates suffering. When the small self tries to find lasting solace in anything, be it a habit, an addiction, another person, work, wealth or spiritual fulfillment, it maintains its role as the driver of the bus of experience, thus making the enlightened perspective into an impossible ideal.

I remember once attending a weekend meditation retreat where on the first night we were instructed to discuss what started us on our spiritual journeys. Everyone was sitting in a circle, taking turns telling their stories. I happened to be in the last position in the circle, and I remember feeling my heart break for so many of these people and the tragedies they'd suffered. Each of them, to a person, was seeking an escape from what life was dealing them, and I couldn't blame them: deaths of spouses, partners, children; addiction to drugs, alcohol, and sex, among other things; losing their jobs; losing their positions in their communities. There seemed to be so much pain and personal tragedy. Finally it was my turn, and I didn't really know what to say. My biggest reason for beginning my spiritual journey was greed. I was curious about Enlightenment, had always had an affinity with life's big questions, and I wanted to find myself Awake in this life. Sure, I'd had my fair share of pain but nothing compared to the seekers in the circle. I was easily the youngest person in the group by twenty years. I didn't want to offend anyone by revealing my seemingly insensitive and trivial reasons for climbing the spiritual ladder. Besides, what kind of Buddhist admits to feeling greedy? So I simply said one word, "Curiosity." That was it.

"Of all the reasons we've heard so far, that's maybe the best reason to start," said the lady brown robe leading the retreat. Suddenly, I began feeling incredibly self-conscious. She reminded me of a cross between an imposing Catholic nun carrying a ruler and Mrs. Eklund, my beloved nursery school teacher. She was ferocity merged with total love. "All of you interested in seeking an escape from your pain might as well leave," she laughed. "You might, over time, not feel your pain as acutely once you begin your practice, but real meditation is about facing the causes and conditions of your suffering with an open curiosity," she said, with an intense gaze. "It is not about seeking an escape. In fact, it's not about seeking anything. It's about facing every single bit of your life: all of your drama, all of your stories, and all of ours, too."

A mixture of fear and pride crept into my awareness. Phrases like, "I kinda' got the right answer," as well as, "This retreat might totally suck," filled my head. But the panicked looks on the faces of those people in the circle still linger with me. It looked like they were hoping for a reprieve but got a metaphorical whack with a stick from a woman none of us could help but appreciate on some level.

"Face your lives," she said. "Face your lives."

It's Not about Bliss

The purpose of a deep stillness practice is not to seek a lowering of our blood pressure, or to get a break from the kids, or to escape our situation. Meditation might, in fact, lower our blood pressure, ease the tension we might feel with our kids, and help us deal with our pain in more constructive ways, but an authentic stillness practice does not allow us to take refuge from life. Rather, it puts us right in the middle of our situation and removes whatever protection we've traditionally clung to in order to defend our selves from its impact. Truly facing our lives scares a lot of people away from meditation when they realize that stillness practice, at this level, isn't about dwelling in states of perpetual bliss. These experiences of unutterable peace and wonder often show up when we meditate, and they are signposts directing us toward the Infinite. Bliss experiences can also help us become temporarily more tolerant of life. We can then experience a greater coolness as our circumstances get hot, and we often find it a little easier to offer open kindness to people we meet. This process of slowing into an ever-deepening relaxation can't help but be good for all aspects of our being.

Yet these benefits are not the purpose of practice, but rather its byproduct. If we're just meditating for any of these beneficial qualities or for the feeling of bliss (which often will arise in the early stages of practice), we can develop a tendency to try repeatedly to reach that particular state that we once had. In the seeking of any state, our attachment to the bliss itself becomes an obstacle to the process of Awakening.

To sustain our motivation, it can be useful to find a group of spiritual friends who are more or less walking on a similar path up the Mountain of Spirit. With a group, we can find support when things dry up in our practice or when we find ourselves in the midst of a cycle of disappointment with our seeming inability to Awaken. I resisted finding a group of spiritual friends as I began my practice because I didn't like groups and I had even less tolerance for organizations of faith. But when I finally checked my resistance at the door and just sat and meditated with others, it made a huge difference in deepening my practice. It helped me to realize that I was not alone, that I was not separate from others, that I was neither above nor unworthy of the experience of community. Most of all, it helped me to see that all things, including both my resistance and my bliss, were just temporary states.

All things, including all of our states of mind, are subject to impermanence. Each of our mental states is bound by time. In other words, they come and then eventually leave after a certain interval. So when we center our practice on something that is dependent on time, such as feeling a certain way, we are asking the ego to lead the way to a false enlightenment. Just as we don't learn everything about love by studying those who are hateful, we should only expect more and more confusion if we let ego commandeer the process of Awakening.

The Rubber Band Effect

Another important realization as we climb occurs when we see that meditation won't necessarily keep us happy. Meditation, done correctly, merely affords us direct and continual exposure to the deep silence underneath whatever is happening right now. Exposure to deep silence reminds us that all things are temporary, including anything we think might make us happy in a permanent way. Any object that the mind seeks in order to gain happiness, such as a new car, a new job, a new relationship, a new religion, or anything else, might put the mind in a state of happiness for a while, but neither our mood nor the thing that fueled the mood will last forever. At some point there will be decay, boredom, exhaustion, or pain, and when this happens the mind snaps like a rubber band back to its position prior to acquiring the thing it thought would make it happy.

The good news, however, is that a stillness practice can, so to speak, change the position of the rubber band. Imagine your right hand plucking a rubber band stretched between your left thumb and index finger. Each pull of the rubber band is like a new distraction that the mind thinks will offer it lasting happiness. In very little time, however, the tension builds as the rubber band stretches, eventually snapping back to its original position. This process can continue in some of us for our whole lives, as if we existed solely for each snap of the rubber band. Stillness, though, mysteriously moves the left hand toward the right as it stretches the rubber band. The snaps are no longer as extreme, and the tension diminishes to the point of a peaceful equilibrium where our happiness is no longer dependent on any object at all. This is how our consciousness evolves: the more still we become, the more we begin to relax the tension of constant seeking and simply allow ourselves to live, consciously, as an expression of a deeper wholeness.

It's important for us to recognize that there isn't any practice that will allow for an Awakening into and through this wholeness unless it involves complete stillness of body and mind. Without stilling the mind, we can't gain access to the perspective from beyond the mind that total quietude shows. As long as we identify with thoughts, feelings, and the things we think will bring us lasting happiness, the rubber band will keep snapping us back into unconscious behavior. Any practice we might choose that doesn't support total stillness will only be a hindrance, and such practices are never able to help us get beyond the constriction of ego in an authentic way.

Truly transformative practices focus on the release of the ego into a profound blending of subject and object where, as we say in Zen, "Form is Emptiness, and Emptiness is form." Loosely translated, this can mean that all things are essentially Infinite in nature, and that Infinity is essentially the fundamental quality of all things. Once we begin to live from a place of stillness, we recognize this Infinity of space in ourselves and everything else. In this still, Infinite space, the rubber band falls away into total insignificance, since from this vastly open perspective, there is no subject and no object—nothing to seek, nothing sought, nothing to avoid, and nothing to fear. All boundaries fall away in this conscious meeting of Infinity. There is neither this nor that, we might say. All is once and forever the One and the many, all at the same moment. Without separation, there can be neither boundary nor separation. There can only be unity. Realizing this, we Awaken.

Death

Die before you die and you shall never die.
—Sufi saying

Now when the bardo of dying dawns upon meI will abandon all grasping, yearning and attachment,Enter the undistracted into clear awareness of the teaching,And eject my consciousness into the space of the unborn Awareness. As I leave this compound body of flesh and blood,I will know it to be a transitory illusion.
—Padma Sambhava

Loss is essentially the end of an attachment. The loss of a relationship to anything, while it may not be permanent, is the same thing: the end, or death, of an attachment. This may be a relationship to another person, to an opinion, to time, to your own body, to the world, to Enlightenment, or to any number of other things. Our relationship to these things will change whether the ego wants them to or not, and our acceptance of the constancy of change can be absolutely terrifying. This situation is an amazingly rich source of pain since ego fears the loss, or death, of its control over our circumstances more than anything else.

Death is inextricably tied to birth in that these two aspects of our conventional circumstance are never separate. No matter what we might like to think, death will come to everything that is born even though we rarely operate with this realization at the forefront of our consciousness. But when we do live with death as a full partner in life, always being aware that our ultimate end is getting closer and closer to us at every minute, we get the chance to live differently. At least our priorities often change. Yet we can watch how ego does everything it can to prevent any type of full recognition, let alone participation, in this fundamental truth.

Instead of allowing itself to deal fully with the implications of an imminent death that it can't escape, the ego ignores and often denies death itself. This is exactly the behavior we see when individuals would rather not go to the doctor for fear of hearing bad news or when we would rather be in denial of the problems a loved one's chemical dependency is causing. The minute the ego can't control a situation, it senses its insignificance. To avoid this disintegration of all the structure that it has built over time, the ego seeks stability in denial.

Why does the ego deny the fact that it can't control everything? Because denying the death of its reign is something it can manage. If the deep and full recognition of death's eventuality were to accurately unfold in our consciousness and an appropriate reprioritization of our living ensued, the ego would start to lose the foundation of its existence.

An empowering relationship with death, on the other hand, means a deep change in business-as-usual. This shift from defense against change into total acceptance of change forces the ego to let go of its managerial and overt controlling tendencies. Here we die to the familiar and open to the unknown. Once this release happens, it's as if we become ripe for the divine accident of Awakening.

While it's true that we're all going to die at some point, as will every other thing in the cosmos, this doesn't negate the importance of any of life's unfolding circumstances. Regardless of the temporary nature of all things, each and every single object that arises in our awareness offers us a direct Path to the Infinite, depending only on if we choose to follow it. Should we consciously approach our living through an intimacy with death? Or, should we generate pain for ourselves and others by denying that death is close? Should we continue the attachment to the status quo of life? Or should we look to see what is beyond it? The Path offered by these choices is always and forever ours to either take or avoid.

If we choose to climb higher by surrendering willingly to the Knowing that all things born into experience will also fall away from experience, we will be forced to look at everything in life as a chance for a serene death in each moment. This conscious and continual surrender allows us to experience, with tenderness, a conscious death of each moment before we experience the death of the body we temporarily inhabit. By truly allowing for this radical acceptance of impermanence, we die before we die and we are offered the chance to authentically experience the expansive and radiant Spirit that embraces and supports each part of our limited circumstance with an infinitely divine grace.

No Fixed Self

Our fixed sense of a self, which we spend so much effort and energy maintaining, is only a creation of our minds. Again, this small self, or ego, is just as a dream—a phantom generated by our minds in order to stabilize the chaos of Infinity. Hearing this is disturbing to the ego since it sees itself as primary to the experience of being a self. To be seen as unimportant means the ego is pushed to the side and is therefore out of work. No matter what it adds to its résumé after Awakening, it will never be rehired at the same salary. To stretch this metaphor further: rather than taking a lateral professional move after this realization, the ego is forced from the boardroom into the mailroom. This relocation means that the ego can still be useful, but it isn't able to use us anymore.

We might uncover a bit of this recognition if we pay close attention to some simple questions. What, for example, represents the "you" in this world? Are you your body? Your feelings? Your thoughts? Your perceived roles? Of course. You are all of these things. But the enlightened perspective shows us that we are actually much more. From the enlightened perspective, you are not what you feel—you are more than just that. Nor are you just your body. You are more than that, too. You are also neither your thoughts, nor your sense of space or time. The real you is that which witnesses all of these things as they arise and cease in your experience. The real you is this Feeler of the feelings, this Thinker of the thoughts, this Hearer of the sounds, this Seer of all that can be seen. The real you is the Audience of the Stage of Mind; a Witness that is aware of all things and is eternally formless, free, and forever beyond the flow of time. It is impersonal, shared equally by all things, Infinite in scope, and forever still. It is the Big Self.

As this Witness becomes more and more recognizable in our experience, the ego's status diminishes radically. When the small, fixed, sense of self awakens into the Big Self, our former way of living, or what some might refer to as "the dream," radically changes. Since death is nothing other than radical change, we can appropriately say that in this Awakening the small self dies to its old role. This death happens in the same way that any awakening from our dreams profoundly diminishes their limited hold on us. Instead of working to rid ourselves of the ego on the Path to Awakening, simply allowing our awareness to expand past ego's grip lets the ego's significance diminish on its own as Awakening naturally unfolds. To be sure, the memory of the egoic dream may live on, but its power over the Witness is lost as long as we stop attaching to the dream and instead attentively watch it play out. Fortunately, we get a chance to do just this as each circumstance, be it good or bad, arises in our consciousness.

Since every single moment offers us a chance to be awake and aware, none of us is ever done with the practice. There is no end point to this work of Awakening. We continually practice stillness so that the witnessing Big Self is continually revealed. No one is ever done with this process any more than anyone is ever done growing, or learning.

As a boy, I had a history teacher who used to say, "No one is ever finished with their education." I found this to be so powerful because it spoke so simply to a curiosity that my parents had nourished in me. I never wanted to stop learning. My teacher went on to say, "Anyone who says they're done, shouldn't be trusted." He was a slight man who smelled of cigarettes and coffee. His hair looked like Einstein's and he would often show up to school with socks that didn't match. His desk was piled high with stacks and stacks of books, and he loved his work. Despite his scruffy exterior, he shined from some place deep within. While his knowledge impressed me, his kindness and sense of humor impressed me more than anything else. He walked his talk, and I appreciated the total lack of hypocrisy in him. He knew that he wasn't finished with his education and that he never would be.

These are great words for any of us to live by, especially as we walk the Path. Knowing that none of us is ever done keeps us from losing our common sense when we meet a spiritual teacher who may not be worthy of our trust. Teachers of worth know that they are also on the Path; they just may be a little further along than their students. They can still fall in the mud. Just as none of us is ever finished with our education, none of us is ever completely Awake.

Rehearsal

A big part of living a conscious life means that we are living fully at every moment, aware and accepting of the fact that at any moment we might die. At this point of experience, everything simultaneously becomes a gift and a mystery. But there is a common spiritual confusion with this *carpe diem* attitude. Some practitioners feel that conscious living means that we should "go for it, because nothing matters." The fearlessness that comes with the go-for-it attitude can be helpful along the Path, but any fixation that "nothing matters" is dangerous unless the mindset is met with a clear sense of ethics and responsibility. This is why an enlightened recognition must be also met with a purposeful relationship to an ethical code. The Precepts arose out of Zen and other Buddhist practices for this very reason. The Old Testament offers us the Ten Commandments, which provide similar guidance, and other traditions do the same. Allowing a deep intimacy with these rules, rather than attaching to them, prepares us for embodying the equanimity that comes with an Awakened perspective.

This embodiment, which we'll discuss in greater detail later, comes from an appreciation for the mystery of life. Consciously participating in this mystery means that we continually look at everything we do as an ongoing rehearsal for our eventual physical death. In this context, every inhalation is a birth, and every exhalation a death. Each moment, like every other thing, is born from a vast and divine Emptiness, lives for a while, and then dies back into the same vastness.

Meditation becomes the conscious enactment of this rehearsal of death, one where our separate sense of self dies to our recognition that we are in fact nothing less than the entire Universe manifesting in this experience at this moment. With sustained awareness, we begin to let go of our tightly held story that we are somehow separate and special. In fact we see that we are all things. Our perspective on death changes as this process shows itself. So, too, does our perspective on life. Suddenly the stuff that we used to cling to and crave, avoid and resist, is truly meaningless when viewed through enlightened eyes that are no longer limited by the lenses of the small self. Uncovering this new clarity, we die to the contracted, ego-driven panic that governs our conventional circumstance. We are thus awakened to all that we truly are as we begin to lead an Ultimate Life.

And yet the losses associated with death can be so very painful. Awakening won't take away this pain. In fact, Awakening never insulates us from life's challenges; it allows these to be expressed more fully in our awareness. Awakening relentlessly forces upon us the grandeur of each experience, and opening to this grandeur gives us each a chance not to get caught by anything. Awakening reveals the inner spaciousness and courage that let us experience everything more completely. We get to meet life's intensity with even more sensitivity, care, intention, and fearlessness. Awakening offers the use of a mind that is neither ossified nor closed, but one that is soft, flexible, present, and open. Because of this, an Awakened mind experiences life in the most dynamic and undefended way imaginable. Tears of grief might flow more freely. The intensity of fear, anger, and passion that we feel in our conventional circumstances might be much more powerful than before we started to meditate regularly. But this enlightened relationship to each birth and death in our experience allows us to meet each circumstance with even more presence without succumbing to any grasping or resistance.

This kind of Freedom is probably best seen in the faces of people who can face life's temptations but aren't necessarily compelled to give in to them. This isn't to say that there is anything wrong with temptation, but when any of us is no longer internally obliged to take temptations on or when we are no longer caught by what they might offer, we are Free.

I noticed this quality in a monk that I knew in Thailand. In his speech, his walk, and the way he ate, there was what could best be described as total ease with it all. He seemed to glide through his days. Nothing seemed to catch him: the local lay female practitioners who thought he was so handsome; the other monks who were in many cases oddly competitive with him; and even what he regarded as the "misrepresentation of the Dharma" by one of the monastery's senior teachers. He simply was free of all of it, and yet totally engaged in living. Like Christ, he seemed to be, "in the world, but not of it."

Non-Reincarnation

Life after death, or life after life, depending on how one looks at it, is one of the more fascinating aspects of spiritual practice since we're not really sure what happens when we die. There are plenty of scriptural teachings to suggest that reincarnation exists. Maybe it does. Certainly, this would make things easier on each of us since we get to live all of this over again and again until we get it right. But aside from faith, scripture, and suggestion, there is little if any authentic empirical evidence to suggest that reincarnation actually happens. There are undoubtedly cases suggestive of reincarnation, but in our conventional world, we just don't have the tools to determine if reincarnation awaits each of us or not. But does it really matter?

I'm sure many of my more traditional Buddhist friends will disagree with me, but to debate whether or not something is true in relation to any tradition, dogma, or scripture misses the most sacred aspects of any great spiritual teaching and certainly misses the point of Awakening into an enlightened perspective. Freeing ourselves from the entire cycle of birth and death is available to us in this lifetime at this moment. No one needs, therefore, to bother with any future speculation of rebirth as we walk the Path.

As we've discussed, when we attach to the faith and religiosity of any wisdom tradition, we diminish its ability to assist us on our climb. This weakening occurs because when we are caught by any attachment our limited egoic view begins to think of itself as something Infinite. For example, consider how the view "I get to live another life all over again" can be a wonderful place for ego to maintain a perceived sense of control over the ultimate chaos of death. The sense that an "I" exists is the very unconsciousness from which we wish to awaken. Awakening, in this sense, is seeing beyond all that the mind, or small self or ego, offers. In the most common views of reincarnation, this delusion of the fixed, and persisting "I" is bolstered by the belief that something separate survives the clutches of death when, in reality, all objects of the mind are subject to time and therefore must succumb to the clutches of death.

On the other hand, the experience of the Witness points to that which in us is never touched by time. Since the Witness can be aware of time, it can't be caught by it. This is perhaps one of the most useful keys in opening the doors of perception, which, in turn, will support our practice at an even more expansive level. Since the Witness can be aware of whatever is arising in the mind, it cannot be caught by the mind. As we uncover this Witness, we are afforded the chance to experience that which is never born and will never die. From this point of infinite awareness, there is nothing to reincarnate, because that which is Infinite in us is exactly the same as that which is, was, and shall always be Infinite in all things. This eternal Infinite, in other words, is never touched by time. In this vast eternal opening, we uncover the already awakened core of each of us and everything else, and we see that everything is perfectly aligned with everything else. When this realization unfolds in us as us, we become a seamless monument of an embodied Awakening that never needs to be reincarnated because it has always been right here, right now ... and it will not move. This Knowing is our practice as well as our ever-present Freedom from which we've never been apart.

Part Two

——

The Summit

After we've begun to climb past the tangle of egoic living, we begin to uncover a clearing beyond anything the mind can grasp. It's as if we've literally climbed past the tree line and into an open space on the other side of everything that used to trap us. In spiritual terms, we are approaching the summit of the Mountain of Spirit.

At this altitude we find that we can objectively experience our felt sense of separation. We are offered an entirely new perspective on life— one that is sourced consciously from total unity. This new perspective is whole, undivided, and intimate with exactly what is happening right now. Participating from this new perspective inspires us to live in ways that are revealed continuously as conscious expressions of engaged wisdom and compassion. Taking in the view from this lofty point changes us forever if we have the courage to let its revelation into all facets of our being.

From the summit, we can see that the ego and all of its activities are oriented in two centers of experience: the mind and the body. All of our pain and all of our pleasure stems from the ego's attachment to these two areas. As the ego attaches to thoughts in the mind and feelings in the body, suffering is born. But through a deepening intimacy with mind and body, we are offered a way out of the limited perspectives of our thoughts and feelings.

The Path leading us towards higher and more expansive levels of awareness shows up when we develop an ability to observe our experience exactly as it is the very moment it unfolds in our minds and bodies. Once we can practice this consistently, we can begin to orient our daily lives from a perspective that simply and silently watches, without judgment, our mental and physical activity, all of which shows itself as performances on the Stage of Mind. From this open orientation, we simply rest as the audience of our thoughts and feelings as they play themselves out on the stage without trying to alter or change anything about them. Instead we consciously surrender to the present moment, without giving in to circumstances. This surrendered meeting of our circumstances gives us a chance to bring our deepest presence into whatever challenges we might face. Once we trust in this conscious participation, we give permission for our psychological and spiritual centers of gravity to shift from the contraction of the small self into a liberated realm of boundless Big Self; from occupation, to presence; from ego, in other words, to the Infinite.

Wisdom and compassion are continually born and reborn here in ways that allow for us to touch lives with complete generosity.

But we need to practice being still in order for this mystery to unfold. Becoming a conscious participant in this kind of awareness comes from discipline and wholeheartedness. As we purposefully expose ourselves to a stillness of mind and body, over and over again, we spontaneously notice that the conventional circumstances of the small self lead us directly to the Ultimate Living of the Big Self. Stillness not only helps us let go, it is the letting go of everything. It allows us to bring the perspective of the summit back into our daily lives. Stillness helps us face our dilemmas and successes with fearless integrity and allows our intentions to be filled with the profoundly rich grace of Spirit. As this grace and ease of Spirit informs our experience, we realize that our stillness is not something we practice only for ourselves, but for the benefit of all things, for all time.

Perspective

4

There is nothing either good or bad but thinking makes it so:
to me it is a prison.
—William. Shakespeare

So the world, grounded in a timeless movement by the Soul which
suffuses it with intelligence, becomes a living and blessed being.
—Plotinus

Key among our efforts to climb beyond both personal and collective suffering is our ability to allow for a conscious opening to the Awareness that is beyond time and mind. To uncover this perspective, it is helpful to imagine that the stillness underneath all that moves is the source of everything that we can conceive in our minds or sense in our bodies. In other words, all things that move are born from and then die into stillness. At the top of the Mountain of Spirit we Know this stillness as the primordial Awareness; the source of everything, including our thoughts and feelings. As the source of everything, it must also be the endpoint of everything, since whatever arises out of it must fall back into it. Whatever is born, in short, must also die. Since this primordial Awareness is the origin of all birth and the destination for all things at death, every single circumstance in the Universe exists as the contents between these two points.

And yet, unlike all the objects, concepts, and feelings that are filtered through the mind and have a beginning and an end, Awareness itself is beyond all of this. As the opening to all beginnings and all ends, it is not bound by anything that can either be born or can die. As the source of all that moves, Awareness can never be anything other than stillness. This silent, infinitely still Awareness has no graspable qualities since it is what is aware of all graspable qualities. It is, as we say in Zen, none other than Emptiness and so offers the creation of all form. It is the stillness that supports the creative generation of all that ever moves, especially our sense of self. This Emptiness is Spirit.

What gets in the way of this realization is the relationship that the ego has with its experience. This is because, like a shark, the ego cannot survive if its not moving. In the face of stillness, the ego is impotent and obsolete. Therefore, in the face of stillness, the ego is only concerned with finding ways to move either toward safety or away from danger. Even the slightest exposure to stillness threatens the ego like nothing else because this experience forces it to recognize its own origin and endpoint. As a stillness practice forces this issue, the ego's personal reality starts to yield to a vast impersonal connection to all things, where an impersonal connection to all things is seen as something that can never be "mine" or "yours." Just as stillness can't be possessed, neither can Awareness. Awareness is totally communal since it can never be owned or possessed. It is always and forever the simple sense of being, which is nothing other than the deeply shared felt sense of awareness at every moment, equally available to all beings, all of the time.

Since Awareness is both present in and the source of all things, it can never separate from anything. It suffuses everything in its loving expanse. As a result of this deep and singular inclusiveness, Awareness has the opportunity to become "aware" of itself through each of our experiences. This awareness of Awareness is something that we might usually refer to as "consciousness." Once we see that our own personal consciousness is merely our awareness of Awareness, we can also recognize that we have a direct and open connection with the Infinite. Put another way, the higher we climb up the Mountain of Spirit, the more we recognize that the summit is built into each and every circumstance.

We can see that essentially we are always on the summit when we become conscious of certain things. First, we need to see how time, like all other things, is insignificant in relation to Awareness. Time may support all of our egoic, or small self circumstances, but since time moves there is no way for it to exist in the stillness of Awareness. Just like the Big Self, Awareness isn't ever born, nor does it ever die. On the other hand, personal experiences are always temporary events, bound by time. Since Awareness is always totally still, and stillness is what gives birth to the entire movement of time, it is at once and in all ways free of time.

This concept is more than a little confusing for the small self, but once we stop grasping at the concept things can become quite clear. For instance, consider how each of us can be aware of a desire for, say, a chocolate chip cookie. If we can be aware of our desire for the cookie, then the desire is an object of our minds. If this desire is an object of which we can be aware, then that which is aware of the desire must be beyond it. So the impersonal Awareness of our desire for a chocolate cookie, through our personal sense of consciousness, automatically goes beyond any desire we might have for the cookie. In the same way, that which is aware of our happiness must be beyond our happiness. That which is aware of our negativity must be beyond our negativity. This realization of our always present, deep, abiding Awareness never can or will be bound by anything—not even our sense of past personal stories or future wants. This is exactly what makes Awareness profoundly and eternally free. No birth, no death—just freedom showing up as Awareness.

While this may sound very much like a sterile mathematical proof, there is a richness in this articulation if what these words point to can be felt rather than merely understood. When we simply practice having a felt sense of where these words point our attention and then we relax in the process, we begin to witness how our thoughts, feelings, and emotions also have no bearing on the nature of Spirit. Each of these things are, like our desire for a chocolate chip cookie, simply objects that arise in Awareness.

As another example, rather than only experiencing the small self perspective of "being angry," we can experience the Big Self perspective of an "Awareness of the sensation of anger." Asking ourselves in any situation, "What is arising in Awareness now?" offers the realization of Big Self since we can only answer the question from the perspective of Awareness. If, on the other hand, we were to ask ourselves, "What am I thinking right now?" there is no potential for Awakening since the small self is given a spotlight on center stage and asked to deliver a monologue about what it believes to be true.

This perspective of Big Self Awareness can be practiced the next time you get into a disagreement with someone you care about deeply. Instead of succumbing to the monologues delivered by the egoic mind, uncover what is arising in your experience with a dispassionate presence.

Don't judge, don't fight, don't do anything to whatever is arising; just practice witnessing your experience. You will notice that the witnessing presence is not caught by whatever emotion might be arising. In fact, you may even be able to see that the witnessing Awareness is totally at peace even though the emotions might be extreme. This allows for deeper and deeper truth to be revealed in any exchange we might have. Responding to our loved ones from this place of openness allows for all of our interactions to shift in an instant from contest to peace.

Living the Awareness that is both beyond time and mind and yet paradoxically their source might sound odd, if not impossible, to the small self. But it is our natural state of being and it is available now, in this life. It is the state of being that exists prior to anything extra that the ego might want to add to our experience in order to make it better or worse. It is the state of being that is simply Aware of what is really happening at any given point in time. This new, infinitely expansive perspective starts to grow past our old psychological and spiritual skin and then begins to inhabit a spacious stillness so vast that it can neither be directly conceived nor articulated. Yet the mystic within each of us can intuit, or Know, that stillness is the source of everything that is true inside and outside of this physical experience that we share with all beings. Consciously meeting this still core of the Infinite is nothing less than resting on the summit of the Mountain of Spirit. Here we are offered an opening to an everyday holiness as we begin to Know beyond the thoughts of our minds and the senses of our bodies that our Path to the Big Self, to the mind of God, is nothing other than this moment, experienced fully.

In Mind: Time and Thought

*Past and future veil God from our sight. Burn both
of them with fire.*
—*Rumi*

*What is troubling us is the tendency to believe that the mind
is like a little man within.*
—*Ludwig Von Wittgenstein*

The only version of time that is infused with Awareness is this
very moment. The present moment, or the Now, is always here. Always.
It is never absent. In fact, there has never been any time other than Now.
Something in the past may arise in our minds as a memory, but it still
arises in the Now. Something in the future may arise in our minds as
anticipation, but even this only ever shows up in the Now. From this
moment, the past extends infinitely. From this moment, the future also
extends infinitely. Therefore, the present moment is forever at the center
of all existence. Just like Awareness, the Now never moves. The causes
and conditions that arise in the Now might change, but the Now itself
is always simply right here. The present moment itself is simply always,
already, forever outside the boundary of past and future, never falling
behind or moving ahead. It is in all ways just this. When we connect with
this present moment with our full attention, we can actually experience
what the Zen tradition calls "No Mind." No Mind shows itself when
the mind lets go of itself and connects spontaneously to the impersonal
experience of the Awareness that exists between each and every thought
that we might have. In this spaciousness offered by the present moment,
we are totally alert yet unfettered by anything personal.

Past and future, in contrast, define our personal versions of experience. Put another way, we might say that our relationship to time is precisely what defines our minds. All of our mental noise and activity, in other words, is rooted in either past experiences or in future desires. Time itself, as both past and future, is therefore nothing other than a series of thoughts that we cling to in our minds. Just like all thoughts, the past and future are moving targets—fertile fantasies to which the ego attaches its many versions of personal meaning. In these experiences of personal meaning, the ego always can cling to so much. In both the personal stories from our past and the personal stories of desire for future outcomes, the ego secures its position in our experience. In fact, ego will even do this dance of clinging to time throughout our entire spiritual journey and everything associated with it. It will do this dance whenever it becomes deeply interested in anything, since this deep interest is simply another form of attachment that diminishes the clarity of our awakening into the fullness of what is happening in the Now.

Unfortunately for the ego, it can't ever find anything to grasp in the present moment. This is because the present moment is not bound by the limits imposed by the scripts and stories associated with either a personal past and a personal future. As the space surrounding our thoughts, the present moment is not and can never be manipulated by our minds.

In order to get a sense of this, there is an exercise that we can do. First of all, find a place where you can be still for a several minutes. Perhaps it's a comfortable chair, maybe a meditation cushion in a corner of your living space, maybe it's in an airport as you wait for your flight. It doesn't really matter as long as you can simultaneously find a place that supports your solitude as well as your ability to stay alert. For this reason, lying down can sometimes get in the way of an experience of alertness since sleep so easily can overtake us when we lie down. After you find a place for stillness, close your eyes and imagine a massive screen on which a film might be shown. Concentrate on the screen, allowing for anything that shows itself on the screen to do so fully. Regardless of the projection on the screen, simply watch it with total relaxation, noting each image as a memory, a judgment, or a plan. Be careful not to offer any evaluation of these thoughts; just watch and note into which category each image falls.

"I miss the times my brother and I would share as we delivered the morning newspaper when we were kids" would count as a memory.

"I can't stand the pain I keep getting in my knees as I sit in this ridiculous lotus position" would count as a judgment.

"I've got to remember to pick up more dog food" would count as a plan.

Do this for a brief time and gently encourage the recognition of the space between the images. Notice with full attention when the screen is blank. Even if this is barely perceptible, keep giving attention not only to the thoughts on the screen but also to the spaces between the thoughts as well. This space between the thinking activity of mind is No Mind. It is also nothing other than the present moment. It is the Now. It is infinite in its nature and comprehensive in its reach both inside of us as well as outside of us. With practice, the recognition of this space between your thoughts will last longer, eventually resulting in the occupation of a central place in your experience.

Recognizing this space between our thoughts, we begin to come to the realization that all past and all future projections within our Awareness are simply sophisticated scripts written by ego as a way for it to remain in a perceived state of control of each circumstance. So time is what allows the ego to attach to things. Without time, there is only the Now—a place where there can be no attachment since there are no thoughts. Experiencing this present moment without thought we awaken to Freedom.

No Mind

An attentive mind is an open mind. An open mind is a surrendered mind—one that neither clings nor avoids—which is the opposite of what minds normally to do. Minds are supposed to categorize and compartmentalize in ways that allow us to create order out of chaos. We get a sense of a surrendered mind when we realize the clarity of experience in the space between our thoughts, where there is no past and no future. We might just as easily call this surrendered mind experience the arising of "no ego" since the ego and the mind are both fueled by past and future.

Similarly, we can interchange ego and mind since both are continually oriented in greed and aversion patterns.

Another of my teachers taught this connection beautifully, and I credit his emphasis on not letting the mind, or ego, abide anywhere with helping many of us along the Path. "A mind that is truly exposed," he would say, "is a mind that is Infinite."

This Zen teaching of No Mind, or what we're referring to here as surrendered mind, is interchangeable with what Christians might easily call "Christ-consciousness." Whatever label we give to a surrendered mind, it can be experienced whenever we witness whatever arises and then consciously orient our participation in life from the space between our thoughts.

To take this a step further, my teacher kept at us, saying that as long as we relaxed in this space between our thoughts, or what he referred to as the place of "no abiding mind," we would be fully expressing our awakened Buddha nature. This confused me for the longest time. How could a mind that doesn't seek anything be something desirable? I enjoyed thinking that my mind was what got me through life, and I thought it would be exactly what would lead the way to Enlightenment. I preferred the idea that my brainpower and my self-image were strong and more than a little competent, and that this was what supported all of my successes and helped me avoid failures. What I didn't realize was that what appears weak to the ego is usually helpful in uncovering the unfathomably rich and infinitely powerful grace of Spirit.

Rather than latching onto opinions, beliefs, and convictions, like any powerful ego should do, I learned from all those hours at the feet of my teacher to open my heart and mind to uncertainty. In order to do this, the teaching suggested that I let listening infuse the talking, humility infuse the knowing, and feeling infuse the thinking. Here again, all of my teachers were very clear. Each in their own way suggested that if we can take all of our understanding and knowing and then trade it in for curiosity and wonder, we are invited to live from and in the liberated space of the present moment.

Any of us can practice this when we run into something that annoys us. Instead of immediately bringing out brigades of internal soldiers in order to defend a certain position, whatever it might be, we can meet our irritants with wonder. We can become curious about our mind state, for instance, as we miss the last flight home after a busy, weeklong business trip; as we forget an important meeting; as we watch our siblings finally find the right mate. When we simply watch our mind state, regardless of the situation, we are expressing an expanded awareness that isn't touched by our annoyance, anger, or even rage. Rather than being irritated, we become curious about our irritation. This curiosity can only show up in the present since its very nature is unattached. Nothing in the infinite spaciousness of open curiosity and uncontracted wonder is anything other than the Now. In this way, when we relax into a direct connection with everything, as everything, in the state of surrendered mind, or No Mind, we become awake in this life that we're experiencing in this moment.

There is a limitless source of power for each of us in this place of curiosity and wonder, in this release into a truly surrendered mind. Since ego's relationship to circumstances is the impediment to this realization, it can't have a hand in managing any part of the process. This does not mean that it won't try to employ even more creative ways of staying in control. One of the most common ways that it does this is to affiliate itself with lots of judgment. Consider how, for example, the qualities of non-aggression and wonder are usually the characteristics that strong egos often judge as feeble and powerless. Yet these qualities of being have the potential of helping us Awaken, since they never seek to control or manipulate anything. Ego, by contrast, is defined by manipulation and will forever be totally threatened by waking up to what is expressed through the experience of the Now, since without time, the ego can no longer grasp thoughts, and without any grasping at thoughts, it can't remain in control.

Awakening to what is beyond time and mind doesn't leave us without purpose, however. Nor does it leave us dead to the thrills of life. On the contrary, the expression of a surrendered mind becomes an imperative to those who cultivate it. Any activity, for example, that is informed consciously by the stillness offered by a surrendered mind is totally dynamic and filled with infinite potential. When we act from the openness of a surrendered mind, our choices start to reflect deeply non-egoic activity. If we rest in this surrendered Emptiness, we can't help but eventually have a felt sense of being at one with all things. Once this felt sense of the deep singularity of all things begins to express itself through us, we naturally live as an offering of both wisdom and compassion in all situations. Living like this we notice that the kisses for those we love become sweeter; laughter resonates within us; the moon and stars sing to us in ways our minds can't imagine; and yet we remain open in the face of the whole, beautiful mess.

Still Caught

Only when we ultimately let go of our attachment to our mind and its activity of thinking can we uncover the ever-present Now. This doesn't mean that we should get rid of any mental creativity we might find or should avoid thought in general. Nor does it mean that having the ability to intellectualize about the Path isn't potentially a good thing. Thinking, after all, isn't problematic unless we become caught by the thoughts. So when we practice letting go all of the time, we become more and more comfortable with nonattachment. The view from this height is one that is similar to what is seen by good parents who continually practice letting go of their children as they grow into and through all of their developmental stages. These parents can gain a certain comfort with the instability inherent in rearing children. They find themselves glad when their babies sleep through the night, when they graduate from being terrible twos, when they graduate from diapers, when they graduate from total dependence to ever increasing levels of self-sufficiency.

Similarly, we should employ the same style of letting go of our habitual relationship to both time and to thought. We do this once we consciously practice sourcing ourselves from the perspective shown to us by the present moment—from the open, impersonal space between our thoughts. Whenever we can let go into this stillness of No Mind, we can't help but be sourced from the Now and we can't help but be supported by the space between thoughts. In this spaciousness, we are again resting at the summit of the Mountain of Spirit.

If we can practice consciously resting at this summit by meeting the space between our thoughts, we tend to notice a felt sense of what's important and what is not. The Infinite shows itself over and over again to be real, for example, while our mind-bound interpretations of what the Infinite offers are seen as unbelievably trivial in comparison. Still, even though we may have had a few of these felt experiences of the Infinite, it usually takes time in order for its meaning to inform our actions in a deliberate way. Although there are great stories of immediate and permanent Awakenings occurring in certain people, it is rare that such a radical shift in awareness can be immediately and permanently embodied. More often than not, Awakening takes patience and a good dose of diligence in order to help us turn our experiential events into actual shifts in the ways that we meet the world.

In fact, one of the major ways that we can actually prevent the enlightened perspective from replacing our limited view is by remaining caught by any of the thoughts and feelings that continue to arise in our minds, especially the ones that accompany spiritual experiences. Again, no matter how deep our realization might be, as long as we remain truly fascinated and enthralled by any part of it, our egos are still caught by an attachment. This will always put the brakes on the process of any authentic Awakening. As long as we are enthralled, captivated, fascinated, or deeply interested by any thought or feeling that comes up, we are engaged in clinging. This clinging is what allows us to be hooked by our minds, and this habitual movement of mind is exactly what defiles the still process of opening to Spirit.

One of my teachers was very helpful to me when I kept facing this very issue in the early days of my Zen practice. Within the first few months of meditation, I started to have some intense experiences on my sitting cushion. The beauty and splendor of what danced in my head while I meditated was beyond anything I could ever put to words, and the feelings of euphoria that came my way still, to this day, give me chills when I recall them. I didn't know what these breathtaking explosions of bliss were, but I knew I wanted them to last and I wanted to have more of them. Then, one day, the internal firework display stopped. So did the bliss. The party had ended, and no one had given any warnings or cries of "last call." For months after the shows stopped, I continued to meditate without any more of the bliss I'd grown so interested in keeping.

When I finally asked my teacher how I could once again summon the bliss to which I'd grown so accustomed, he just smiled and said, "Could it be that your interest in having your experiences continue is the kind of attachment that keeps us spiritually stunted?"

I just stared at him, knowing that he was right. My craving for more of these amazing states prevented them. The whole of my practice shifted at that point from a place of trying to acquire more bliss, to a practice of letting go of it and everything else.

Still, I find that there is a question that often arises at this point for many practitioners: Wouldn't life be boring if we were to let go of the things that engage us? Perhaps. But asking ourselves what we would be like if we weren't so captivated by the usual stuff can also lead us to liberation. Who, for instance, would you be without all of those scripts and story lines that the ego delivers? Who are you, really? Are you more than the objects of your clinging? Whatever your answers might be to these and other invitations of self-inquiry will always lead to the very source of who we always have been, beyond the places that still catch the ego.

Along these lines, one should keep in mind that not being captivated is not the same thing as being shut off from life. Allowing ourselves to be insulated from the fullness of any circumstance would be the ego averting any impact of the Infinite that a situation, thought, or feeling might present. Aversion or any denial of what arises is just another form of false security for that in us which is small. Not being captivated or caught by anything, on the other hand, allows us to experience whatever situation shows up with a greater depth and a more comprehensive sense of freedom. Not being enthralled allows us to meet everything with all of our fullness, instead of letting our minds limit what we meet. This non-clinging Awareness helps us meet all of life without any compulsion to judge anything in our experience as either positive or negative. We just let what is be what is, and then we let the resonance of our whole, unattached Big Self be there for everything, as everything, in each moment.

In Body: Feelings and Emotions

The heart of man is nearer to the Truth than his intelligence.
—Aurobindo

God is in me or else not at all.
—Wallace Stevens

If you haven't wept deeply, you haven't begun to meditate.
—Ajahn Chah

Just as with time and thought, the mind generates scripts to
be delivered on the Stage of Mind that are specifically associated
with physical feelings and emotions. We can use the same course of
examination as we have before to see that feelings and emotions are little
more than deeply held energetic states onto which we project our stories.
The ego adheres to many of these feelings and emotions, especially the
intense ones, with tremendous energy. But since feelings and emotions
are simply objects of attachment, we have the opportunity to radically
diminish their hold on us. While feelings and emotions are often deeply
held by each of us, they are still objects of mind that we can, with
practice, choose to meet consciously, instead of indulging or avoiding
them. Just like everything else, any object of mind is both interdependent
and temporary. In addition, if we look at any object deeply enough, we see
that it is mysteriously Infinite at its core. At the summit of the Mountain
of Spirit, our view allows for a shift in our perspective that uncovers the
Infinite experientially, thereby giving us a chance to meet our lives in ways
characterized by increasing levels of openness.

We get a sense of this openness when we deconstruct the senses and
perceptions of our bodies. Feelings occur when the mind interprets the

physical energetic manifestations within the body. As an example, a woman on her cell phone in line at the local café bumped the stroller in which I had packed my daughter, causing my freshly made latte to spill down my pants. For those who haven't experienced this, hot espresso drinks spilled down our pants will bring on intense and immediate feelings of discomfort. Emotions register themselves in the mind in the same way, except that rather than merely having a physical component to them, they incorporate psychological and energetic variations as well. The latte that spilled down my pants, for example, briefly carried judgment and blame with it, such as: Did that woman have to be so careless? Did that latte have to be the temperature of lava? Luckily, meditation practice can help lessen the intensity of situations like these. Judgment and blame can actually fade quite quickly if we become keenly aware of our mind's activity in the middle of spilled latte incidents. Forgiveness and even humor can show up once we see that despite the differences between feelings and emotions, both are always simply egoic activity meeting the fullness of our bodily form. With more and more practice, we begin to see that no matter what we experience, be it elation or depression, or anything else, bodily experiences are nothing other than felt energetic patterns that register and then get interpreted in the mind. Seeing this activity for what it is frees us from responses to life that are solely rooted in the contraction of the small self, thereby allowing us to move through the world with greater ease.

Feelings as Thoughts

To get a little technical, feelings are deep thoughts. Consider that all of our sensations are energetic bodily states of various levels of intensity that are interpreted and then given a contextual meaning by the mind. For example, if you feel pain, what is actually being noticed by the mind is an intensity that corresponds viscerally to some memory of discomfort. This memory carries with it all of the results of this previous discomfort, whatever they might have been. Because of this baggage, the pain we experience is an imputation, or a script, that ego plays out as something to avoid. The energy from ego's resistance to this circumstance is a thought we've been conditioned to refer to as "pain." Put another way, pain is the name we give to an intense experience that we are trying to avoid. The avoidance of the intensity gives rise to the mental interpretation of the event as negative, and this negativity manifests bodily as a contracted sense of desperation. While our feelings may vary substantially, this process of recognition followed by interpretation followed by varying degrees of grasping or avoidance applies to all feelings and all emotions. This isn't to say that our felt sense of things isn't real. Of course our feelings are real. It's just that our perspective from the summit of the Mountain of Spirit shows us that our feelings are inextricably linked to egoic patterns of greed and avoidance.

As odd as this might sound, feelings are simply objects of mind that manifest in the body. Any object of mind is simply a thought, and at the summit none of us is caught by thoughts or anything else. So it's not that feelings aren't felt or that we meet our emotions with a cold disregard. Rather, we see that the stories we give our bodily senses are ego-authored projections. Any body sense, seen through this lens, is only temporary. Nothing more, nothing less. Feelings arise like everything else in Awareness. But at their essence, they are born out of Emptiness and they eventually die back into Emptiness, just as do all other things in the Universe.

Maybe this is a little heady and obscure, but underneath all of these words there is a rather hopeful message. Basically, we are free of any physical or emotional hindrance if we can just recognize the tendency of mind to grasp and thereby consistently impede the fullness of our potential experience. By observing the mind's impulse to grasp and label all of our feelings, we are offered a chance to be free of the mind when we rest in every experience as a conscious Observer, Seer, Audience, or Witness of all that arises.

To give this point some context: At one point during a retreat that I was leading, one of the practitioners approached me in tears, telling me about both the pain he felt in his back and the pain he still felt in his heart over a marriage that had ended nearly ten years previously. He described his physical and emotional trials in great detail and told me how his therapist suggested that he meet his pain fully while neither avoiding it nor judging it, just as I'd been suggesting he do during our retreat.

"My discomfort is just a deep thought," he kept saying while I remained nearly silent during our exchange.

The next day, he and I met again, and it was as if I were looking at the face of an entirely different person. His eyes sparkled, he wore an authentic smile, and he seemed to be sitting with less difficulty.

"It's amazing," he said. "When you stay in the fire of it all, and you don't move, you just witness the whole thing. The stuff you don't need burns away."

We bowed to each other and he left the room. Then it was my turn to cry. What a gift to be able to watch this simple heroism show up in his life. He had seen through his mind's interpretation of his thoughts, giving space for deep authentic peace to reveal itself.

The Middle Way

From the infinitely open perspective of the summit, we realize that we are not what we think nor what we feel. From a limited, egoic view, we are simply an attachment to the activity of our minds, always believing we are only what we think and what we feel. In other words, the very things that arise in the mind are precisely what we are in that moment, yet at the same time we are much more than what is arising. In *The Heart Sutra*, we chant that, "Form is Emptiness, and Emptiness is form." Put another way, we are here in human form, yet we are simultaneously infinite Emptiness. Negating this Infinity is at the core of all the thoughts that give birth to our pain and suffering. Negating our conscious expression of Spirit perfectly describes the prison from which we seek to escape.

So in a way this realization renders Descartes's famous statement, "I think, therefore I am," as the articulation of our fundamental delusion rather than an articulation of anything close to authentic existence. If we are defined by thinking and feeling, we are then clinging to the mind, which is exactly what obscures Awakening. If, on the other hand, we blew the translation, and Descartes was actually suggesting something closer to, "There is consciousness, therefore I am," then he's pointing us directly toward the summit of the Mountain of Spirit. In other words, if we are aware of our awareness ("there is consciousness"), and we allow this awareness to support the recognition of our own existence, we come to the experience of "I am." This "am-ness," or Presence, or Being, is the very same thing as what we've referred to as the Big Self: the uncontracted, always present, timeless, primordial opening that is who we ultimately are. We are here in this mental and bodily form, yet at the same time we are only awakened Emptiness. Regardless of how we might translate Descartes, our practice is to walk this razor's edge between the relative truth (form) and the Ultimate Truth (Emptiness). This tightrope of a Path, with the relative on one side and the Ultimate on the other, is what in Buddhism we call "the Middle Way."

Most of us do our best to let the Ultimate extend its boundless clarity into our relative, often messy, conventional circumstance. At least this is where the Middle Way points us. Instead of being trapped by our feelings, the Middle Way shows us that we can become free of our attachment to them as we watch their arising and their ceasing. From this place of open observation of all that is going in our experience, we are consciously resting in Emptiness, or what we might just as easily call "No-thing-ness." When we are no longer caught by things, peace informs our walk as well as our work.

Even if the label "No-thing-ness" confuses the mind, it is important to remember that "No-thing-ness" is inseparable from the flow of "Everything-ness", including our feelings. It goes beyond and yet brings along the flow. As the still source of all things, Nothingness, or Emptiness, or Awareness, is unchanging and always already present at every point of this flow. The flow itself, as well as our feelings, are born from and die to this Source. Walking the Middle Way occurs when we align ourselves with the felt sense of this Source as we go about our day. For example, when we consciously witness our joy when we cheer on our college football team; or when we are consciously witness our pain when our significant other says something that cuts to the quick. Walking the Middle Way, while tricky at times, is nothing other than letting observation infuse and inform our participation in all aspects of a life that builds itself from a spacious and deep connectivity.

The Truth

Awakening into an enlightened perspective happens when we intentionally open our hearts and minds and let go of all thoughts and feelings that relate to a separate sense of what we've always known as a *self*. This self isn't anything fixed. It is our mistaken belief that this sense of "I" is the cause of all pain. The source of our suffering isn't that we have an "I," or an ego, but rather that our ego's clinging keeps us blind to our natural state of boundless grace atop the Mountain of Spirit. Ego isn't the problem; rather its fixations and its inertia are what prevent the Divine from shining through us.

The deep, felt sense of grace in our bodies that often accompanies a profound spiritual opening to Truth is often blissful. So, it is common for a practitioner's ego to identify any profoundly expansive feeling with Enlightenment when in fact the experience is still confined to the perceptions of one's individual body and mind. Just because an experience feels as if the ego has been transcended doesn't mean that it has. Experiences of total self are constantly confused with experiences of no self, yet in terms of Awakening, the difference is profound. Confusing childlike innocence, for example, with Enlightenment gets us into trouble, because childlike innocence is not outside the bounds of ego but rather totally subsumed by it. Children see, in other words, the Universe as an extension of a "me" that gets to define what is "mine," while the enlightened among us have let go of this form of clinging. To an Awakened person, the me and the mine have given way to a vast sense of undivided awareness we might call "All."

I remember when a woman got upset with a teacher giving a Dharma talk on this topic. Basically, he was emphasizing that the gift and curse of adulthood centers around our ability to reflect on our minds and bodies. This reflection allows us to go past mind and body if we don't attach to any part of the process. "Little kids," I remember him saying, "can't do this like we can."

"Kids are always better at it than we are," the woman countered after his talk. "Isn't that what we're trying to do here? Reclaim our childlike states of innocence?"

He gave an interesting response saying that "While childlike states of innocence are beautiful to experience, the experience is never anything other than a pointer to what is beyond the experience itself. It's not that the Infinite only extends outside of us. It extends within us as well. As such, this thing we call me is like a screen door to the Universe, swinging open and closed, never really keeping anything in or out. So it helps to recognize that any state we might reach is simply pointing us in a certain direction. For any of us to cling to any thought or feeling of what Awakening might be like merely sets the small self up to manage our search for a deeper spirituality that we've mistaken for childish egocentrism."

It is critical for the sincere practitioner to realize that Enlightenment mustn't be confused with the feeling of a state of bliss or the emotions that might accompany these sensations. Enlightenment shows up when both the mind and body are dropped from the experiential continuum. Mind and body, in other words, are seen for what they are: temporary experiences, whose versions of truth are always and forever partial. This realization unties and extends past all boundaries of thought and feeling. It's as if a divine transplant occurs, exchanging our fixations with what is beyond fixation. As strange and as threatening as this may sound to the ego, this shift is the way we begin to embody an enlightened Illumination.

Having said this, our felt sense of this Illumination is both an invitation to the party of Awakening and a simple reflection of our individual sense of Truth. It is not the Truth itself any more than our image in a mirror is real. Any felt sense of the Truth beyond name and form invariably points us directly into the light of Awakening. Your sense of Truth is important, but it isn't the whole story. In fact, your sense of Truth, as well as my sense of Truth, is always partial. Our feelings and emotions are centered and oriented in personal experience, yet they are only an expression of our most basic fixation on our own egocentricity. On the other hand, authentic spiritual practice systematically exposes our egocentric limitations to the clear light of Truth. Awakening to this light cannot be understood as a personal experience, since the latter inappropriately confines the Infinite to the boundary of our own personal thoughts and feelings.

While egos might bristle at any mention of Truth (*Whose Truth? Truth is culture bound! Truth is relative!*), it is important to recognize that we are only pointing toward the Infinity that gives birth to every form and mind-identified version of Truth. It is beyond any egoic script that might sound like: "That was the enlightenment experience that I've been waiting to have. I guess I'm done since it feels like I've been successful in letting my ego fall away." It is beyond any attachment that might suggest that there is no such thing as Truth since any version of Truth is only a relative experience. The Truth that Awakening offers up is beyond all relativity. It isn't mine, nor is it yours, nor is it anyone else's. It is that spark of divinity that shimmers in all things whether we consciously recognize it or not. It is the brilliant chaotic Uncertainty that surpasses any categorization or tradition, whether or not we want to comfort our egos by attaching to labels like Hindu, Muslim, Christian, Buddhist or Jew. It is a Truth that goes beyond and yet brings everything along with its expression. This is equally everybody's Truth, and, if we're ready to receive it, we'll find that it is always showing itself at the core of everything that we might ever think or feel.

Being the Expanse

One of the biggest parts of our practice, then, is to neither indulge our feelings nor avoid them. We should just meet them with a committed openness so that we can witness them and therefore become free of our attachment to them. This doesn't mean that we don't feel anything. Becoming numb to our feelings isn't the work. Being free of our attachment to our feelings usually means that they become both more instructive and more vivid. But, our relationship to everything that we feel becomes much less limiting. Whether our felt experiences are enjoyable or not isn't the point. The important matter at hand is how we are able to function in the world with Awakened bodies and minds.

We really have two choices: we either show up in the world as a contracted reflection of whatever our experience might be, or we can be the expansive awareness of whatever experience arises. From the contraction, our feelings and emotions work closely with ego in order to move us through the world. In the contracted state, our feelings and emotions that are brought about by our personal experiences with pleasure and pain, gain and loss, praise and blame, along with fame and shame, get to be the determiners of how we live in the world of circumstance. By contrast, from the uncontracted, Awakened context, our feelings and emotions are witnessed and experienced from a spaciousness forever beyond ego's reach. When feelings and emotions, as well as ego's management of them, can be watched instead of grasped, we are employing a mind and body that are Awake. This shift allows for us to watch our feelings and emotions from the impersonal perspective of the

Big Self. To the extent that we can practice this nonattachment in relation to our feelings and emotions, this allows for a different kind of resonance and connectivity to arise with each moment thereby delivering us into a precious Ultimate Life.

Presence

5

*Lift the stone and you will find me; cleave the wood
and I am there.*
—*Jesus Christ*

He who knows himself, knows God.
—*Muhammad*

Presence shows itself most often as a simple expression of full awareness. Almost everyone has had the pleasure of being in the vicinity of people who carry with them a certain magnetism that can't easily be described. There's just something about them. More often than not, this kind of energetic authority is seen by the ego as charisma, or what a Hindu practitioner might call *shakti*. Regardless of its name, any being that embodies this presence radiates a certain clarity that we can't seem to ignore. It's like when I'm watching my cat stalking something in the backyard and I can't take my eyes away from what he's doing. The same applies to any of us if we are fully engaged in what we are doing. If, at any point in time, we are resting in deep attention, it will always have the potential of pulling mysteriously at a part of anyone else nearby. Especially when we stalk things in our backyard.

The fully present among us can't help but be compelling. The space that they occupy speaks to something special within us: our own, most sacred sense of Being. If we're alert, we can sense this energetic field within ourselves, even as we do even the most mundane of life's work. We can uncover our sacred presence as we water our plants, brush our teeth, eat our meals, wash our dishes, or pay or bills. All that we need to do in order to live from this space is pay full attention to whatever it is that we are doing.

One of my most memorable experiences of presence occurred when I first stepped into the kitchen at Green Gulch Farm Zen Center. The staff busily prepared breakfast for the community; I helped with the zucchini muffins. As I grated the squash, I couldn't help but notice the precision and care offered by each of the participants in this culinary dance, all of which was in total silence. It was as if each person were having an inter-subjective, or telepathic, experience with some type of spiritual Big Chef that called all the shots, all at once.

One of the cooks in particular was so amazingly focused on slicing strawberries that I couldn't take my eyes off him. There was nothing unnatural or forced about what he was doing. It just appeared that the entire process of strawberry slicing was an expression of this guy's whole being: his activity was careful and yet carefree, focused and yet open, free of anything extra. Without any reservation whatsoever, he gave every bit of himself to the slicing of these big beautiful strawberries, as a gift to all of us. I, on the other hand, was distracted by his grace and kept nicking my knuckles on the grater. As silly as it must sound, a deep longing arose in me to be able to do something, anything, with as much presence and care as the guy slicing strawberries that morning. I wanted, in that moment, to be able to live from that type of fullness.

This mental and physical orientation toward living fully shows up in our experience as a weaving together of wisdom and compassion in all that we do. Our full attention to the present moment and whatever it offers is wisdom, while any of our participation that is guided by this full attention to the present moment is compassion. Putting these together, like hands meeting for a prayer, allows for a different kind of relationship with the circumstances of life. All things that come from this meeting of wisdom and compassion become a holy and celebratory way of living. Our participation from this place is the unfolding of our Ultimate Life. In this spacious unfolding, all things become recognized as miracles of the Universe's constant creativity. From here, there is nothing left to do except smile and bow.

In Mind: Wisdom

If the doors of perception were cleansed, everything would
appear to man as it is, infinite.
—*William Blake*

The nature of God is a circle of which the center is everywhere
and the circumference is nowhere.
—*Empedocles*

As the audience, or Witness, of the illusory and repetitious charade of ego on the Stage of Mind, we suddenly have an empowering choice offered to each of us in every single situation that we might encounter. In this choice we always uncover a chance in each moment to surrender any and all forms of attachment. Wisdom comes from our ability to watch without judgment and therefore see through the various levels of our clinging until we are confronted with the profoundly obvious Truth that every thing that can be conceived is merely a ripple in the totally unified, oceanic expression of Emptiness. Truly seeing that all things are an expression of this Oneness is wisdom.

From the summit of the Mountain, all things begin to take on an entirely new meaning and assume a position in our consciousness in ways far different from what we've always known. We've previously touched on how all things can be seen as having three defining qualities: every thing is temporary; every thing is interdependent; and every thing is ultimately an expression of the Infinite. The realization of this makes the ego, as well as all the other constructs of our minds, rather trivial. Every thing, including ego, becomes largely insubstantial in the face of the expansiveness of the Infinite Oneness. But we don't just dissolve into bliss at this recognition. Nor does our "infinite wisdom" show us that nothing is of any importance at all. Life itself, from this perspective, is never meaningless. On the contrary, recognizing the temporary nature of all things, the interdependence of all things, and the empty or Infinite nature of all things can inspire us to live our lives with intense courage and compassion in every situation because the Knowing of this Truth frees us from the habitual orientation built and serviced by the small self.

When we begin to rest in this Truth, as this Self beyond the self, we can freely participate as the wisdom that is revealed by that which witnesses all experience. Then we can start to source our lives from an inexhaustible supply of fearless availability. From the Witness, we wisely recognize that we are free to choose how we will respond to any and all circumstances that might arise. Instead, for instance, of being bound by the usual responses to the constant threats and desires offered in our life situations, we begin to see another way to operate—one that is generous to everyone involved, including ourselves. When we fully re-center our consciousness in the formless, inclusive, and groundless space of the Witness, we become free of all things because we begin to see that we are all things. It is at this point that we begin to offer a presence to the entire Universe that is nothing less than the unattached and enlightened grace of Being.

The Eighth Sense

Another way to refer to the Witness is to call it our "Eighth Sense." By this I mean that we have our five senses of our physical experience: those of sight, sound, taste, smell, and touch. Then, in our mental experience, we have our thoughts, which can be counted as our sixth sense. Unlike the Western idea that suggests the sixth sense is some supernatural representation of insight, Eastern cultures soberly suggest that our sixth sense simply encompasses the activities of mind such as thinking, emotions, opinions, intuition, and the like. For our purposes here, we will look at the sixth sense as an Eastern culture might. But we can notice another aspect of our mental experience once we see that all of our mental activity exists and is bound by something truly fundamental. No thoughts, emotions, opinions, or intuition could ever exist without the container of time. Without past and future, there would be no sixth sense therefore, we can call this perception of time, of past and future, our seventh sense.

In order to be clear, we should probably point out again that time and mind cannot really be separate since our thinking can only exist as an expression of past events, future outcomes, or judgments therein. This means that the sixth and seventh senses dependently co-arise with each other, as Buddhists say, in every one of our circumstances. If our mind is not aligning itself with either past or future, it is resting in the present moment. And any mind fully engaged in the present moment is Awake since it wisely refrains from grabbing hold of anything linked to a past or a future. Because it is free of time and yet fully engaged it is a conscious expression of the vastness of Spirit.

This vastness is exactly where the Eighth Sense, or Witness, shows up in experience. The witnessing awareness of our Eighth Sense allows for each of us to watch everything and is always present in our consciousness. We can become aware of the Eighth Sense easily. First of all, pay attention right now to your breath. Is it an inhalation or an exhalation? Does your breath flow smoothly or does it feel constricted? Are you in agreement with what's being said in this book? Or are you doubtful of its usefulness? That which is aware of both the body and these mental positions is the Witness.

As another example, consider your longing to fall in love again; or to Awaken; or to understand why the world is the way it is. Whatever your deepest longing is, allow for it to fill your experience right now. What exactly does it feel like, and where is this feeling arising in your body? Don't lean into the longing or push it away, just be intimate with the feeling without grasping it or avoiding it. Feel it completely without judging it as positive or negative. Be fully with the feeling. Meet it with your full attention. That which registers any kind of felt sense of experience right now as you do this is the Witness.

To take this a step further ask yourself, "What am I sensing at this very moment?" Then open your awareness up to whatever you are sensing. Let the question itself guide you to that which is aware within your experience. Are you tired? Confused? At peace? Tense? Relaxed? Distracted? Simply be aware of the unfolding of everything that comes into being in each moment with a deep, nonjudgmental, and unattached curiosity. As you consider these words, continue to be aware of what you are experiencing. Maybe it's an unsettled feeling—maybe a resentful or frustrated feeling—maybe you are witnessing a sense of being truly open. Again, the "noticer" of all these things is precisely what we can refer to as the witnessing Eighth Sense that radiates equally on all things. It doesn't evaluate, it doesn't adjust, it doesn't move. It is simply aware. As such, this very Witness can be realized as an ever so slight contraction of the very Spirit that gives birth and offers a final resting place to all things in the Universe.

We should review this critical point for a quick moment. If we realize Spirit as a vast, all-encompassing Awareness, we can then look at our consciousness as the awareness of this Awareness. In other words, consciousness can be seen as Awareness experienced through each one of us. Similarly, the Witness can be seen as Spirit realizing itself through us, as each one of us. By this logic, Spirit fully realizes itself as itself the moment we Awaken. In short, when that which is totally impersonal is consciously experienced personally, we are shown in that moment the Summit.

This may sound overly esoteric and intellectual, but this is actually the point where realization can begin to show up and support us in the ways that we live each day. When we simply practice witnessing with our Eighth Sense all things that arise, we become free of our attachments. Watching our experience allows us to begin to dis-identify with all the mind-created things that distort our experience of life. This is wisdom that leads all of us to the heart of Awakening.

The Ninth Sense

Just as the Eighth Sense is the felt sense of Awareness that is the Source of all things, it is also our ever-so-slightly contracted sense of this primordial Source. When we put our Witness to use, we see that it is the Awakened space that welcomes the very arising of all things. On the other hand, this Eighth Sense is not a thing at all. Calling it "ours" doesn't express its true nature. Still, even though language can get in the way here, we do our best to give it a name in order to talk about it and point out that this Eighth Sense is the most fundamental link to the totally expansive, impersonal, singularity of Awakened Emptiness.

Perhaps calling this Awakened Emptiness the "Ninth Sense" is a creative, albeit limited, way of expressing its inexpressibility. But unless we recognize that the Ninth Sense can't be "sensed" with either the body or mind, we can get in trouble, since the ego is just trying to turn Spirit into something it can grasp. Things are born out of the Ninth Sense and therefore can't begin to adequately qualify or quantify its majesty. Since this Ninth Sense cannot be qualified or quantified by the body and cannot be categorized or understood by the mind, it really isn't even a sense at all. In fact, any experience of the Ninth Sense only points us in its direction by reminding us of its constant presence underneath all creative expressions of the Universe. The subjective experience itself, in other words, is exactly *not* the Ninth Sense at all since the Ninth Sense can't really be contained or objectified, just like none of us, despite our egoic efforts, can control or manage Infinity.

Yet this doesn't mean that the Ninth Sense is missing. More than a feeling, a sense, or an intuition, the Ninth Sense is the fundamental quality of the entire Mountain of Spirit as well as its climbers. It is the exact Awareness in which all experience, including the Witness, arises and falls. It is the essential, impersonal, quality of feelings, sensations, and intuition, just like light is the essential, impersonal, quality of any image we might see projected on a movie screen. The Awareness that infuses itself into and springs from the Witness allows even the Witness itself to fall away. Nothing is outside of this Awareness. It is Truth. And it is the timeless origin of each and every moment of our experience no matter what our particular state of consciousness might be or how close we are to realizing its impersonal grace. Whatever name we choose to point to this awakened spaciousness that is infinitely inside and outside of all things, it is never anything other than the awakened totality, the Deep Singularity, of everything all the time. It is always available to us in each breath, at each tragedy, at each of our kids' successes and failures, at each of our lonely moments, in darkness, and in the inextinguishable, blinding light of the expansive and clear Truth of Being.

The Ninth Sense is Spirit, and it expresses itself in everything and in every way *as* everything and every way.

Capital "K" Knowing

When the Eighth Sense reveals itself from the tenderness of the Ninth Sense, we give our experience over to what we might call a "conscious awareness." We have previously called this Knowing. Using the capital "K" implies that it is an unattached version of recognition, far different from the regular, attached, egoic, lower case "k" knowing that categorizes, compartmentalizes, and evaluates our experiences. Knowing is consciously sourced from the Ninth Sense, and the Witness is nothing other than an unattached Knower. The "attached knower," on the other hand, may simply be seen as the ego. So while the Witness and the ego are not separate, it's critical to recognize that they are not the same. Because the Witness can observe the activity of ego, it is always beyond ego's limitations and actions.

While the Witness isn't an object of the mind that can be known by the senses of the body or by the constructs of the mind, it can be experienced by itself as itself. To be sure, words can get in the way at this point. There is not much that we can really say about the ineffable since doing so only limits the experience as an attachment to a thought. The Witness is simply a name, a concept, a template we throw over an experiential Knowing that can't be grasped. The name is only a thing that points us in the direction of the Path up the Mountain. And the Path is the continual surrender of all things, even of the concepts that support an ever-deepening understanding. Despite the fact that we don't want to turn any of this into an intellectual exercise, we can say that by following the Witness to its source, we Awaken.

Those who have fearlessly walked the Path before us point this out in their teaching. The Buddha, for example, suggested that attachments fall away as soon as the ego and its structures are witnessed, when he says, "House builder you have now been seen; you shall not build the house again." Christ does the same thing telling us that witnessing our interior shows us that which is beyond the ego when he says, "Greater is he that is in you, than he that is in the world." Teresa of Avila tells us that in our still observation of all that is, we see that, "All things pass; God never changes. Patience attains all that it strives for. He who has God finds he lacks nothing: God alone suffices." Plotinus tells us even more directly to "Withdraw into yourself and look... cut away all that is excessive, straighten all that is crooked, bring light to all that is overcast, labor to make all one glow or beauty and never cease chiseling your statue, until there shall shine out on you from it the godlike splendor of virtue, until you see the perfect goodness surely established in the stainless shrine." Aurobindo also suggests, "To have a developed intellect is always helpful if one can enlighten it from above and turn it to a divine use." While Sri Ramana Maharshi carries this a step further when he suggests that instead of indulging in mental speculations about Enlightenment, each of us should devote ourselves to witnessing the "here and now, to the search for the Truth that is ever within you."

The shared gift of these sages was to map this process for us so that we might climb to the top of the Mountain of Spirit on our own. Doing so shows us that this Witness, this Eighth Sense, this direct connection with Spirit, can be realized as what's underneath, above, and throughout all experience. As such, the Eighth Sense, like the sky, like God, doesn't move. It's just there, like a "stainless shrine." Always. It doesn't make a sound, but is rather the source of all sound. It is not familiar to our bodily senses, since it is the source of all sensation. As the source of all things that arise within us and without us, it cannot be said to have substance. In fact, it is forever, the vast and totally still space between and around all substance. It is the all-encompassing Source of an Ultimate Life. It is Spirit. It is the Now. It is Awareness. It is the Truth that is always within you, waiting to be uncovered as your most sacred presence. It is the radical, unquantifiable fullness of Emptiness that both surpasses and embraces all form.

Aligning ourselves from this clear, unattached space beyond time and mind becomes a practice of perpetual Knowing. Orienting our actions from here, we see that this space is not "empty" in the conventional sense, but is a total and complete fulfillment without any boundary; a placeless place that is totally complete; an openness where nothing is lacking. It is a seamless monument to the still presence that always and forever shows itself as a divine expression of wisdom.

Relating to the Knowing

At some point on the Path, we find that we are in an unsettling place where our minds begin to realize that they don't have the capacity to take us any further. It's as if the small self has been busy extending a board over the side of the ship of consciousness, but at some critical point the small self suddenly recognizes that it is the one who must walk this plank. This realization is devastating to the small self, and yet the reality of deep spiritual work is that Awakening to what is forever beyond the small self can't be understood by the small self. Stillness helps us have the experience that points us directly toward this Knowing. This Knowing is an infinite opening of wisdom rather than a contracted compartmentalization of intellect. It's not a conceptual understanding, but instead a readiness for the spiritual bloom that comes from a radically different relationship to our conventional circumstances. Unfortunately for many of us who are deeply interested in the intellectual aspects of spiritual work, Knowing this flowering blossom has nothing to do with an intellectual or mental connection to anything. Rather, this precious bloom has to do with letting go of everything even remotely related to the mind.

The Witness arises at the point where the Awareness meets our surrender to whatever is going on this very moment. Our letting go into and from this witnessing perspective allows for enlightened presence to flow spontaneously from all aspects of us. We then become, as some have said, a presence that offers an appropriate response to all circumstance. Maintaining this presence means that we simply commit to an intimacy with our lives. Each time we notice ourselves caught in thought, which is merely the ego reading a script from the Stage of Mind, we can simply witness that activity without judgment. This is the Path.

On the other hand, if there is judgment mixed into any of our experience, we are veering off the Path. Judgment creeps into our experience when the ego starts to act as the unattached Knowing of the Witness. Our clue that this is happening is the recognition of resistance in our bodies. Resistance, or negativity, is the sign that the effortless grace and defenselessness of the Witness has given way to the ego. The ego can never be an impartial, disinterested observer since its reason for being is to protect and preserve its own sense of command and control of everything that goes on in our lives and in the lives of others.

How plugged in we are to this unattached state of Knowing depends almost entirely on the depth of our practice of stillness and how this stillness informs each moment. As we've discussed, tremendous support can come from teachers with integrity as well as a community of spiritual friends. Ultimately, however, Awakening totally depends on our commitment to becoming fully aware of all that moves in our conscious awareness. This practice never ends, because as long as we are participants in the life and death experience, there will always be more to which we can open ourselves, as well as more we can release.

With this point in mind, I should point out that as I've traveled, I've met some amazing spiritual masters but I haven't met any people that were fully "cooked." The most profound people that I've met were always living the recognition of the deepest aspects of Spirit intentionally as they existed in the world of form. In other words, while they all exhibit signs of deep peace, they are always on the lookout for their own clinging. This is why we call the journey along this Path "practice."

Our Path to Enlightenment in this very life is repeatedly offering to support us. We only have to be willing to let go of our attachments, especially the ego's attachment to itself. Awakening is never relative to what and how much our egos can manage, understand or know about the practice. In fact, it is better to put the emphasis on "not knowing." An Awakening depends on the small self's ability to let go of what it thinks it knows. It's not about collecting anything or getting anywhere, but rather about dropping everything and being still. Awakening is only relative to our ability to neither grab nor avoid anything that arises in each moment. Because of this, getting to the Summit has precisely nothing to do with the ego's role as the "attached knower," and precisely everything to do with relaxing as the empty, unattached Knower, the Eighth Sense, or Witness. Form evolves, Emptiness doesn't. Enlightenment consciously opens our experience of form's constant evolution to the still Knowing of Emptiness in each moment. Living from this place changes lives, including our own. On the other hand, if there is an allowance for ego to determine what is and what isn't Enlightenment, then there is no Awakening, but only more delusion disguising itself as Truth.

In Body: Compassion

Those who see worldly life as an obstacle to Dharma see no Dharma in everyday actions; they have not yet discovered that there are no everyday actions outside of Dharma.
—*Eihei Dogen*

Too often, people think that solving the world's problems is based on conquering the earth rather than touching the earth, touching ground.—*Chogyam Trungpa*
By showing grace to you, by my own power, I have revealed to you my highest form.
—*Bhagavad Gita*

If we source our sense of being from the Witness instead of the ego, our action as well as our orientation in the world changes. This change occurs largely because our surrender to what is offers each of us a profound clarity in any circumstance we might find ourselves. This clarity works to connect us to our Ultimate Life, and in the process we become much less attached to our contracted sense of self. This flowering of deep openness allows us to see something profound. Openness to the Oneness of Spirit supports our recognition that the many is also equally representative of Spirit. Compassion is truly seeing that the multiplicity of Spirit is reflected in each and every thing in the Universe.

I once heard a spiritual teacher say that we can look at compassion as an unattached version of love—a love beyond hatred, jealousy, or possessiveness. When we bring presence into our bodies, compassion shows itself as an empathy that arises for all beings regardless of how the ego might judge any of them. From this view, we see each sentient being as a reflection of ourselves, and we see that their experience is inseparable from our own. This deep commonality with all things arises within the expanding context brought on by our stillness practice. Quite simply, recognizing the totality of this connection is the birth of wisdom. Any action that is consciously sourced from this wisdom shows itself as compassion—a love beyond any grasping.

We've discussed how any participation in circumstance, as long as it is grounded in the full witnessing of the event, will come from the vast and powerful source of all things that we've called Spirit, the Ninth Sense, and Emptiness. All of these names point toward and reflect an infinite openness. As such, any action sourced from this place can't help but be unfathomably loving. This love will also be freely given without any attachment to compromise the offering. When we act in this way, we change the world by becoming a point where the typical delusion of separation is ended and where Awakening can resonate in the hearts and minds of others as they experience the compassionate expression of their true nature through us.

Relationships

Among the richest areas for practice is relationship. Many of us, whether we are in a committed relationship or not, tend to have our connections with people inform most if not all of what we do. Romantic relationships, work relationships, as well as friendships and family relationships, can pull us from a Big Self expanse back into a small self contraction with amazing speed. They can also open us in the other direction if we know how to let them help us evolve into deeper levels of consciousness.

In a broader sense, the tendency for relationships with people and with other things to dominate our consciousness reflects the fact that there is nothing other than relationship in our experience. Relationships are things. All "things"—from thoughts, to material objects, to interactions with partners and other people—are interdependent. Therefore, our relationships are examples of our deep connection with all aspects of the Universe. Consider how anything we might come across in our experience, be it a material object, an opinion, a feeling, a judgment, a memory, or a plan, is born out of Emptiness. All things arise out of this stillness and are given meaning when our minds attach to them in some way. The mind may like what is arising, or it may hate it. Regardless, at this meeting of mind and object we have what Buddhists refer to as "birth." This birth is not only the birth of a thing; it is also a birth of our relationship with this thing. The big question at this point for any of us on the Path is: "What will inform our relationship to this new birth, arising in our Awareness?" Will our relationship be informed by wisdom and thus become an expression of compassion? Or will our relationship be informed by grasping and thus become an expression of greed?

It is critical to remember that not one thing in this Universe acts in isolation from anything else. All things exist interdependently. Furthermore, things are always temporary. Relationships are born, and, like everything else, will die at some point. This is because death always awaits everything that is ever born. Moreover, all things have the Infinite as their core nature. When we recognize that all things, once again, are interdependent, temporary, and yet Infinite at their core, we see that all relationships are interesting ways of studying ourselves since they offer our egos so much in the way of attachment.

For example, we often want our relationships to be free from outside influences and to be permanent, even though this goes against the most basic laws of the Universe. Still the ego tries its hardest to stave off the eventual entropy that all things must face. I can recall the first time I met my wife. At the time, I was involved with someone and not very happy with how things were going, yet I wasn't looking to get out of my current situation. But after only a few minutes of conversation with my wife-to-be, I realized that something powerful had happened. She satisfied each part of my checklist: she had a great sense of humor; she was brilliant; she didn't have any chemical dependency issues; she liked the ocean; and it didn't hurt that she was so gorgeous that I stumbled over my words. Most importantly, I discovered that she was clear about the fact that all of our time in this life is borrowed. This fact, she said, "makes kindness key." After six weeks of dating, I asked her to marry me, and she agreed. But in our discussions of what our partnership meant, we have both grown to accept the fact that as much as we love, admire, and respect each other, our relationship, like all other things, will eventually end. One of us might die, or the relationship might, for some reason, no longer be able to sustain itself. We also know that the relationship's sustainability depends on what both of us do and don't do. And finally, in our wedding vows, we agreed to protect each other's solitude so that the Infinite might continually support the conscious expression of our love—even when I leave the toilet seat up, and she leaves her clothes in a heap on the floor.

In our most intimate relationships, we discover that feelings of love affect us on both the physical and the psychological levels. This means that love always carries a tremendous amount of weight in our consciousness. During sexual intimacy, for example, all of us are given an opportunity to get brief glimpses of a deep, formless, empty, and nondual union with another being—a union that reminds us that there is depth and unspeakable beauty beyond the confines of the physical nature of the small self. We go from separation to union, and in the process of our conscious sexual expression, our small self awareness can yield to something much more expansive. But these experiences, like all other things, are only fleeting reminders. Repeating the physical process in order to establish some kind of permanent, ecstatic grace only brings temporary relief from the basic unease of being separate.

On the psychological plane, love can similarly work to mask our pain by creating powerful distractions. This masking process is typical and may appear normal to most people, but in order to cultivate an enlightened relationship with another person, we must be careful to watch ego's dance in this realm. A connection rooted in "romantic love" is based on the dualism and separation inherent in attachment. Rather than sourcing our behavior from a deeply unified sense of Awareness, the dualism of lover-and-beloved arises and suddenly, "I am here, and I want that person over there." In this psychological container of separation the only place for a relationship to evolve is into a perpetual state of negotiation between two entities tied to their senses of separation. In this space, we are always in a contracted, defensive, and unenlightened state, giving only if there can be some form of getting in return. After some period of time the intoxicating, initial bliss of romantic love eventually wears off. This fading of romantic love will forever be the case, since this circumstance, like all others, is born as an experience in time, which means that it is always fundamentally temporary.

Intimate relationships are continually challenged by this fact: initially they give us a glimpse of the Infinite's shine, only to give way to the fog of what appear to be diminishing returns. The speed with which this can happen can shock and amaze us. Seemingly without warning, "Things aren't like they were when we first met," and because of this sense of lack, "the thrill is gone." With the thrill gone, what's the use of pursuing the relationship any further? Of course, maybe things can be salvaged, but often couples stay together only because they are able to distract themselves through shared activities involving their kids, or because they give each other overt amounts of "space" where intimacy dies or takes on superficial meaning.

This unfortunate situation is one that many of us have experienced. Sadly, any relationship rooted in attachment will eventually become heavy for us, and its weight hinders the expression of the love that we initially may have felt. The psychological and physical energy that used to arise with our loved one's presence now gets drained from us. It is as if we are riding on a wildly spinning merry-go-round where our emotions violently toss us up, down, and around so that we soon find ourselves exhausted from the ride, unable to even reach for the brass ring. Other aspects of our lives suffer because so much of our time is spent trying to remain stable in the midst of all the instability. Our friends don't like being around us because we throw our emotional baggage around mindlessly. And yet despite all of the misery, the ego is at home and in charge as long as its sense of pleasure is either enhanced or threatened. This is exactly why the ego craves romantic love. With all of its endless supplies of pleasure and pain, the negotiations surrounding romantic love guarantee that the ego gets to call the shots.

The good news is that there is a way off of this not-so-merry "ego"-go-round. What's more, getting off this ride doesn't mean that we can't have romance in our lives. In fact, the essence of romance shows up whenever we consciously ground our relationship in the recognition of what is Infinite in ourselves and our partners. This Infinite, or Ultimate, Love is compassion, and it is something that we can cultivate once we learn to stop judging ourselves and our partners. Compassion is born in ourselves and others in this non-judgmental space. Letting go of judgment always creates room for an expansive, all-inclusive love to reveal itself in our experience. There is no merry-go-round to ride in this openness since this sacred version love comes from the spaciousness beyond any greed or aversion.

Accepting yourself and your partner totally and then acting only from that place of deep surrender supports compassion and the felt sense of this opening is experienced as a type of love that is never limited by egoic negotiation. Living this compassion doesn't mean, however, that we should do whatever the other person wants at the expense of our own sense of peace. Denying our desire is merely an attachment to not being intimate with either ourselves or our partners. Instead, the work for each of us is to consciously meet our partners in each circumstance that arises and to be ready to dance: resisting when conscious resistance is an expression of generosity, and pulling him or her toward us when a doing so is a conscious expression of generosity. Without a conscious push and pull, there can be no spin. Without any spin, the beauty of our dance diminishes. On the other hand, once conscious exchanges of generosity occur, a divine version of the tango is expressed for you both to enjoy. Of course, this dance is shared at different levels of intensity with different people in our lives, but ultimately we can love and dance with all beings in just this way. With practice, it is possible to truly see and accept each being that comes into our experience exactly as that being is in this space and time, and so carry on and celebrate the sacred dance of compassion.

The Pain Cycle

Whenever relationships are discussed in the context of spiritual practice, most of the questions concern unhealthy attachment. Whether we are conscious of it or not, dysfunction continually offers the ego a place to hide. For example, the ego would much rather attach itself to the known quantity of bad relationships than deal with the unknown aspects of healthy ones. Healthy relationships built on compassion require profound surrender, and surrender is something that the ego will do anything to avoid. The small self simply wants to be in charge of everything and everybody for all time. Surrender is the opposite of this impulse. But healthy relationships require space on the dance floor where absolute familiarity is jettisoned for a never-ending exploration of what is completely unfamiliar. Ego will resist this lack of control and begin to act from its typically defensive position. Threats to its control generate resistance, and activity that arises from resistance to what is will both inflict and perpetuate pain. Once pain arises the ego will start to move in any way that it can so as to evade, or worse, sabotage the experience.

For a moment, consider that the only way for ego to keep its job in the face of peace is to create war. In other words, the most threatening circumstance to ego is the conscious surrender to living intimately with all that arises in the present moment. Love relationships that consciously cultivate non-possessive compassion are perhaps the most profound threat that ego will ever face. In order to avoid this final assault against its sense of power and control, the ego will create cycles of pain through evasion as well as sabotage in order to keep its job. For the ego, misery is a far better choice than the Mystery.

Even in the face of its self-created cycles of pain that can destroy everything, at least the ego can stay relevant. Every one of these pain cycles, by the way, is a form of addiction, and every single addiction that we might ever deal with is caused by ego's constant avoidance of what it perceives to be pain. Again, whether it's a relationship to a person, a thing, a substance, or an idea, we use the compulsive clinging of addiction as an attempt to stabilize the perceived chaos of living authentically.

But, if we can realize that the only thing that can ever feel the agitation of resistance is the ego and we can bring the intense, relaxed, observational presence of the Witness into the middle of that experience without indulging or avoiding anything, then we can radically change our relationship to the agitation. From this place of deep presence, we can center our entire being in the eye of every circumstantial hurricane with total fearlessness. This is exactly the way that each experience we have, positive or negative, becomes an invitation to Awaken.

Still, cultivating the presence to stand in the clear light offered by the eye of any of life's bigger storms takes practice. We must have the courage to surrender continually to whatever is happening in our circumstance, whether or not it feels good. From this place of surrender, we then can respond with compassion to whatever shows up in life. We keep surrendering over and over again, whether we are sitting in meditation, grieving the loss of someone we love, watching the birth of a child, or marveling at the evening stars. We never stop practicing the compassion that spontaneously expresses itself as we begin to show up consciously for our lives.

We must never stop showing up. Even when we have had an unsurpassable, penetrating, and perfect Awakening experience, we keep practicing. There isn't an endpoint to any of this practice and this Path of Awakening. We don't stop once we get to the summit. The meeting of wisdom and compassion is nothing other than a gentle repetitious grace of meeting your life without clinging as it unfolds in each moment. It's a debilitating and harmful mistake to view anyone's enlightenment experience as an endpoint where she can get off her meditation cushion and go do whatever she wants since she understands that everything is just an illusion. Authentic practices, teachers, and communities can keep us from falling into this trap. Besides, the Witness itself offers us the opportunity to be free of the tight mask of personality and the prison of time and mind. This freedom means that we can be real, normal people, walking in the world without anything extra added. In Awakening out of our cycles of pain, we simply become ordinary. Ego hates hearing this, of course, because it always wants to distinguish itself as something or someone special. Those among us who are truly Awake, however, are simply and breathtakingly ordinary. The experience of enlightened Awareness is just the beginning of a life whose spiritual center of gravity has a chance of undergoing a profound shift toward deeper and broader expressions of wisdom and compassion.

Authentic Communication

Communicating either with those not familiar with the Path or with those who reject it outright can be challenging. Unconsciousness is just about the most contagious ailment that humans carry, but Awakening doesn't depend on another's ability to share each step with us along the Path. Rather, Awakening can only ever depend on our ability to relate to our own experiences, regardless of who is involved or in what state they might be. Sometimes, the challenge of another's unconsciousness is exactly what our practice needs in order to keep us on our toes. Meeting up with another's contracted self is a great opportunity for us to actively practice openness. We do this like we would with any circumstance: we meet and communicate without greed or aversion from a place of total relaxation. This meeting and communication offers whomever or whatever we encounter both our full presence and the spontaneous compassion that comes with it. But as this encounter is going on, we need to be aware of the intention behind our communication. Are we really trying to hear the other person, or are we trying to manipulate him into changing something about himself? Are we really trying to see the other person as he is, or are we trying to get something from him? If there is any move on our part to achieve a particular outcome from our meeting, our words and actions become reflections of resistance, and we miss the opportunity to Awaken with the other person.

Whenever our intention comes from a place that is resisting or wanting to change something about what is, we can immediately run into trouble. Our intention greatly influences the way we use language with each other, so being mindful as we use our words can be amazingly helpful in communicating from a truthful place. Our words are the sharpened edge of the sword, so to speak, that can either cause great harm or can cut through the veils of delusion, thereby unleashing great beauty upon everything. It all depends on whether or not our intention is informed by our small selves or our Big Selves.

Take a discussion with your favorite teenager, for example. If your communication with them can come consciously from your deepest, most generous intention, and your words are chosen skillfully, there is a much better chance, though no guarantee, that they will be able to hear not only what you are saying but also the care that infuses your connection to them. This type of situation can yield outcomes that benefit both sides. On the other hand, if your communication with your favorite teenager is fueled by a desire for some kind of personal gain or control, there is much less of a chance for a win-win situation, let alone Enlightenment. This is partly due to the fact that teens, in my experience, are at the high tide of egoic greed and aversion. Their unconsciousness is worn as obviously as their stylistic choices. In fact, much of their unconsciousness seems to be consciously part of their style. Regardless, like all other beings, teens are looking for some way out of their unique mixture of arrogance and fear. When our intention is clear and we are speaking to them from our Big Self, we can make connections that authentically bridge the gap between self and other. Even if we are disappointing our favorite teenagers, their anger, fear, and grief is infused with a reflection of our care, thereby keeping in short supply the ingredients for all-out war.

No matter the situation, it's helpful to remember that our words are powerful. Our spoken language is the functional push and pull of any activity of our minds. Generous thoughts yield opportunities for caring words, while selfish thoughts yield opportunities for word-induced suffering. In spiritual work, we often find that regardless of their meaning or orientation, words get in the way of our ability to articulate any truly transformational event or activity. Still, these experiences beyond our articulation can have profound impacts on us. When our minds generate a series of thoughts around our experience and then systematically assign words and meaning to these thoughts, we usually fall short of adequately conveying the mystery of our experience.

This clumsiness happens because our words are the way we articulate mind, and the most profound spiritual experiences transcend the mind's boundaries. This gap leaves the mind groping for signs and signifiers with which to communicate meaning. Words are what our minds create in order to participate in the arena of circumstance; in contrast, profound spiritual experiences can take us to the source of this arena. So our language can leave us feeling like we've been asked to repair a watch with a truck mechanic's tool set. Some rare individuals have a gift for being able to point practitioners verbally into the eye of Spirit. But, those who are best at it merely point us in the right direction. They are careful never to allow us to confuse their words with what their words are pointing out. This is part of what makes these teachers so great. Great teachers, in whatever their form, recognize that words often amplify our spiritual clumsiness, and so they stay silent, rightly believing that their presence and silent intention can communicate more generosity than their words. This silent presence is very difficult for egos to accept, which explains why most spiritual seeking can be so short-lived. Egos are not interested in anything revolutionary unless they can control the experience. When we learn to communicate in a way that isn't bound by ego's selfishness, our ego is forced to get out of the way of a white hot clarity of intentional generosity. Exposure to this flame of magnanimity has the potential to change ego's relationship to everything, since everything starts to reveal itself as an expression of exactly what is beyond the scope of anything ego can grasp. This kind of communication may or may not involve words or sound. But for those ready to communicate from and as Spirit, a deep, silent connectivity awaits them.

This kind of silent, selfless communication is something the ego will do its best to avoid since it is being invited to do nothing less than purposefully lose everything that it deems necessary for its survival. Because of the ego's oversensitivity and defensiveness, we need to be careful about the way we speak and connect with both ourselves and others as we progress down the Path leading us beyond its constraints. More often than not, we want to be gentle as we support others' expansion. Once in a while, it helps not to be so gentle, but even in our not-so-gentleness, our intention needs to come from a place that inspires communication filled with compassion and care. Careless expressions only serve to bolster egoic dominance in our circumstances.

In careless expression, we can watch all sorts of problems arise, especially in our intimate relationships. Individuals, for example, wanting to convince their partners of the rightness of their position are simply allowing the ego to get back into a managerial position for both individuals in the partnership. This process is tricky, because once we start questioning our lives at the deepest level and expanding into an ever-broadening sense of self, we can't really fit back into our old skin. We have begun to face our moments courageously as they arise, and we find it unnecessary and undesirable to go back to participating in life from a contracted place of fear. Because of this courage and commitment, we tend to resist others' pushes and pulls back into our old ways, and this new way of living threatens everyone around us who isn't on this Path—especially those who are most significant to us.

In my experience, I've seen two things happen to intimate partnerships faced with situations like this: either the presence of Awareness brings the couple closer together and the relationship becomes a sacred spiritual practice, or Awareness becomes unbalanced, leaving one participant on the Path while the other gets lost, thus driving the partnership apart. Either way, things won't stay the same as long as there is an intentional commitment to Awaken by one of the partners. Staying together in this capacity is difficult unless absolute attention is paid to an authentic generosity directed towards the relationship itself. This generosity doesn't guarantee that the relationship will survive in the traditional sense, but it does mean that both parties will be more conscious no matter what happens. If a couple can continue to dance together spiritually, the relationship will be oriented around a more expansive, intentional, generous, and enriching consciousness. If the couple splits up, both people still have an opportunity to orient their lives around a more expansive, selfless consciousness either alone or with a partner who may be a better match. Whatever the case, the big message to all of us is that it is unnecessary to wait for someone to join us in our intentional journey along the Path. Ultimately, we as individuals are the only ones who can take the steps anyway. Waiting for another to walk with us distorts the whole experience by generating even more attachments to various imagined outcomes of the journey. Engaging fully in the process whether alone or with a partner is the work.

In taking on this challenge, we have a chance to provide an amazing service to our most intimate partnerships (and everybody else) when we Know that people are not their unconsciousness. It can be so helpful to take the time to notice how our partners, like everyone else, are always so much more than what is small in them. Continually recognizing their essential greatness helps nourish our compassionate communication. This doesn't mean that we should stay with our partner no matter what they do. Leaving one's partner, in fact, might be the best choice, since it might give him or her a better opportunity to Awaken. Whatever the decision, it helps us to recognize that no one can embody compassionate Awareness and simultaneously remain completely caught by the ego. Partners will ultimately need to choose for themselves whether to remain unconscious or to allow an unattached Knowing support the expression of their own liberation. We can encourage and help our partners make this latter choice by being as aware as possible in all aspects of our relationship and then participating fully from this presence. Again, no matter what the outcome, the world will be more conscious because of our fearless and intentional commitment to clarity and love.

There will be more grace and ease for all of us in our day-to-day lives if we remember that the work of a committed practitioner is threatening for any ego. We can expect friends, family members, and life partners to act out unconsciously at times since they can feel challenged by our practice and its expression. The important thing is to witness their resistance without letting our own egos get caught by their unconsciousness.

One of my teachers told me that I should always be thankful whenever an opportunity for Freedom shows itself. She went on to say that whenever those closest to me generated any resistance either in me or in themselves, I should "be present for it with [my] whole body and mind... especially when things get really difficult." If we are totally alert when tension arises, every personal challenge becomes an opportunity for us to open beyond the boundaries imposed by our attachments to our histories and expectations. When we are truly alert, we can learn to welcome all challenges, all resistance, and all negativity that might come our way since it shows us yet more stuff that we get to release in order to continue walking the Path. With increasingly less baggage to carry, we have a chance to learn not to let ego corrupt any offering in any moment by pointing fingers, getting defensive, acting judgmental, or blaming anyone in any way. From this open perspective, we see that we do not need to react to anyone's sense of lack, since we see that we are all actually beautiful expressions of fullness.

A tall order? Perhaps. But the only way not to succeed in this work is, as the Buddha says, not to start and not to continue. As long as even one person follows the intention for a compassionate evolution, the whole Universe changes. As usual, humanity will always experience difficulties, but just as the Universe itself is expanding at an ever-increasing rate, so too more and more people across the globe have the chance to recognize that our very survival is interconnected with all other aspects of the planet. Amidst all of the cries of desperation, compassionate people will begin listening in an unattached way to what is at the center of all the pain experienced by themselves and others. Their listening is the key, since hearing and witnessing the cries of the world is always the unattached recognition and acceptance of things as they are, and it is this recognition and acceptance that allows all beings to be generous with each other.

Evil

In our meditation group, the study of compassion invariably brings up discussions that explore evil. How is it that we can be compassionate for people who wish to do us harm? How does one, from the enlightened perspective, make sense of the tragedies that keep happening in the world? How can we possibly be compassionate to those who are polluting, abusing the poor, or invading other countries?

These are all great questions, but among the first things we should be careful of as practitioners is to not fall into the trap of trying to understand everything in terms of right and wrong. This dualistic arena lets the ego become a self-righteous gladiator. Looking past our personal sense of right and wrong enables us to experience the impersonal and profound love of God. We let this experience come through us by simply letting go and then acting from this place of release. This letting go of surety goes against a very deep, habitual momentum, but releasing the desire to make sense of anything gives us the opportunity to experience a deep intimacy with all events. This intimacy reveals the profound stillness that compassionately embraces all beings. Regardless of our preferred wisdom tradition, we can embody compassion with practice.

As much as the ego would like us to make sense of the cries and horrors of the world, making sense of them misses the point. Making sense of anything puts us right back in the personal experience of mind, as opposed to the impersonal depth of peace. Making sense of things sets up mental views that beget clinging, and clinging is precisely what leads to tragedy. Getting intimate with tragedy, on the other hand, as well as the intense unconsciousness that we call evil, merely allows us the chance to experience a nourishing stillness in our relationship to whatever the tragedy or evil might be. We see that tragedy leads to evil, and vice versa. This view takes us away from the pain embedded in the move toward attaching to any form of rage, sadness, meaning or understanding. An open, undivided wisdom develops in us as we begin to respond in compassionate ways to whatever type of horror might present itself.

As difficult as it might be for ego to process any of this, God, or Spirit, has never been separate from history's ugliness. The ovens at Auschwitz, the killing fields in Cambodia, the machetes in Rwanda, the camps in Darfur, and the attacks on 9/11 all had an equal presence of the Infinite. On 9/11, Spirit manifested as each of the rescue workers, the secretaries, the cops, the firefighters, as well as the hijackers. Everyone involved gave gifts that day to each other. Even the perpetrators of deep unconsciousness gave millions of people the opportunity to uncover Spirit in all its chaotic, unsettling, profoundly ungraspable glory. The same applies for any event that ego labels as evil. This isn't to offer an excuse for all the harm that has been caused by deeply attached egos. But any tragedy can remind each of us that an opening to God is always available.

From the Awakened context, God is not separate from anything, ever. In fact, ego shows its folly any time we think that God is outside of our experience or that we are in any way separate from Him. For us to think that God is "out there," and that we are somehow separate from His presence is precisely what generates the egotistical attachments that perpetuate fear. Fear is what leads us directly into the fires of hatred. This deeply held delusion of our separation from Spirit is what has created all the pain that humanity has ever experienced. Attachment to a felt sense of separation from others is exactly what lit the ovens, stacked the skulls, tortured the innocent, maimed the children, and flew the planes into the towers. This attachment is also what elicits the passionate reactions to all of it, and it is what allows us to harm each other in every case.

Our compassion is unleashed on the world when we realize that God, or Spirit, or Infinity, or whatever name we might give to the Absolute is never separate from anything. Ever. As much as ego will resist Spirit's conscious expression in this life, letting it happen is key to unlocking our freedom from all of our suffering. In the middle of all the horror, Spirit shines its compassionate light equally through all of it, offering us each a chance to surrender to what is happening and a chance to act from an unattached and compassionate place. At the same time, ego, both singularly and collectively, can refuse Spirit's offering, preferring, as it always will, attachment instead of surrender.

It is important to note that when egos become collective in their contraction, consciousness evaporates. The greatest of human tragedies manifest that perfectly respectable people have done unconscious things when their minds and bodies become attached to particular perspectives. Evil, then, is a label that we can give this behavior as long as we see it as an extreme version of attachment born out of a profound contraction of ego around any opinion. Spirit, or God, can be recognized as precisely what is beyond all of this: an expansive Presence of Infinite Knowing of whatever this moment offers. As such, Spirit is absolutely and totally beyond any mind-identified concept of right or wrong, good or bad. This recognition reveals a truth that we rarely consider: in each moment we all have the potential to embody this infinite and compassionate grace of Spirit or to embody an horrific evil generated by the small self's contraction.

So in the middle of any of our horrors, when attachment manifests in unspeakably destructive ways, we also can witness unbelievable acts of compassionate presence and selflessness. We watch breathlessly as the selfless enter hell so that others can live. We see strangers in positions of incredible personal risk reach out to help those in harm's way. We see ourselves hold each other, simply because the Infinite within us manifests as a beautiful and divine expression of deep connectivity. Our spiritual cores are exposed to each other, and we effortlessly offer the beauty of touch that lets each of us know that we are all part of one deep singularity, now experienced as the summit of the Mountain of Spirit. There is no part of God that is not here on the summit. Everything is simply Spirit. When we become intimate with life in this way and consistently engage in nonattached witnessing of our experience, all of us become better listeners and can help all beings realize the divinity of simple and mindful compassion as well as the freedom brought on by the all-encompassing and unattached love that is God. When we can do this consciously, we effortlessly offer a wise presence that embodies the compassionate answer to prayer.

Practice

6

When the Buddha is gone, look to the Dharma as your teacher.
Make the practice your teacher. The Dharma and the
Sangha will be your teacher.
—The Buddha

Do not shout thy prayer publicly, nor yet speak it low in
secret, but seek between these a middle way.
—The Koran

I will now close my eyes, I will stop my ears, I will turn away my
senses from their objects, I will even efface from my consciousness
all the images of corporeal things; or at least, because this can hardly be
accomplished, I will consider them as empty and false; and thus, holding
converse only with myself, and closely examining my nature, I will endeavor
to obtain by degrees a more intimate and familiar knowledge of myself.
—Rene Descartes

When we begin to integrate wisdom with compassionate activity in conscious ways, we practice. Usually we assume that our spiritual practices need to happen only on our meditation cushion, or in our church or synagogue, or on our prayer rug. While all of these circumstances can help support an opening to the view atop the Mountain of Spirit, limiting our spiritual connection to the forms and ceremonies of the Path diminishes our connection with the Empty, Spirit-infused reality that is our whole life. On the other hand, if we can see that Spirit is always already here with us and everything else all the time and that we are never separate from any of it, then our entire life can become a deliberate manifestation of Spirit. As we do this, we come to realize that Spirit is never only "out there," listening or talking to us from a place separate from us. Instead, we must uncover within ourselves the Knowing that Spirit is exactly what is both listening and doing the talking *as* us, *as* this very moment. In other words, there is nothing that is not Spirit in action. If we operate, therefore, in a way that puts Spirit or any of its divine grace outside any part of our experience, we will forever limit ourselves to lives of separation. This is the ego's realm, oriented perpetually from its erroneously perceived sense of lack. Living from this place of lack can only work to inhibit the full experience and expression of the freedom that Spirit always delivers us in infinite abundance.

In order for us to receive this gift, we must practice opening ourselves to its offering. This means nothing other than consciously engaging each thing that arises in our awareness with total relaxation in both mind and body. If we can look at our total relaxation as a manifestation of stillness in body and mind, then we can begin to realize a profound and limitless source of power. Real relaxation means we do not resist what is happening either in our minds or in our bodies. This absence of resistance allows for a letting go of our habitual drives, thus opening us to stillness. We stop clinging to judgments and other scripts authored by the ego, while at the same time we face everything and avoid nothing. This is what an intimate meeting of life is, and it happens the moment we can slow down to the point of consciously surrendering to exactly what is happening right now.

In my experience, some of the most memorable moments of this kind of quietude came in the early morning when I would sit in meditation with a large group of other practitioners. I can recall initially sitting on my cushion with a chattering mind, only to watch it slow down over the course of several minutes of silence. After the initial period of zazen, we got up for a few minutes of walking meditation, and then we would sit back down again for a second period of zazen. Like clockwork, the second sitting gave rise to a deep relaxation that lacked any kind of resistance or want. It was as if someone had shut off a noisy fan that had been buzzing in my head and suddenly I could recognize the silence underneath everything—a silence that was always there, just covered up by the noise of my mental activity.

Even in the midst of great activity, this stillness is present, and it can show up whenever we are truly still. Stillness, like Spirit, is never separate from any aspect of either our circumstance or our Ultimate Life. In fact, stillness is the actual felt presence of just this Now, as well as the infinite Emptiness that is the source of all things. Stillness is our letting go into silent Awareness. Stillness is the surrender to Peace. It is also the groundless ground, the pathless path, and the fruition of every spiritual quest for the deeply felt oneness with absolutely everything in the Universe.

In Mind: Surrender

Repeating 'Thou, Thou,' I became Thou in me, no 'I' remained.
—The Mundaka Upanishad

Things are not as they appear, nor are they otherwise.
—The Lankavatara Sutra

Come out of thy meditations and leave aside thy flowers and incense!
What harm is there if thy clothes become tattered and stained?
—Rabindranath Tagore

Several traditions equate surrender with renunciation. This is an appropriate way to look at surrender as long as renunciation isn't seen as a denial of anything. Denial, after all, is merely an egoic avoidance. Another mistake occurs when surrender is interpreted to mean "giving in." In fact, giving in is just the opposite of fully meeting whatever the present moment is offering. Unlike authentic surrender, giving in means that we create an attachment to something other than what is being offered in our experience. Giving in runs away, while true surrender stays put, opening itself to exactly what is happening without moving an inch.

Consider a difficult exchange with the person to whom you are closest. Let's say that the communication is filled with negative emotion. Your body feels almost hot, and resistance pervades your experience. It is a real battle, where the other person is being unreasonable—at least in your view. Giving in to the other person would mean you decide that, in order to preserve the peace, you will let him have what he wants. You will offer him what he has asked for even though it means that you will be making, let's say, an unjust sacrifice. But you'll do it in order to be a good person, or a good spiritual being. "It is the compassionate thing," you say to yourself, "to surrender to the needs of others." Unfortunately, this action is neither compassionate nor supportive of the other person since your giving in exacerbates his unconsciousness as well as your own.

There is tremendous confusion around this topic. Being clear about it, however, can easily set us up for an authentic Awakening. The script that most of us cling to on this topic is the one that attaches the idea of surrender to a white flag being waved by a battle-worn individual or group. The definition from an Awakened perspective, however, implies a letting go of the battle and of its participants. In other words, surrender, in the spiritual sense, means a letting go of all things in order to participate more fully with all things.

In our example, real surrender to the conflict with the person we're closest to might involve standing firmly, peacefully, and lovingly in our place while not giving in. For that matter, real surrender might also involve walking away from the whole conflict. Regardless, surrender is a way to open to the totality of any situation we might face. Despite our adversary's protests, we get intimate with his feelings as well as our own, with his words as well as our own, with his attachments as well as our own. In doing this we open ourselves, and from that open space we can offer responses that make all parties more conscious.

Really letting go, or authentically surrendering, only occurs when there is full release into the present moment. The instant that there is the slightest grasp of any script, opinion, or other mental construct of either past or future, there will be an opportunity for ego to offer its resistance. Once this happens, we erroneously avoid what's happening by succumbing to our habitual tendencies, instead of fearlessly surrendering deeply into the present moment and whatever it might bring.

The Stream

A teacher once told me that real spiritual practice was analogous to quieting life's stream. Meditation begins to slow the flow of everything in our lives. As the rush of life's stream begins to lose intensity, we can observe the stones upon the riverbed that impede the free and unobstructed flow of our living. As the flow slows down, we become keenly aware of every eddy, every whirlpool, and every rapid. What's more, we can see the causes and conditions that lead to all of the obstructions to the simple flow of our life.

Recognizing the stones, branches, and all of the other junk that divert this flow can be uncomfortable for people, to say nothing of making a commitment to removing these impediments from the stream altogether. But the systematic clearing of this timeless flow of life is the work of Awakening. With practice, stillness shows each of us what we don't need to carry any longer. It points out what gets in our way and reveals what we've been hiding from. This forces a choice for each of us: we can either go on as we have been, keeping ourselves limited and small, or we can roll up our sleeves and get to the real work of clearing our mind's detritus from our stream. Choosing to unblock our life's stream can't help but offer us deeper and deeper levels of clarity. This clarity forces another choice upon us: we can either face or reject what is being offered. If we reject what shows up, we are avoiding what is being offered, and thus limiting ourselves. On the other hand, if we fearlessly and repeatedly face our circumstance exactly as it is being offered, we open to what is mystical and great not only within the experience, but within all things, including ourselves.

Let Go

A practitioner at a retreat that I was leading challenged me to simplify Awakening into as few words as possible.

Amazing, I thought silently, *we are always looking for ways to speed up the process.* Of course, I was including myself in this commentary since I had asked basically the same question of my teacher some years earlier. The response that my teacher gave me was immediate.

"Let go," he smiled. "That's it. Just let go."

I didn't really know what to make of his answer. It sounded pretty silly at the time—a way of avoiding responsibility and a path to becoming something more like a couch potato than an Awakened being. Still I trusted something about him so I just let his comment marinate my brain, hoping against hope that his words might cause something to shift.

I decided to offer the same response to this inquisitive person on our retreat, but I embellished it a little. "Let go, and then step into the world informed by this deep release," I said.

Letting go of our attachments and acting from a place of spontaneous clarity and spaciousness is the activity of all Awakened beings. This simple yet revolutionary routine means that in order to stop our suffering, all we need to do is practice the intentional, moment-by-moment releasing of everything.

This lets us take in the view from the summit of the Mountain of Spirit. It reveals our core essence as being that which is beyond time, beyond feelings, and beyond thought. We are none of these things. Rather, we are the awakened space that infuses, sources, and informs them. This awakened space in the middle of everything arises as one identical Knowing that each of us shares with every other being, just as we are all equally inseparable from Infinity.

Let Go of Even More

It can be helpful to know that, regardless of our situation, whenever we make a decision, we always have three options: 1) we can leave the circumstance, 2) we can act to change the circumstance, or 3) we can completely surrender to the circumstance. There really isn't anywhere else we can possibly go. Even if we decide not to decide, we're still making a decision—one that is really just a disguised version of leaving or turning away from what's going on. Since avoidance of any kind is a form of attachment, it can only provide temporary relief from what is causing us distress and may even work to increase our pain as well as the pain of others.

On the other hand, if we decide to change the situation and we act from a place without any attachment or negativity, we are doing enlightened work. Acting from this place of deep surrender is always compassionate since it supports a deepening of consciousness for everyone involved. At the same time, we need to be careful. Often the actions we offer in order to change our situation are tainted with self-interest. Just as with avoidance, this type of self-centered action usually comes back to us in the form of more suffering.

Surrendering to any situation, however, offers nothing less than a perfectly appropriate response to whatever circumstance in which we find ourselves. This, again, doesn't mean that we buckle under the circumstantial pressures we encounter. Nor does it mean that we sit on our cushion, or worse yet on our couch, and never take any action. Instead, it means that we consciously act from the openness of deep surrender. When our action springs from this place, we end the cycle of suffering that traps us all. Our consciousness begins to shift once we're off of this ride since we are no longer bound by any limitation of our past history, our future wants, or anything else that might arise in our minds. With disciplined practice, this unfettered Awareness of our personal situation shows itself to be deeply impersonal and ultimately free of any hindrance whatsoever.

This simple way of being even applies when disaster strikes us. If we can't leave the disaster, and we can't act to change it, then the only choice left for us is to surrender to it and act from the peace that arises from the letting go of even more. This is the work of committed practitioners who meet their circumstances with grace and ease no matter how difficult things may get and then commit to fully engaging the life in front of them. Suffering in any situation arises only when ego fights against what is actually happening. The ego of the committed practitioner might identify with any number of circumstances, but because the practitioner has brought surrendered presence to the experience, the ego can do little more than impotently rail against whatever it sees.

Surrendering fully to what is happening and then engaging the world from that place of openness allows for us to witness the entire experience and participate more consciously in life. This moment-to-moment surrender doesn't change any given disaster we might face, but it changes our relationship to the disaster at the most basic level of our consciousness. This shift in our relationship with our pain pushes our experience from the confines of circumstance into the openness of Ultimate Living.

The practice of letting go dissolves attachment at a radical level. Attachment is the cause of suffering, so surrendering attachment essentially offers us, as the Buddha taught, "the end of suffering." This doesn't necessarily mean that we will never experience pain or discomfort ever again. In fact, we might find at times that things in our lives hurt tremendously and go very poorly. But whether things are going well or not, at the summit we are conscious of the fact that all judgments are merely evaluations made by the ego. Knowing this, we no longer get caught by them as easily. When we let go, our consciousness deepens. In the process of this deepening, we find that there is little concern about any of ego's activity, least of all its judgments.

Really letting go can take lots of patience and practiced repetition, however. When our release is partial, we often find ourselves in a spiritual purgatory since ego resists surrender at all costs. During the process of surrender, the ego is continually being marginalized as it is exposed to the light of our consciousness. The last thing the ego ever wants to do is let go of anything, so when we practice letting go over and over, we are answering the call that the ego wants us to ignore.

In Body: Stillness

The meditative mind is silent. It is beyond thought...[T]he meditative mind is the religious mind—the mind that is not touched by the church, the temples or by chants...Meditation is not a means to an end. It is both the means and the end.
—*J. Krishnamurthi*

Be still and know that I am God.
—*Psalm 46*

In walking just walk. In sitting just sit. Above all, don't wobble.
—*Yunmen*

Awakening to the Truth beyond name and form involves little more than a continual uncovering of the stillness that is always present. It is forever both within and around all things in the Universe. Awakening to an enlightened perspective, therefore, embodies this ever-present calm. But we need to consciously and continually practice our uncovering of stillness and quietude, since neither will be realized unless we deliberately weave surrender into our intention to wake up. Practicing stillness can be a challenge for most of us on the go, especially since it takes time, commitment, and patience. Most people who I've met who are engaged in this great process have, at one time or another, realized that there is no shortcut to stillness except, quite simply, not to move either mentally or physically. This may sound obvious enough, but its application can get difficult, since being still and quiet goes against much of our conditioning.

Stillness can't be apprehended, nor can it be acted upon—that would be moving toward what the mind conceives as stillness. The mental attempt to "go after" stillness is like yelling in order to find silence. Stillness can't be found by moving toward or away from anything. Rather than attempting to grasp stillness, we need to practice creating opportunities for it to show up. Otherwise, we won't wake up. We need to be the very stillness we wish to find. Stillness reveals itself when we physically and mentally practice the stopping of what we are doing.

This repeated stopping of the activities that come from body and mind is the practice that leads each of us to realization of the still nature of Spirit in each of our circumstances. Our practice of stopping uncovers the countless invitations to surrender to stillness even while we are in the midst of great activity. Grounding the entirety of our Being in this place of total "non-movement" is what we practice when we meditate. From this Empty field of deep silence, we can watch our experience of being a person take on a strikingly ordinary tone. We begin to live from a place of absolute simplicity, and we offer the world nothing extra—only an Awakened presence that deeply touches all things that come near its radiance.

Avoidance vs. Stillness

There is a difference between consciously aligning our lives from stillness and not feeling any need to get out of bed in the morning. A commitment to stillness doesn't mean that we should absolve ourselves of any directed activity. This is simple laziness, which is nothing other than avoidance, and avoidance is an attachment to something other than what is arising in the present moment. All practitioners can fall prey to their attachment to nonattachment. This clinging to nonclinging impedes Awakening as well as anything else on the Path and is quite a common ailment among even the most experienced of those who meditate. It is possible for any of us to grasp at our sense of the Absolute. Even those of us teaching can find ourselves attached to our teaching. Instead of still seeing ourselves a students of the Dharma who happen to be a little further along the Path than the people who see us as teachers, we can begin to think of ourselves as being beyond the need to practice. Being wary of this hazard deepens our practice as well as our approach to expressing ourselves fully through conscious living. But the fact remains, whether we are attaching to the

Absolute or to the world, we are still locked into, and caught by, the cause of all suffering—attachment. In the end, these and all other forms of clinging are what force us off the summit and back down the slopes that we've previously climbed, thus preventing the unfolding of Awakening.

One of the most important conversations I have ever had with any of my teachers involved this issue. During a silent retreat, I had an experience in meditation that left me in a state that still, even after all these years, leaves me breathless. It was like I'd just melted away, and what was left was just the shimmer of life and the Knowing that this shimmer was, for lack of a better term, me. It was an experience similar to ones I'd had years before I ever started to meditate, but this event left me even more off-balance. All things in my awareness seemed to exist in a certain poignant disarray. All that I witnessed was within my Awareness, which was nothing other than me. Paradoxically, it was as if nothing mattered since all things were imbued with beautiful and boundless grace and yet all things were filled with meaning. For several days, this state of deep, silent awareness carried itself through my sleep, my eating, and my sitting. The chores that I did around the meditation hall each morning became less of a concern, and I started to miss areas that I normally swept clean. But I didn't care. At one point I even chose to sleep through morning meditation since nothing really mattered to me. I was filled with a certain feeling of open completion; nothing needed to be done. Everything was forever finished.

I lingered in this spaciousness as I approached the door to my teacher's sitting room before one of our meetings. There was the distinct sense arising within me that, for the first time, there were no questions to ask him. There was only the shimmer. I felt nicely stuck in this expansive state of consciousness. I entered his room, bowed to the alter and then stepped sideways, positioning myself directly in front of him. I looked into his eyes and was amazed at how I felt totally anaesthetized to any gain or loss, honor or disgrace, praise or blame, pain or pleasure—there was no ego to be found. Returning his stare, I paused for a moment. I then bowed deeply to my teacher, who sat perfectly upright in full lotus. After my bow, I adjusted myself into a position that awkwardly mirrored his while his eyes kept staring through me. I didn't feel scared or on edge like usual. I didn't worry about appearing like I was progressing along the Path. I just sat, reflecting my teacher's presence, quietly wondering what could be better than for me to stay like this. How remarkable it seemed that I was so unattached, unbothered, uncaring, and unmoved by this life. *Surely this must be it*, I thought. *I must be done.*

"Not if you're looking to awaken beyond name and form," my teacher said. I'd either accidentally lost control of my inner-dialog, or he had just read my mind. Both seemed equally plausible. Suddenly, all my bliss started to drain from me like water out of a bathtub. I started to get apprehensive and more than a little bit fearful. Where was all of my openness going? Within a few seconds, it felt like a balloon had popped and all of my hard-won freedom was gone.

"You can't stay there," he smiled.

"Why not?" I asked. "Isn't that the whole point?"

"Living from deep stillness is not the same as clinging to deep stillness." Then he smiled, and as usual, it felt like I was totally exposed in his presence. "We call this attachment to nonattachment 'Zen sickness,'" he said. "And there is a cure for it." I was amazed. No words. Then, just like the moment before when I thought he'd read my mind, he said, "Get to the zendo on time each morning, and make sure that your sweeping improves. Do all of this with your full awareness and don't get distracted by the feeling of stillness. It will make a difference to everyone."

I remember humbly bowing to him. I felt so much gratitude knowing that he'd helped push me back on the Path just when I was about to get lost. He showed me that having no ego is not the goal of my meditation. Rather, using ego as a tool, instead of always getting tooled by it, is the result of a committed practice. No matter what, we continue to practice nonattachment in order to awaken for the sake of the whole. Practicing stillness means that we must take the experience of a still mind, which is the same thing as a witnessing awareness, and infuse it into and through every bit of activity that we do, no matter how we might feel about it. We simply, and consistently, let go of all things that show up. We don't grasp experiences because they feel like Enlightenment, nor do we avoid them because they don't. We just practice nonattachment.

Any one of us can practice this kind of letting go when we do anything that turns off the chattering mind. I've noticed this to be particularly true in those individuals involved with extreme sports, since the excitement of their activity takes them, for a little bit of time at least, out of their habitual identification with thinking. Other kinds of athletes also know the importance of stillness when they are in the midst of intense activity. Put simply, their experience of being in "the Zone," as they say, is the same open stillness that we experience in meditation. In this openness there is no longer an identification with the mind's activity. A mind that isn't caught by habitual activity is one that is still. Mental silence arises spontaneously as we practice any activity where we are totally present with what is happening. In these moments we can recognize a depth and beauty of experience that is entirely quiet, void of any articulation, absent of any movement. No movement means no time. No time means no thought. No thought means stillness. Stillness means no ego. When the ego perceives a loss of its voice it predictably will fight the stillness since it will equate stillness and the silence that it brings with its own death.

Yet there are three things we can do in order to keep the ego's fear from pushing us back down the Mountain of Spirit. First, it helps to commit and recommit to a disciplined stillness practice in order to break the massive inertia of ego. Whether you want to sit or not, you just do it. Whether it makes you happy or tense isn't the point, you just do it. Second, it helps to have a deeply realized practitioner to add structure, focus, and guidance to your practice. Find a teacher who knows what they are doing and whose words and actions correspond with your internal sense of integrity. Third, it helps to associate with a community of individuals who are also committed to the intention of Awakening. Meditating with a group is an amazing way to ground a stillness practice since everyone is there for everyone. This togetherness amplifies what resonates most deeply for all participants, and if those involved are climbing the Mountain, its beauty can't help but be revealed.

Sit Still, Be Quiet

Unfortunately for our greedy egos, awakening to an enlightened perspective cannot happen without stillness. You might be one of those exceedingly rare individuals who awakens without the support of either a teacher or a regular stillness practice. But the Enlightenment that the mystics and sages speak about can only ever show up through stillness. As much as our egos would love to have it their way where they can manage the entire process of Awakening, authentic transformation, from the narrowness of the small self to the spacious Ultimate Life of the Big Self, happens only when meditative stillness becomes part of our more active lives. Sadly enough for our overachieving egos rushing to Awaken, meditation is the shortcut, since meditation is stillness, and stillness is the unbounded estate of Enlightenment.

In Nepal, I once heard a Tibetan teacher lament over how his western students were always interested in shortcuts to Awakening. The teacher told us that when he would explain that the fastest way to Enlightenment was meditation, his students would always look so disappointed.

"Why can't you in the West just sit still and be quiet?" he asked with a chuckle. "Stillness and silence are the only way to Awaken to what's real. It can't be done with a pill."

He paused for what seemed like minutes. Those of us in the audience knew that behind his smile he was very interested in making sure we heard his next point.

"Any shortcut or pill other than stillness merely desensitize us to the Truth," he went on. "Pills make us less aware, not more aware. Because of this they don't truly make us still. They just help people mistake being numb for being Awake."

I loved his points. There was no way around it. Without stillness our climb up the Mountain of Spirit stops. Without stillness, there is no way to study the movement of the small self. Without studying the movement of small self, we will remain confined by it. This is what the Buddha called "delusion."

"Study your mind, your ego, your self, whatever you want to call it," the teacher said with eyes that seemed to be on fire. "Otherwise you won't ever Know the open expanse of Awareness. To avoid this practice of stillness is to be busy wasting time."

The teacher, at that point, laughed again. His smile showed tremendous love for the teaching and for us, but I could tell he wasn't interested in people wasting his time either. It was a relief for me to hear the teaching hit hard like this. There was no evasion in his delivery, there was no riddle in his offering. His points were as clear as direct sunlight.

"Pay attention to what's going on in your experience right now," he continued. "Watch your self. Always."

He then leaned slightly forward, rolling prayer beads in his hand. Every eye simply stared at the teacher, and a palpable stillness seemed to descend over the room. He then smiled again as we all recognized the booming silence.

"The whole point of a meditation practice," he whispered, "is to continually expose an internal, still alertness to all that moves. That's it."

Conversations at the monastery's lunch tables that afternoon were lively. I happened to like what he said. Others felt that his words didn't seem so compassionate. I guess they were right if we think of compassion as making egos feel comfortable. This guy was going straight after our egos, doing his best to turn up the heat. He wanted our small selves exposed to the light of our deepest Awareness. I walked away feeling like it was important for me to engage a practice where I would just shut up and sit still.

When we eventually decide to sit still and shut up, we find that we can relax more deeply and we can let the stillness that begins to inhabit us inform each circumstance. We notice that there isn't a separation between the consciousness of meditative awareness and the consciousness of everyday awareness. They are "not one, and not two," as the Zen saying goes. In other words, we start to see that while the Big Self never moves, the small self is all that ever scurries in any direction. Yet the Awareness of both the Big Self and the small self is precisely the same. We can recognize this open Awareness regardless of any state that we're in, no matter how active we are, since it is always present. It's never not right here. As these words fill your experience, you are Aware of them, the imagery that they elicit, perhaps some resistance they provoke, maybe generate agreement, or some confusion. They are all objects of this Awareness. No matter how stormy or peaceful our life gets, the Awareness of life can be recognized.

Our work is to be this Awareness in all of our circumstances. Be deeply and totally conscious in whatever you do with your body. Witness your mind state in every situation, whether it is calling an employee to task, setting an unpopular limit with your child, kissing your significant other, or gazing at the miracle of a flower. Be aware of all of it. Teaching and practice show us that Spirit is all right here, right now, showing itself as this timeless and ever-present Awareness that we all share.

It is important to note here, once again, that living from this Awareness means that we see that the ego is not the problem. The ego is not wrong. It isn't separate from the Universe's divine nature. Its activity, on the other hand, clouds our potential to Awaken, always attempting to block the shine from our deepest Truth. As we've discussed, the ego is merely the protagonist on our own personal Stage of Mind. We tend to get caught up in the ego's dramatic skill and then live out our circumstances as if the stage play were not only what is real but also what should define our lives. We are most likely to get trapped in this unconscious approach to life when the scripts for each circumstance are well written, since this is exactly the condition that leads us to live in denial.

This denial can show up in spiritual traditions as well. For example, any approach that advocates clinging to scriptural texts as the best way to awaken to Truth might well lead its adherents down a confused path. Attaching to anything religious, like anything else, is always at the core of ego's mission. In essence, if ego is allowed to manage its own belief structure, we can rest assured that we won't Awaken. The same thing applies if, instead of just being a witnessing presence, we are trying to adjust or alter the ego's performance on the Stage of Mind. Manipulation and adjustment, in all its forms, comes from attachment, and attachment supports what is unconsciousness. If we are trying to manage anything the ego does, we are simply allowing the ego, with all of its limitations, to sneak into this process from the back door and, at least temporarily, scuttle our chances at realizing the unbounded Truth that stillness offers.

This is why our meditation practice is so important. By definition, stillness is the absence of movement. Any egoic activity, whether it is remembering, planning, judging, or manipulating, is simply movement. Any kind of doing, any kind of wanting, any kind of avoiding, any kind of adjusting, is simply movement. Movement of any kind, no matter how subtle or overt, denies stillness. In order to open to this stillness, we can recognize that the process of authentic realization involves not pushing or pulling anything, especially the ego. Rather than doing anything to the ego, practitioners only have to try to witness consciously its arising in their experience. We must be alert "to all that moves," as my Tibetan teacher said. That's it. When this happens, stillness begins to inform our internal life, the ego is metaphorically seen as "the man behind the curtain" who is manipulating an illusion of the Great Oz—and this shocking realization changes our world.

In this moment of insight, the Great Oz is seen as a simple charade of what's real: a benign projection of the small self that we've come to call our "personality." Although the personality can be very useful at times, it isn't grounded in anything other than the ego's many attachments to thoughts about how to stay in control of everything and fend off all threats. In fact, the personality itself is merely a psychological embodiment of a vast collection of self-authored scripts that articulate how things need to be in order to stay alive. Upon recognition of this state of affairs, we have a chance to realize that there is never a need to do anything to the ego. No need to control it or push it out of the way. We just have to see it for what it is: an illusory projection that constantly creates other illusory projections that center and source themselves from its attachments to things it perceives will keep it safe and full of pleasure. Once seen, we radically diminish the ego's hold on our circumstance because it can't control the Big Self. It is at this point that the Big Self, or Ultimate Life, or Spirit, truly begins to recognize its birth in all things. From this openness, there is a dis-identification with anything egoic for each of us. In this moment, the ego's activity is deeply recognized as incomplete and thus an entirely new relationship with the ego evolves as we cultivate an ever-deepening Awareness in our practice of stillness.

It can be a surprise how often we can acknowledge that stillness underlies every aspect of living. Even in our busy schedules, we can "check in" with stillness. It's a wonderful practice to simply ask yourself throughout the day, "Where is the stillness now?" With this practice of inquiry, we can find stillness with greater and greater regularity in ways that deepen our experience of spacious peace. This can be especially helpful when we find ourselves in the midst of conflict, panic, or pain, since the practice cultivates a calm mind. Calm minds always have a greater tendency toward responding to any situation with wisdom and compassion.

Awakening begins to offer itself whenever we do not indulge the ego's habitual patterns of control. So learn to stop moving and begin to experience the part of you that is still, and then let this experience inform everything that requires movement. Don't walk. Don't run. Don't even indulge the mind as it swings like a monkey from thought to thought. Just be still for a while. This is especially challenging for successful people who believe that their striving is what allows them to achieve their goals, and that the achievement of these goals is what defines them. But achievements are not a complete picture of who we are. Achievements are what the ego uses to prove its validity, and this is precisely the way ego must always and forever be. Always. This isn't to say that striving is bad. It's not. Neither is the ego, for that matter. But striving and ego are inseparable. So we study the habits of our ego-driven small self with our full meditative attention at every moment, and begin gently to let go of all the scripts associated with our behaviors. From this release, we engage life. That's the work. But it requires endless supplies of fearlessness, since stillness and studied awareness will radically alter the ego's sense of control over our lives.

Just Sitting

As heady as all of these words might strike us, pointing to Infinity is fairly simple. In fact, everything is Infinity, so there is no way to avoid it. Knowing this deeply, all things change to reflect our realization, and we begin to inhabit a different place of being. Just sitting still ignites a mysterious process. It's not unlike water of stillness being poured on the dry sponge of the contracted, always moving small self. The more stillness, the more the small self expands its form into an uncontracted Big Self. Once this expansion begins to occur, we become more intensely aware of everything that arises in life. In fact, the whole world can open us up to an intense fire of Freedom. As we soak our contracted sense of self with this timeless and boundless communion with everything and then allow all of our action to come from this infinitely expansive and fluid place, we can't avoid becoming profoundly helpful. This helpfulness spontaneously expresses itself as we become what Buddhism refers to as *bodhisattvas*.

But bodhisattvahood won't necessarily come if we are merely excellent at meditating and accessing marvelous and dramatic states of mind. States won't enlighten us. They arise and cease like everything else. They are bound by time and can offer the mind a nice playground, but no matter how great any meditative state might strike us, it is not Enlightenment. It might point us in the right direction, but no state that can be achieved can be considered complete Enlightenment.

On the other hand, our relationship to the intensified presence that comes from meditative practice and its resulting states can work to create a space for a deeper humanity to unfold in each of us. In this way, our meditative states support the behaviors we manifest in the world. Thus, our states have the opportunity to evolve into traits. All we have to do is practice being still and then integrate its offerings into our activity. When this experience of deep stillness of mind and body arises in awareness, we are acting from a spacious release. Once we can consistently act from this release, we simply exist as this release and we are no longer anything other than a single point of Awakened consciousness. We are just sitting. And while this whole experience may be felt as a "single point" of stillness, it is also simultaneously recognized as universally comprehensive and vast.

As committed as we might be, meditation is tough on most of us. Practicing stillness is the physical act of reaching toward the Infinite that creates an opening into the Awareness beyond the boundary of our minds. Enlightenment is a slip or fall that fundamentally changes the way we meet the world, while our stillness practice throws banana peels all over the floor. "Enlightenment is an accident," as we say in Zen. "Meditation makes us accident prone." Becoming accident prone causes intense stress to the mind and body. In many cases, our minds do what they can to avoid stress during meditation by sabotaging the experience. This sabotage happens in any number of ways: perhaps sleepiness is brought on; maybe physical pain shows up, or even constant mental noise might flood our experience. Regardless, letting patience inform our sitting can help lessen the impact of these impediments.

Some time ago a group of senior monks at the Zen Center were sharing lunch and rather animatedly discussing problems that they were facing in their stillness practice. A friend and I sat at the adjacent table and listened, amazed that people who had embraced a practice for decades still had difficulty on their cushions. We chewed our food quietly so that we wouldn't miss any of the conversation.

"My knees still kill me every morning," said one middle-aged man.

"Wait until your hips go," responded a smiling woman who must have been in her late sixties.

"I still deal with intense grief," said another monk. "It always surprises me when the tears come up over the loss of my son. Twenty years ago and it still crushes me every once in a while."

I couldn't believe it. After all this time, all of these monks still had to deal with small self issues such as physical and emotional discomfort. Was there any hope for a guy like me who had been sitting regularly for a comparatively short time of only five or six years?

My friend then wisely pointed out, in between bites of green salad and brown rice, "But they don't seem caught by any of it." She was right. They didn't seem to be the least bit worried.

"More for us to let go of," said the most senior monk at the other table, a lady who wore her baldness with amazing dignity. This beautiful bald woman then started to laugh from some place deep within. It was like a song of forgiveness.

Practice for even the most experienced meditators will always and forever be just that: a practice. None of us will ever be finished with this work. We won't arrive at some endpoint and be done attaining stillness, since the Universe will keep moving, always showing us that there is more to meet. More grace and resistance to observe and then release.

This observe-and-release practice helps us not only recognize the traps and snares of our lives, but it also has the power to move us beyond them without causing harm to anything in the process. We cultivate a mental and bodily awareness where any and all resistance to stillness can be exposed and then addressed. Our freedom from meditative obstacles requires patience, compassion, and a dedicated use of the Witness in whatever state we find ourselves.

Just sit. There are a number of ways to do this, and much to the chagrin of my Zen teachers, I don't believe there is a right way to do this. I devoted years to getting my legs in just the right position and getting my posture to reflect my dedicated intention as much as possible. This sincere and continuous effort has served me well, and I will always feel deep gratitude for what I was taught. I don't regret any of the training. But as a teacher, I've found that the body's position matters less than the intention behind the meditation. We can consciously meet our lives at any time, from any place, in any mind state. Ultimately, there doesn't need to be a technique for this to occur. Just sit down and be quiet, over and over again, and watch what happens. Teachings, teachers, and groups of spiritual friends will help this process along, but ultimately there isn't anything that isn't meditation as long as we are dedicated to Awakening. Regardless of our sitting posture or our ability to attain certain proscribed states of consciousness, the non-action of simple stillness is the Way.

However, it is important to know that until we commit to sitting still with our full body and mind, we will not be ready to assimilate what awaits us as our practice deepens and expands. This isn't said to discourage. But the enlightened perspective cannot unfold in any transformative way until we are ready for it. In order to get ready, we need to practice completely letting go of the old habits of the small self that have governed our lives. Only when we're ready to release our mental narratives that define our past, and any deliverance we think we might find in the future, can we expect Enlightenment to find fertile ground in this body of ours. In the process of practicing stillness, profound insights may show up at any time or at any stage of our work, but what the insights point to can't truly inform us unless we can integrate the expansiveness of the experience. Meditation will always deepen our stillness, and the level of stillness we attain will always determine the extent to which our insights will resonate. The more we practice stillness, the greater our capacity for integrating our insights in meaningful ways.

And how do we stay focused and engaged in this whole process? Inspiration for sitting still can come from a number of sources. But it is always helpful, regardless of our deepest reasons for sitting, to recognize that the thing in us that doesn't want to meditate is the thing keeping us from Enlightenment. A great question to ask ourselves when we don't want to meditate is, "What do I want more than anything else in the time that I have left in this life?" Once you truly ask yourself this question, watch what arises from within yourself. Watch for any and all forms of resistance and grasping, and know that this is nothing other than the activity of the small self fighting for its very survival against the threats posed by the Big Self's eternal offering of Freedom.

The Deepest Inquiry

As we learn to stop moving, we come to the realization that there is a largely unfamiliar part of us that has never and will never move at all.

Re-familiarizing ourselves with this space is an amazing, often tear-filled homecoming into grace. The mystery is that we are individually and collectively each quite homesick for this place of grace, and that homesickness shows itself all of the time. Most often it happens when our individual egos experience a feeling that something is wrong, that something is somehow either lacking or too much, or of a deep anxiety about our circumstances. Sometimes we even feel excruciating psychological or physical pain. This makes us feel either a need or a compulsion to reconnect with grace. Whatever the case, if in meditation we follow these egoic senses to their origins and we constantly uncover "who," or better yet "what," exactly is feeling them, we will put ourselves on the Path that leads us directly into a home where we are forever able to live as an expression of grace.

In this open and timeless expanse, where we experience the openness of the Big Self, we find that there is absolutely nothing that we don't have. There is a profound absence of need. We find that the Universe infinitely supports us at every moment. What's more, this return to our deepest essence generates an unlimited supply of compassion, since the boundary between self and other is gone. As we begin to trust in this death of our old relationship to the ego, we begin to live out a stable consciousness of boundless love about which all of the enlightened among us have spoken, taught, and written. Here again, we aren't compelled to kill ego, but rather we allow for our spiritual growth to expand past it. We do this spontaneously when we stop grabbing for lifelines and start realizing that we're complete exactly as we are in our oceanic experience; we lack nothing, and we are already the goal and the destination of all we've ever sought. We see that we are what is doing all the seeking and that we are always right here, living full lives in our own skin, in this life. Once this happens, we've learned not to let our mental habits cover up or mute the deepest resonance of what we really are: a perpetually divine expression of Infinity.

Part Three

——

The Return

Living in the world after we have seen the view from the summit is something we cultivate carefully. It is both an integration of the timeless into the boundary of time and an integration of the Absolute with all that is limited.

When we eventually realize the Truth shown to us at the summit of the Mountain of Spirit we uncover a wisdom that we've always Known, that we've continually heard as an echo and seen radiating from all things. The view offered as we Awaken shows us that there is nothing lacking, nor is there any excess. There is complete balance and perfection in the Universe. Once we can let this realization permeate our being, we can begin to offer action rooted from this spacious, formless singularity that extends past but also brings along that which is limited in us. An orientation from this openness offers wisdom. Activity consciously sourced from this full recognition of wisdom can't help but manifest as a continual and effortless expression of compassion for all beings. Bringing this wisdom and compassion together allows us to stand in the face of unconsciousness and meet it in each instance with an appropriate response.

This quiet strength steadily guides our descent from the Mountain of Spirit and brings us to a home that we have never left. Returning from the spiritual summit back into the world, we begin to weave our realization into a life that engages all experience on all levels in ways that continually broaden and deepen our life experiences. Returning home, there is the potential to radically alter the ways we participate with others. Being in the world from this orientation integrates our Big Selves with our small selves and so allows for helpfulness to be expressed through all we do. Since we see that we are intimately connected with all things and that there is no need for us to be anything or anyone special, our actions begin to take on sacred meaning. Everything we do is now considered as an offering for the sake of everyone and everything else in the Universe. From here, powerful realizations arise, showing us that our descent from the Mountain of Spirit never just serves our personal needs. Instead, the view as we return from the summit reminds us to serve the world and everyone in it with selfless, spontaneous presence.

This is the moment when we find ourselves awake in this life, ready to live out the promise offered by spiritual teachers from countless traditions throughout time.

Clarity

7

*Do not divert your love from visible things. But go on loving
what is good, simple and ordinary; animals and things
and flowers and keep the balance true.*
—Rainer Maria Rilke

*In the heaven which receives most of His light have I been; and have
seen things which whoso descends from there has neither
knowledge nor power to recount.*
—Dante Alighieri

The map is not the territory.
—Alfred Korzybski

When we can truly see the incompleteness of our basic sense of
separation from things, we have a chance to uncover the great
unity offered through a life lived consciously. But in order to
make our realization helpful and our practice relevant, we must learn to
allow the splendor of the Big Self to dissolve the small self's limitations.
Doing so, we can become increasingly clear about how we must engage the
world. But just because our perspective has shifted in major ways doesn't
mean that problems won't arise.

For example, getting to the mountaintop and taking in the view
most certainly does not resolve everything about us into a timeless state
of perfection. Confusion and harm can result if this perspective simply
reasserts the small self sense of "I'm Awake, but those people don't have
a clue." Living from this place is a life still divided, and a life divided is a
life of delusion. In order for any view from the summit to support a life

of unity, our practice must align itself with a purposeful integrity. Are we, for instance, doing all of this meditation for something beyond the ego, or has the ego hijacked our practice for its own gain? If the latter is true, it is entirely possible that we might have a deep experience of awakening and yet cling to the belief that our view from the summit is exclusive or "ours." Rather than being an expression of interior and exterior luminosity, a crippled Awakening limits its span to an interiority that is mistakenly realigned to fit the neediness of the ego.

Individuals with these false Awakenings fill the spiritual marketplace. They may be charismatic, brilliant, and disarming. Yet as teachers they perhaps haven't fully dealt with the shadow elements of their personalities, thus leaving spiritual gaps in what would otherwise be an integrated whole. To be fair, all of us need to pay attention to this. When we stand in the light of awareness, shadows are revealed. No matter how hard any of us who lives in the world tries, we can't escape them. We can only use the practice to undercut the power that our shadows hold over us. Looking honestly at all of our darkness, at all of our negativity, at all of our unconsciousness, and never flinching as we meet all of it diminishes our shadow's subconscious hold. Unfortunately the traditions don't always do a good job of helping this revealing process take root in their communities. Sex scandals, criminal activities, and financial improprieties show up all the time in the spiritual arena. Most likely all of this will continue as long as spiritual leaders and their communities collectively let their egos grasp onto all of their glowing press releases. A good dose of Western psychotherapy in conjunction with deep spiritual work might do a better job at preventing this kind of abuse. Authentically integrating what is best from spiritual traditions along with what is best from psychotherapy might prevent further destruction of communities by enlightened egos that always lose sight of their most sacred responsibility: to not cause harm.

No matter where we find ourselves on the Mountain of Spirit, being Awake in this life happens only when we live from a place of integrated clarity. This occurs only when we get past our preoccupation with satisfying the perpetual cravings of ego. Practicing this clarity in each moment births an intention to act from the freely infused Knowing that supports all of life's situations. This integrated perspective frees us from the sense that we are caught either by what life provides or fails to provide. Coming down the Mountain, we see that even though we are in this life, we are not bound by it. Integrating an enlightened perspective with our day-to-day living reminds us that anything in our experience that we recognize as mine or yours is merely a thought tethered to an egoic need for satisfaction. Watching this clinging play out in each of our circumstances helps us to make choices that integrate, align, and source our living in the world from a deeply impersonal and generous space. From here, all life that we touch becomes imbued with a deep lucidity.

Being clear with ourselves and others can take on many different forms, but mostly it reveals itself through decreasing our habitual and compulsive need for personal recognition. Our drive to "be somebody" gently falls by the wayside of our newly conscious life. Instead of allowing the ego to manipulate circumstances that let it leave its mark on things, we align with an even deeper impulse that leaves no trace of a separate existence. For example, when we walk through an art museum, we may experience something in us that refrains from damaging any of the beauty. It's not something we need to think about or manage. It's just the way we orient our walk through life. Here we actually begin to see and Know the beauty of all existence even when it isn't so pretty. A sacred wish, at this point, arises within us to leave the blessing of this beauty for everyone to enjoy, and we want nothing in return for allowing this to happen. The reward, we Know, has always already been there.

This kind of participatory clarity allows us to dance with life, and this dance supports a commitment to simplifying our participation in the world so that we don't harm. Indeed, we become agents of deeply compassionate change in the world—change that doesn't generate war but rather shows peace, since we see that we *are* the world and the world *is* us. The committed integration of this recognition within our day-to-day activity creates a space where all beings can potentially join the dance that always expands in the direction of all that is helpful.

With a little attention, each of us can notice that our lives have been filled with individuals who have either consciously or unconsciously engaged their activity from this type of elegant simplicity. Pick any heroic act of selflessness that you have seen: in it you will recognize this dance of deep clarity. Perhaps you know someone who put herself at risk to help another. Perhaps you have seen tremendous personal sacrifice in order to make sure that others might live better lives. Perhaps you've witnessed someone give so that others might have. The legacies of these people live on within us and without us, and at the confluence of within and without we can always uncover clarity. In this space, between within and without, we find our Big Selves. When we inhabit our Big Selves, we stare through the eyes of God.

Intention

> *To find, know, and possess the Divine existence, consciousness and nature and to live in it for the Divine is our true aim and the one perfection to which we must aspire.*
> —*Aurobindo*

> *The most important thing is to find out what the most important thing is.*
> —*Shunryu Suzuki*

What is it that truly drives us?

Uncovering the radically honest answer to this question and then committing our thoughts and actions to its realization means that we can live from wholesome intention. Of course, there can be confusion surrounding this type of inquiry, but if we allow our intentional questioning to penetrate deeply enough into our experience, we can uncover all that we will ever need to continue along the Path to Awakening. The important part is uncovering what we really want.

As an example of how this can go astray, consider the cliché of a middle-aged man who, for some reason, is driven to trade in his old car in order to drive a sleek and stylish car. What drives him to do this? It may have been his dream since he was young to own a car that can go very fast. Maybe he wants to reward himself for successes that he's garnered. He might even feel that with his new car he's better able to communicate a deep truth about himself. Or, he might feel a sense of lack somewhere and the new car seems like just the thing to compensate for, all jokes aside, his perceived shortcoming. Any of these reasons has some validity, but what truly drives him to make this choice? For that matter, what truly drives any of us at our most fundamental level? Whether it's a new sports car, a new girlfriend or boyfriend, a new group of friends, or a new spiritual path, all of these examples simply act as weak bridges of connectivity to the perception of a more meaningful or at least more pleasurable life. Regardless of its cost or perceived purpose, the intention behind any accumulation is to fill the void that always accompanies the feelings of separation generated by our egos.

The good news is that once we see that no matter how many things we add to our experience, a personal void inevitably appears. We may even see this truth early on the Path. In fact, it is often the very situation that starts us on our spiritual quest in the first place. Yet once we reach the summit, we are allowed to stare into the Source of all that makes us who we think we are, and what we uncover is precisely what has never been missing; what has always been right here; what lacks nothing, and burns in each and every heart and mind of each and every being. Our descent down the Mountain is made easier if we maintain the courageous intention to meet this internal fire wherever it burns.

This intentionality is key if we truly wish to Awaken in this life. Learning to question our intention in everything we do helps this process along by keeping the small self and all of its activity from reclaiming its position of dominance, thus dragging us back down the Mountain altogether. If we can keep close to our deepest longing and question it fully as it arises, we are offered a chance to participate in life as the Big Self. Asking simple, self-scrutinizing questions—such as, "Is what I'm about to do a generous move, or not?" or, "Is this a loving move, or not?" or "Is this helpful, or not?" or "How much ego is involved in this decision?" or "Is there any clinging going on in my mind or in my body?"—can keep wisdom and compassion at the forefront of the way we exist in the world. Letting these types of questions guide the choices we make in each of our circumstances spontaneously uncovers our deepest intention. Finding our deepest intention supports the clarity that profoundly enhances the ways we meet each experience in each moment. Most teachers suggest that we sit on our cushions and meditate until we uncover our deepest, most generous intention. I think this is a great practice. I also think that allowing our deepest intention to reflect the attitude and nature of non-harming, will keep us going in the right direction on our descent.

This intention not to harm is the birthplace of compassion. As long as an intention is not harmful, compassion is born out of the fertile field of conscious presence. If, on the other hand, ego begins to attach to any outcome of the intention, no matter how wholesome the intention might be, then both the potential for compassion and the potential for an open approach to meeting all that arises will be limited to a contracted and perpetual series of egoic negotiations. Some traditions like to call these entanglements *karma*. If we look more carefully at the implications of this tangle of egoic give and take, we can see that as long as there is self-concern mixed into our activity, there will never be enough room for much generosity or love in any given situation. When our thoughts and actions are not grounded in the free expression of generosity and love but are instead rooted in the tangled greed of personal gain, we ultimately generate suffering for ourselves and for others since we have allowed the ego to climb back into the driver's seat. In this position, the ego always alternates between clinging to its desires and avoiding its pain. Whenever we find ourselves in this place of greed and aversion, we are living from the small self. Recognizing this tendency and consciously practicing the intention to let go of it frees us from its grasp.

No Division

When we let an unattached intention of peace for self and others inform our actions, we naturally and effortlessly become helpful. On the other hand, letting our actions come from a place other than one of nonattachment is the work of ego. This activity will inevitably show up as some form of unconsciousness that feeds on both itself and on the unconscious activity of others. This kind of activity is the root of greed, hatred, and delusion. Despite what we perceive as our best intentions, any self-serving thought is a divided thought, split between a self and something else. Division that manifests as activity will enhance our contraction and generate tangled lives.

Good intentions can go astray the moment clinging enters into their manifestation. Any of us can see this happen, for example, when we attend rallies or marches for particular causes. Advocates of peace can, and often do, become agents of violence when they cling to their agendas. Absolute certitude gives birth to violence even if the certitude is peace itself. When this happens, we become the darkness that we wish would cease.

Despite the sincerity of their practice, many well-meaning practitioners still cannot see how anyone can act from an intentional place of surrender in the face of situations that generate personal outrage. In fact, they resist this teaching with an intensity that continually impresses me.

"What about all of the evil in the world? How can we fight unconsciousness if we're constantly surrendering?"

To these and questions like them, I usually ask, "Wouldn't the antidote for a lack of consciousness be a concerted effort to increase the consciousness in ourselves and others?"

Practitioners usually continue to resist this prompt, which is fine, but resistance is where our unconsciousness is most at home. Intentionally increasing our levels of surrender is the activity that fuels an increase in non-resistance, and this surrender is where awareness is most at home. This continuous surrendering doesn't mean that we should roll over to whatever challenges we face. Instead, when we return from the summit, we let our responses to unconsciousness be sourced from intentional clarity. This sourcing is exactly what shines light in what would otherwise be completely dark. Letting go of the attachments that push us into positions of outrage helps us take the form of intentionally conscious action. Action that comes from an unsurrendered place, on the other hand, is the kind of activity that begets war and only creates more pain in the hearts and minds of the people who share with us the experience of life and death.

To help illustrate this more completely, let us revisit the concept of evil. Consider that the word "evil" is itself merely a label given to an egoic judgment, while the root of the judgment itself comes from a lack of consciousness. Evil, as an accusatory label, can be applied to either side of any conflict, depending on one's perspective. Consciousness, on the other hand, is beyond ego, so it enfolds both sides of any argument. Letting the space beyond ego inform our intentions has a huge impact on all circumstances and therefore has the potential to reduce the amount of evil in the world. We start practicing this spaciousness with ourselves and then share our practice freely with others. In this way we stop whatever war we are fighting.

Similarly, when any of us refers to a situation as a "problem," we limit our circumstance to whatever our mind's definition of problem might be. When we cling to any definition, we are doing nothing less than writing a script for ego to deliver on the Stage of Mind. As long as we see any situation as a problem, we've lost an opportunity to Awaken to what is exactly beyond ego's ability to grasp. This realization can be hard for egos to take since it radically diminishes their influence in our lives. But when we rest in the realization from the enlightened perspective that there are no problems, we discover that more peace and clarity are available to support our thoughts and actions. When we return from the summit, we see that all situations, regardless of our perception of their desirability or undesirability, are noticed as circumstances that offer us direct connections to Awakening. The perspective offered from this realization can't help but increase consciousness and decrease the amount of evil we see as well as the number of problems we encounter. From here, any problem becomes a circumstance that shows us a direct path into the heart of realizing Truth. Our job is to take that Path, knowing full well that it is always there.

Although this Awakened perspective on evil and problems may be difficult for our small selves to accept, the state of the world is simply the state that it is in at this moment. Sure, there are situations that need our full and immediate attention and compassionate activity. But if either our actions or reactions to the world don't come from a place of deeply generous intent, then we are fueling the tangled negativity that generated the situation in the first place.

In a peace march relating to the United States' involvement in Iraq, my wife and I were amazed at the venom being spit by so many people who claimed to be agents of peace. Human likenesses were burned in effigy, placards proclaimed that one or another of the Bush administration feasted on Iraqi babies, and those that spoke at the rally used language that most of us would try to prevent our kids from hearing. Despite their wishes for peace, they were fighting internal, ego-driven wars. Instead of the assembly being for peace, it was at war with war. The moment we allow for ourselves to cling to a position against anything, we are divided, and in division we let the ego take us to war. This doesn't mean that we have to allow for injustice to flourish without responding appropriately. Protest can be very effective, especially when we don't allow the ego to co-opt either our intentions or our responses. Meet those opposed to your view, and by being clear and present, you won't let their unconsciousness ignite your own. Instead, embody the peace you wish would fill the space between and among all the sides, and then act with complete generosity.

So what might this look like? How might an enlightened person, someone who has returned from the summit, intentionally engage the world? She would meet each moment with relaxed intimacy, a quality no different from generous intention. Then she would let her actions come from that place of radical openness. This intentionally surrendered action would allow for an appropriate response to anything that could possibly arise. She would therefore be a helpful agent of clarity and peace even in the face of madness. The clarity she expresses would also allow compassion to be expressed for all sides of any conflict. Each step that she might take, each move that she might make, would come from the wisdom that we are all divine expressions of Spirit. Most of all, a modern day Buddha would not attach to anything in any part of this process. Ever. In this way, the Enlightened sages among us show up as the very peace that resonates deeply in the hearts of all beings. Sometimes, they will show up as a helpful hands to those in need. They might also set clear but compassionate limits by which their children can live. When they give themselves over to a cause, they never let anger or bitterness harm anyone, including themselves, in the process. Whatever the situation, those who are Awake in this life continually live from their deepest expression of love and care for every single being in the Universe.

Nothing Personal

As we come off the Mountain of Spirit, we recognize how little about us needs to be defended. This is because we have begun to build lives out of our realization of Emptiness. This Emptiness is the Source of everything. This Source, once again, is totally still and gives birth to all that moves. It is an eternal, unmoving Awareness that generates everything that evolves. It has no opinion about anything, no judgments, no beliefs, and no convictions. It is neither happy nor sad and is concerned with neither gain nor loss, neither praise nor blame, neither pleasure nor pain. These, after all, are personal concerns, and Emptiness has nothing to do with any of these things that we recognize as being personal. There is no I, you, we, or they associated with any part of Emptiness—and no mine, yours, ours, or theirs. Nor is there, oddly enough, anything missing from it. This Empty Source, this Spirit, is exactly beyond all form, and as such, it is beyond anything that can be confined.

This formlessness and boundlessness means that Emptiness is forever untouched by the constraints of everything that we could ever know as personal. How then, if we were truly grounded in the radically open Source of all things, would we ever interpret any comment or action as a personal affront? If we realize that the self isn't a fixed entity but just an open expression of this Source, what would there be to defend? Imagine the freedom of knowing that there was never a need to take anything personally. Imagine the implications of Knowing that ultimately there is nothing to own, control, or possess; that everything is totally out of your hands.

Yet this realization also shows us that while everything is out of our hands, all we might ever need is within us. This may sound puzzling to the mind, but those returning from the Mountain forever Know its Truth. The realization of impersonal awareness arises spontaneously once we begin to study everything about our experience that is personal: our motives, our desires, our memories, our dreams, and our resistances, as expressed on the Stage of Mind. As we practice paying attention, all of these personal things are brought under an intense scrutiny, and the stillness uncovered by meditation integrates itself into our lives. Rather than our habitual place of reference being our personal unconsciousness acting on our mind-made stage, we can start with a stillness practice in order to orient each experience around our ability to watch things impersonally, especially our unconsciousness and fear. The same impersonal opening in us can be helpful as we meet our pain and suffering. Instead of allowing negativity to kick us around, the practice of stillness offers us a chance to become grounded in the conscious presence that can observe the negativity and yet remain forever free from it. The more we practice watching from the audience of our experience, the more this profound awareness shows up as an entirely new option for us, regardless of our state or situation.

But simply being able to recognize negativity does not mean that a person is enlightened. Although seeing one's past and future creates a space for an open awareness to reveal itself, recognizing this isn't the end of the journey. Rather, it's the beginning. The clarity brought on by the continual study of all things personal, however, inevitably brings up questions surrounding the core of all to which we could ever cling. This is a natural process that each of us goes through as we mature over the developmental stages of life: we go past our childhood, for example, yet bring it along as we mature. In spiritual work, we go past the unconscious tendencies of the small self, yet we can bring the small self along in a supporting role as we evolve into a conscious expression of the Big Self.

Clarity points out that our attachment to the ego and everything it generates becomes increasingly unimportant. Clarity also shows us that our old ways of living begin to lack the seductive pull they once had. The old concepts and habitual pieces of psychological inertia can't handle the Big Self that dutifully saps the small self's attachments of their energy.

The great Zen master Eihei Dogen commented on this process of Awakening by saying, "[T]o study the self is to forget the self; and to forget the self is to be enlightened by all things." Or, to use our earlier metaphor: the observation of the Stage of Mind offers an awareness from the perspective of the audience; and this observing awareness allows for us to be free from our attachments. Deep spiritual work is simply our study of the source of our awareness in order to let go of the concepts our ego has authored that prevent us from opening to the Truth beyond its grasp. So we might better describe the process by saying that the subjective or personal nature of our experience is released, or even forgotten.

None of this means that any of us has to disappear and fade away from participating in life. The dishes can still get washed, the lawn mowed, the party attended. We just do it without our deeply held habits of self-concern. Instead of our typical mode of operation dominating our experience, we open to something bigger that frees us. We notice that where the "I" is the subject, and the "me" is the object of our activity, an opening shows up that offers a place where nothing is bound by any habits of "my" sense of either time or the ego's performance. With this release of identification with your past, your future, and your mental activity, there is a profound recognition that all things are simply one undivided whole and that you are nothing other than this infinite unity. What's more, our meditation continually reminds us that the free expression of this deep singularity is only ever blocked by our unconscious attachments to the things that we think define us.

No Judgment

*Things derive their being and nature by mutual dependence
and are nothing in themselves.*
—Nagarjuna

*Among the great things to be found among us, the
Being of Nothingness is the greatest.*
—Leonardo da Vinci

Descending the Mountain means that we are able to engage each moment in life from an unattached position of discriminating awareness rather than from a position of judgment. It can be helpful to think of discriminating awareness as simply the recognition of whatever presents itself to us without any positive or negative mental evaluation. Judgment, on the other hand, involves the ego's assessment and appraisal. For example, as I began my meditation practice years ago, there were times when I would finish my morning meditation and then think, *Wow, that was a great meditation. I hope I can do that again this afternoon.* This egoic evaluation was metaphorically putting clouds in what otherwise would have been an open, blue-sky mind. In my contracted striving to recreate my personal judgment of what was great, I inhibited the expansion I'd tasted in the first place.

As an example, we might consider the ocean again: water vapor differs from waves, and waves differ from water beneath the surface. Yet vapor, waves, and deep water are also inherently the same thing. Recognizing their difference and their similarity without evaluating them as good or bad is exercising our discriminating awareness since there is no clinging involved. On the other hand, if we were to say something like, "I hate this... the waves suck today... no sense in even trying to surf," the ego is attached to an outcome that it can't manage and has therefore offered its negative evaluation.

Discriminating awareness, on the other hand, shows us that the various permutations of water are simply permutations of water. Whether at the stormy surface, or in the stillness of its greatest depths, water offers all of us only one constant essential quality of wetness. There are no preferences in this evaluation, nor are there any attachments. Metaphorically, wetness and Witness are the same. In other words, wetness is equally available to all parts of the ocean, just like the Witness is equally available to all parts of our experience. No matter what state we're ever in, no matter what our circumstance or our life may offer, no matter what our depth of realization, we see that this immediate experience we call Being is always and forever expressed as one simple essence: Awareness.

From this view, all things have a certain holiness to them that transcends whatever label the ego might like to apply to whatever it sees. So while there may be no point in trying to surf when there are no waves, there is nothing to hate about the situation once we come off the mountaintop.

The only option for any of us, once we begin to see through our judgments and then let go of them, is to act from an inherently open place of discriminating awareness. A key implication of this orientation is that we have to make sure that the Freedom born from the enlightened perspective is extended to all beings without any reservation or evaluation. This means that radical, even revolutionary, personal action needs to be taken in order to support the expression of this teaching. Our practice of Enlightenment needs to involve not only sitting still but also letting that stillness consciously inform all of our mental and physical activity with total generosity. This can be a paradox on the level of mind and one that gets lots of climbers into trouble. Seekers, for example, are usually only looking for a way feel good so they cling to the ego's definition of good rather than rest in the discriminating awareness of Spirit. Experiences of profound states of meditative bliss, for example, will be judged by the ego as something to preserve, thus defiling the experience. This craving for bliss fuels resistance to anything that gets in the way of its recurrence.

Resistance leads to evaluation and then judgment, and the doors of judgment close on Awakened awareness.

The way out of this trap is to recognize it as a trap. Practitioners should repeatedly meet the experience of the life they are given without resisting anything, and then act from this place of openness. This unattached way of meeting life prevents the ego from evaluating and then going after or avoiding anything. As this ego-free meeting informs practitioners' lives, they can begin to embody an enlightened awareness. Put another way, practitioners see that all things and all situations are beyond the limits of ego's view. At the same time, they see the need to integrate or "improve" life by bringing conscious awareness to it, so that the wisdom and compassion inherent in this integration can spontaneously meet any situation.

This is how Awakening changes the world. It gives us more options rooted in generosity so that our choices work for the sake of the whole instead of for only ourselves. As opposed to allowing for us to stay on our meditation cushions or in our monasteries, this Awakening actually directs us to participate fully in the world with a committed purpose. Getting beyond judgment shows us that we can live in ways that are helpful, and this helpfulness naturally shows itself when we inhabit a perspective involving no fixated resistance to anything. From this place of nonattachment, all attempts to change the world become expressions of ease and balance, and they are amazingly powerful since they neither cling to nor avert anything. Being in the world in this way resonates in the hearts and minds of all who can watch this compassionate expression of Spirit in action. But in order for us to ground ourselves in this space, we need to Know the Infinite deeply. We can never grasp at judgmental certitudes and expect to be helpful at the same time. This is a key component in the actions of people coming down the Mountain. When they are open to the wisdom offered by discriminating awareness, they can burn with an embodied helpfulness and tender attention that the world always needs. If this recipe is followed with care, whatever comes out of the oven, so to speak, offers up one amazing taste. Rather than compulsively judging, compartmentalizing, categorizing, and evaluating things, a cooked practitioner sees that there is variation and unity all at once.

No Complaints

My first day of kindergarten was interesting. I wasn't yet five years old, and as my parents began to leave me in my new classroom, I noticed that my mother was crying. *Why in the world would she do that?* I wondered. As time progressed, so too did the depths of our dinner conversations, and since the school was parochial, I eagerly shared biblical stories with my parents that had been offered up in class. I remember being obsessed with the stories of Jonah inside the whale, Job's really bad luck, Abraham nearly killing his son, and especially Cain beating down his brother Abel. This last story had real significance since I was always beating down my brother Mark, and I was worried that I might be punished by God if I wasn't careful. How scary it all was, and yet for some reason I couldn't get enough of it.

What really shook me, however, was the 23rd Psalm's phrase, "I shall not want." I spent my days wanting all sorts of things, which couldn't be good if the Bible was always right. If only I'd known that in Hebrew the words were *lo echsar,* which translates to something close to "I shall not lack," I might not have been so judgmental of myself. Regardless, the idea that I shouldn't want led to tremendous guilt on my part and an interesting teachable moment for my mom and dad.

As it turned out I was afraid because I really wanted the new Munster's lunchbox. Since wanting went against this teaching, I thought that there was little doubt that I was going to burn in hell. At least that was my interpretation of my teacher's evaluation of the Bible. My parents tried to play both sides by telling me that it's important to be satisfied with what we have, but that it's fine to wish for things. But then they confused me when they told me that hell doesn't exist unless you create it for yourself—pretty Zen for a couple of Protestants! The next thing I remember, I was going to a different school where I got to play with frogs, worms, clay, and I got to learn about dinosaurs. While I never did get the Munster's lunchbox, I was given an amazing introduction to my spiritual life, since my parents taught me about how to hold off on judging myself as a way to avoid suffering in a self-created hell.

Without any formal training in the teachings of Enlightenment, my mom and dad were Buddhas in this moment. They pointed out that "not wanting" (or at least knowing that I was not lacking) is the key to freeing ourselves from the tangle of judgment and evaluation. When we can recognize these traps and snares, we can uncover a deep satisfaction. Wanting is absolutely normal. Spiritual enlightenment, on the other hand, is anything but normal. We have all of this biological apparatus affixed to our bodies that supports our cravings as well as our revulsions. This constant leaning back and forth into and away from whatever we judge to be valuable or unsightly is the main activity of being a person driven by egoic attachment. We do this all the time, but this is just our habitual inertia. Getting free of it and eventually embodying something much greater takes a deep commitment to stillness. If we don't move, we inevitably come to the realization that there is a space between our judgments that offers the amazing expanse of Freedom. In this expanse we suddenly lose the need to insist on anything being a certain way. We suddenly find that we have nothing to complain or *kvetch* about since everything points us into the confluence of those streams that flow directly into our deepest, most sacred sense of wonder. As we begin to find comfort in this wonder, it becomes our home. In this home we find ourselves Awake in this life.

No Preferences

"Whenever you feel a judgment arise in your awareness, you are feeling the ego's energetic pull," the Zen teacher said to a group of us in the meditation hall.

It was late in the afternoon and I was tired, worried that I might fall asleep during this lady's talk. I wasn't bored with what she was saying, I just wanted a little sleep.

"Any preference," she went on, "can show us where our attachments are."

I began to perk up at this comment. Could my judgments help me recognize, and better understand my ego's pull? Could my preferences do the same thing?

The fog of sleepiness began to fade a bit as I considered her comments. I was judging all the time, and I had all sorts of preferences. But something about what she was saying made sense at a level that was new to me.

My hand shot up after the talk concluded. I asked, "Are preferences the same as judgments?"

"I think it's helpful to see the ego as the sun in a psychological solar system. Preferences are like small planets that have an observable gravitational pull. Judgments are planets as well; they're just bigger, and therefore have more pull."

This seemed so elegant. So simple. I bowed to her in gratitude.

"Then how do we free ourselves from all the pull?" came another question from across the hall.

"We're free from any and all forms of judgmental or preferential pull, when we can integrate the recognition that we are at once the unlimited entirety of the Universe and a limited egoic solar system."

She paused and let this sink in.

"All things that orbit around you," she went on, "start to shrink when seen from the enormity of what you really are. You'll sense this the more you sit. And then it is my hope that you'll let your enormity express itself through your life."

She started to giggle, and then bowed to us, leaving us to make friends with our enormity without any preferences.

Commitment

8

*The only difference between us is that I am aware of my natural state,
while you are bemused... We discover it by being earnest,
by searching, enquiring, questioning daily and hourly, by giving one's
life to this discovery.*
—*Nisargadatta Maharaj*

*Those who enter the gates of heaven are not beings who have no
passions or who have curbed the passions, but those who have cultivated an
understanding of them.*
—*William Blake*

If you gaze long enough into the abyss, the abyss gazes into you.
—*Friedrich Nietzsche*

The commitment to walking along the Path of Awakening challenges us in ways that most of us don't expect. Truly dedicating ourselves to anything is hard work, but this is especially true for this process. Devotion to deep spiritual work is perhaps one of the most treacherous areas for any of us to explore since it involves nothing short of an all-encompassing promise to live our lives as profound expressions of the Truth that all the great spiritual teachers, whether they be Muslim, Jewish, Hindu, Christian, Buddhist, or anything else, have been pointing out over the course of human history.

What is it that those among us who are returning from the Mountain—who are truly living the confluence of wisdom and compassion—use to guide their every response to conventional circumstances? The answer is simple: they vow simply, wholeheartedly, intentionally, and continually to live in ways that won't harm. But this vow not to harm can be a challenge since enacting this profound promise extracts many of the things our egos have tucked away in our consciousness and forces them into our immediate experience. This exposed living means that we can no longer hide from either what is false or from what is True. We are forced to show up and face our lives.

As we attend to our lives, we live intimately with the fact that we can cause harm whenever we act from a tangled web of clinging. Whether we are clinging to something that we believe will benefit us or even to the teaching of non-clinging, we can cause damage to ourselves and to others. So how do we stay aware of our clinging? Many traditions have guides: the Buddhist precepts, the Biblical commandments, the Hindu Yamas and Niyamas all help us expose even our most subtle attachments and our deepest secrets, thereby supporting the continual development of an undefended and truly open spiritual life. While this doesn't necessarily mean that we have to show anyone what we'd just as soon keep private, it does mean that we can no longer keep anything hidden from ourselves. We find ourselves in a situation where there is no way to avoid either our past or our future. Committing ourselves to living from this place of radical honesty means that we use our Eighth Sense to study continuously everything that we cling to in life without judgment or evaluation. We see the stories from our childhood that still might be keeping us from living more fully, and in the seeing, we uncover the tools needed for freedom. We uncover the pictures we've painted that represent ideal futures, and in the seeing, again, we dis-identify with any future attachment and can become free. This seeing and freeing helps us to live a life of greater expanse, depth and integration.

Because there are so many situations that can offer impediments along the Path, authentic spiritual work connects itself with ethical frameworks that support continual and conscious surrender of the objects and ideas that can keep us from Realization. For instance, Buddhist practitioners should be intimate with not killing, not stealing, not lying, not abusing intoxicants, and not misusing sexuality. While a great deal can be said about the interpretations of these precepts, they can support a deepening of any traditional spiritual practice. This is because in our vow to remain intimate with these precepts, we can consciously live from a place of nonattachment in relation to the things that generate our most intense psychological and physical desires. This isn't to say that we must accept being governed by rules, which, if broken, cast us into a hellish realm from which there is no escape. On the contrary, it is most healthy and helpful to look at these ethical structures, regardless of our preferred tradition, as guideposts rather than edicts along the Path. Edicts, after all, are merely imposed attachments. But with our commitment to openness, each precept can act as a bridge, rather than as an attachment, that leads us from the prison of the small self to the freely integrated expanse of the Big Self.

Showing Up

Only a Buddha with a Buddha realizes enlightenment.
—*Lotus Sutra*

All real living is meeting.
—*Martin Buber*

When I see that I am nothing, that is wisdom. When I see that I am everything, that is love. And between these two, my life flows.
—*Nisargadatta Maharaj*

When there is a meeting among beings grounded in the commitment not to harm, Spirit enriches everything. This enrichment happens because unattached Knowing supports the dissolution of clinging with its infinite field of helpful compassion. In any place that is consciously free of clinging, there is a chance to meet, as we say in the Zen liturgy, "an unsurpassed, penetrating, perfect Enlightenment."

This opportunity occurs whenever we consciously and fearlessly show up for all that arises in our circumstance without flinching. Our ability to show up to our lives is automatically enhanced as long as we consistently refrain from certain behaviors: from attaching to our desires; from overindulging; from avoidance; from resistance. Showing up also occurs when we are diligent in our practice, when we pay attention to our lives, and when we communicate with care. As we live like this, everyone, including ourselves, is offered a continuous blessing. When there is neither a push toward nor a pull away from anything and we commit to leaving nothing out of this intimate meeting of exactly the life we are given in this moment, we live as a conscious expression of non-greed and non-aversion.

Living like this offers a continually appropriate response for all of us. An appropriate response to this life is nothing other than an engaged and integrated Awakening.

Appropriate Responses

The Chinese Master Yunmen referred to the most profound Buddhist teachings as simply being "an appropriate response" to the circumstances of our lives. Any time we see egolessness in action, we are looking at an appropriate response. Whenever we can watch someone act without wanting anything in return for his or her action, we are seeing an appropriate response in action. Essentially, an appropriate response is participation that arises from a space of non-resistance. Unlike the reactions of resistance offered by an ego that thinks it's enlightened, an appropriate response is unimpeded, open and unattached to any outcome or agenda, just like any of us might return a heartfelt smile or help someone who is struggling with his grocery bags and car keys. Since any of us can meet our circumstances like this as long as we show up to what is really going on in our lives, each of us can express the Awakened capacity that has always been available underneath all of the interests of our small selves. This is what is meant when the sages of today as well as those of old say that we are already enlightened.

One of my teachers would point out that his teacher, Shunryu Suzuki, used to say, "Strictly speaking, there are no enlightened people; there is only enlightened action." This understanding makes all of us vessels of Enlightenment, whether we are conscious of it or not. Whether we are beginning our climb along the spiritual Path, we are at the summit, or we are returning down from the Mountain, all of us can commit to offering helpful responses that won't generate suffering. When we live in this way, whatever another's action (or reaction) might be, the ego's needs are taken out of our intention, and we take care of our vow to not harm.

To be sure, I don't know if any of us, regardless of our commitments and good intentions, can avoid harm on a technical level. Even taking medicine, for example, harms the bacteria that we're hosting. Eating harms whatever our meal happens to be, and even in compassion we can harm another's sense of what's right. But what helps guide our decisions is our answer to the question that we're exploring here. A practitioner who is integrating the depth of Spirit into his life will always ask himself, "What is an appropriate response to what is arising in this situation?" This question and its answer cannot reveal themselves unless we're clear about our egoless intention and our commitment not to harm. A great litmus test here is to consider if we, for example, are acting from a place of generosity for the whole or in a way that either indulges our greed or our aversion. Acting from a place of generosity puts us into a space where intimacy with our experience continually supports deeper levels of non-resistance and, in turn, deeper levels of conscious behavior for all of us.

The Vows

It took me years to commit formally to a practice. Something about me just thought that the whole idea of taking vows and committing to a way of living was merely window dressing to mask the seriousness of one's practice. So I chose to sample a bit here, a bit there, read a little of this and a little of that, thus gaining vast amounts of experiential square footage. I had traveled to where the ancients had taught and sat with masters in different cultures and countries, but I hadn't formally taken on the vows. It got to the point where people around the Zen Center were surprised to learn that I had not gone through the precept ceremony. I laughed it off and made some comment about how I simply was too much of a renegade to settle into the dogma of any tradition.

Preparing for the Jukai ceremony, as the Zen tradition calls it, is a pretty big deal. It's like a bar mitzvah or confirmation for grownups, except your parents have no part in the decision-making process. To begin with, you have to decide whether or not you can abide by ten precepts. First, no killing. Second, no stealing. Third, no misuse of sexuality. Fourth, no lying. Fifth, no abuse of intoxicants. Sixth, no slander. Seventh, no praising self at the expense of another. Eighth, no attaching. Ninth, no harboring ill-will. And tenth, no abusing the Buddha, the Dharma, or the Sangha. Next, one has to decide on a teacher to act as one's guide in the process. Finally, one has to hand stitch a bib-like replica of the Buddha's patchwork robe called a *rakesu*. None of it held much appeal for me. I was more interested in getting to the meditation hall, thank you.

One day while scrubbing pots in the kitchen, one of the long-time bib-wearing monks asked me about my reasoning.

"So why aren't you interested in taking on the precepts?" my friend Lynn asked.

For the longest time I silently continued scraping oatmeal out of the bottom of a giant pot. I wanted to answer her honestly since we had grown to be close friends, but there weren't any words coming.

I stopped what I was doing and looked in her eyes. She returned my stare still smiling. There was something so disarming about her. Maybe it was that she had seen so much in her life. No doubt, she could fill a book with stories from her time as one of only a few female photojournalists in Southeast Asia during and after the Vietnam War and then barely escaped Phnom Penh as the Khmer Rouge rose to power shortly thereafter. She also had seen just about every single concert of merit in the 1960s. I especially loved hearing about her time at Monterey Pop and Woodstock.

"I don't know," I said in response to her question. "It just feels strange committing to the Path like that."

"How do you mean?"

"Isn't a vow just an attachment in spiritual clothing?"

She started to smile. I knew I wanted to be as skillful as possible in this conversation since she'd gone through her own Jukai ceremony some twenty years before. I didn't want to offend her, but I wanted to be honest regarding my doubts.

"I think that formally committing to a practice could involve a lot of clinging," she said. "But it hasn't worked that way for me."

All thoughts of oatmeal-caked pots had vanished at this point. I wanted to know what exactly she meant since I had so much respect for both the way she lived and the way she wore her Buddhism. She was authentic, grounded, funny, engaged, and kind. She was on her way home from the Mountain of Spirit while I was somewhere in the middle of my climb. This had become obvious in recent months, and I wondered if I was missing something that an honest and clear commitment might bring.

"I decided to take on the precepts," she began with a note of seriousness, "because I wanted to go deeper. I knew that everything I had ever achieved in my life came out of fearless commitment. I wanted to see what fearless commitment might bring to my spiritual life."

"But doesn't living by these rules limit you?" I asked.

"Not in the slightest," she said. "Then again, I have never looked at them as rules. They are my guides, my clues to living well. They remind me how to stay clear and focused on showing up to this life."

I was all ears. This was the first time anyone had even come close to helping me see the value in taking on vows. She then started talking as she continued with the pots.

"I have a dresser on which there are a few objects that remind me of what is sacred. One is a picture I took of Jimi Hendrix burning his guitar. Another is a picture of an ex-girlfriend who became a nun and was later killed in Central America. Another is a piece of the Berlin Wall. And most important of all, is a downy feather I found at the beach when I was a kid." She smiled.

"Why the feather?" I asked.

"Because throughout my life, it has reminded me not to rush. If I walk by it too fast, it gets caught in the current of air that this big body of mine stirs up, and it falls off my dresser. To be honest, I can't believe I still have the little artifact. I kept it in my beat-up wallet for years and forgot about it. But my point is, for me the precepts have been like that feather. I now live in a way that doesn't allow me to blow past the things that I should be paying close attention to."

"So no more sex, drugs, and rock-n-roll?"

"I'm just more caring and mindful with all of that. Of course, I still enjoy my wine, women, and song. But I don't cling to any of it. Nor do I avoid any of it."

We finished our work together, and the signal for us to get back to the meditation hall sounded shortly thereafter. For the rest of the day I sat with her words.

The next morning I approached the senior Dharma teacher and asked to speak with him. He and I talked for some time about the conversation I'd had with Lynn and I soon realized that I was ready to take my practice to a new, more committed level. I began sewing my *rakesu* within days and within two months I took the vows. While deciding to formally commit to living according to the precepts is not a prerequisite for Awakening, doing so has made a significant difference for many people. Despite the fact that I don't formally identify myself as a Zen Buddhist, the decision to jump fully into a particular practice certainly helped turn the heat up on my practice, making the Path at once more obvious and more available.

Choice

Grapes want to turn into wine.
—*Rumi*

When making your choice in life, don't neglect to live.
—*Samuel Johnson*

When we begin to commit ourselves to integrating the teaching into our lives, we become clearer about how we can consciously choose the ways in which to meet each situation we face. For example, we know that our preoccupation with satisfying the needs of the small self only leads us into trouble. We begin to see that anything in our experience that we can recognize as personal must be tied directly to the satisfaction of ego. This helps us to realign our lives in ways that are deeply impersonal, and as a result, all the life that we begin to touch becomes imbued with the expansiveness of Spirit.

At some point during spiritual work, practitioners recognize that each situation in life, no matter how glorious or horrific, offers an opportunity to Know the deep choices that come from the realignment of our intentions from the shallowness of the small self to depth and Infinite nature of the Big Self. Practitioners recognize that everything in their life, in every way, conspires to put them in a position of absolute, Enlightened potential, depending only on how they choose to respond to whatever arises in their awareness. Practitioners then see that all that is needed is to choose fearlessly to surrender into Awakening at every possible opportunity.

These opportunities for intentional surrender are always ready to meet us if we are ready to commit to meeting them. They show up as everything, in every moment, and when we give them our full attention, a new life awaits—one that is inhabited by a deep peace regardless of whatever circumstance might arise. Choosing to show up consciously helps all of the successes and pain of our past and all the hopes and fears of our future to fall away as insubstantial monuments of an inherently unstable way of living. This falling away doesn't diminish our glory or our pain, but we suddenly aren't subject to being caught by these feelings when we make choices from a deeply conscious place. The Big Self doesn't need the praise nor does it feel the blame from anything or anyone, and this nonattachment enables us to begin to forgive and to take full responsibility for the way we live in each and every moment.

Choosing this way of living means that we enter into a life of an integrated openness where blame and victimization, like all other egoic stories, lose their grip on our experience and fall away from what is real in us. Once this happens, we realize that there can be no Awakening of any authenticity unless we choose to let go of any and all traces of past grievances against all people and all situations. When we become free of blame and forgive, we begin to open ourselves to all beings, just as a mother opens her arms to receive her child.

But along with this openness that starts to inform our every step comes a recognition that we can never rely on anything. Openness and forgiveness show us that ego can't count on anything except change. As frightening as this may sound to the ego, this realization means that our choices become guides into a surprisingly beautiful realm of total potential, rather than expectations tied to finite outcomes. This realization brings about an equanimity that supports the grace and ease of a deeply felt surrender to the mystery and wonder of all aspects of life.

No Shortcuts

I've mentioned that I began my meditation practice asking teachers if there might be a shortcut to any of this work. The answers I got all came down to what I've so often repeated in these pages: simply practice a deep surrender into stillness and then let your activity consciously arise from this place. The thing in me that wanted the shortcut is the thing in all of us that wants to manage the experience of Awakening. No matter how great our teacher, how extensive our reading list, or how supportive our spiritual friends, no one can do any of this work for us. This means that we must orient all of our choices around the generous intention of letting go of everything, including whatever spiritual flavor we like the most. This takes courage, fortitude, and discipline.

If we find ourselves in situations where we just can't let go, we're in good company. Even the Buddha himself went through a rather significant process of clinging when he began to deny his body through extreme asceticism as a way of reaching what his ego defined as Awakening to Truth. His intention was to get past the desires of the flesh by starving it into submission. The problem was that his choices were killing him, thereby undoing his intention of becoming Awake in this life. Over time, a realization arose pointing out that this denial was yet another attachment, and as such, it was an inappropriate response to what was being offered. He chose to let go of his attachment to this particular view, and the surrender of this view allowed for an even deeper opening within. The Buddha's experience offers each of us a great lesson on how we are led astray when the process of spiritual evolution becomes ego driven. Whenever we think that some activity, vow, or choice will show us a shortcut to Spirit, we will perpetually miss the mark, or "sin," as the archers of old used to say. All spiritual work, be it meditation, chanting, prayer, silence, or anything else, is offered to us so that we can ultimately see that we are not separate from God, nor have we ever been. God, like the present moment, like our breath, like our beating heart, like Infinity, is always right here.

If there is any attachment to the idea that freedom exists as any external circumstantial form instead of as an internal release, then enlightened awareness will be profoundly hindered by ego. This hindrance is exactly what forces us into the role of seeking. As long as we perceive enlightenment—God, Allah, Brahman, or Spirit—as existing outside of our experience, we will never Awaken to the Truth from which our experience originates. Similarly, if our intentions and corresponding choices are driven by anything other than deep generosity for all beings, we are hindering everyone's potential for this very realization. If there is a deep longing to Awaken arising within you, this is wonderful. But do not get caught by this longing. Don't deny it and don't look for shortcuts, but rather choose to become intimate with the wanting. Then vow to live a life from that open, surrendered observation. Living in this way, of course, is infinitely supported when we sit still with a committed generosity of purposeful choosing, when we don't harm, and when we can allow ourselves to be deeply curious about every circumstance that we meet.

Unhooked

Choosing to become intimate with Awareness requires a constancy of both attention and intention. Neither the attention, nor the intention, is a fixed entity, and yet they can easily become attachments if we aren't careful. On the other hand, if we don't get hooked by them, they can be seen as manifestations of surrender supported by the ever-present Awareness of Spirit. This practice of being unhooked is exactly what keeps our vows from becoming rules that generate fundamentalist blindness. Allowing this free-flowing dance of ever-present Awareness to guide our choices radically diminishes the strength of ego's grip on our responses to life.

Someone who lives in the world unhooked by any of its challenges embodies the flow of Spirit. Each of us can practice unhooking ourselves whenever we are feeling ensnared by something. Say, for example, that the clerk in the hardware store is taking an excessive amount of time with one of the customers in front of you. You find it frustrating, unprofessional, and rude that they should engage in all of this happy talk when there are so many sprinklers to fix. This situation is a gift because you can, with just a little bit of witnessing, see that you are hooked by the circumstance that you face. You've even judged and labeled the people involved in holding up your sprinkler repair duties. All that is necessary for you do, and this might be difficult at first, is recognize the hook fully and become intimate with every aspect of its sting. Do not, however, indulge the feelings of negativity. Simply get curious about them. What exactly do they feel like? Where are they most intensely felt? Let your reaction, whatever it is, become the subject of an intense, non-judgmental scrutiny. Then identify your feelings—not with internal descriptions but instead with the single, silent observational "Wow." This process forces us to watch, wonder, and wow at our experience. Doing so lets us off of the hook and into a conscious dance with precisely what hooked us.

Good spiritual teachers are great at showing us what hooks us and what we use to hook others. Straightening out the barbs, so to speak, by inviting these hooks to dance with us always points us in the direction of Truth. "Whose Truth?" hooked egos love to ask. But it's the Truth that doesn't belong to anyone. No one wrote it in a book, nor has anyone ever codified it in a methodology. It neither depends on any religious tradition nor on anything else because this Truth is the very "thingness" of all things. It goes past everything and yet gives birth to everything. Always. It is beyond time, body, and mind, and therefore can't be identified with any of the senses. We can give it names, but these just point to it. When the discovery of this Truth arises, there is an authentication that resonates, thereby allowing for the formless, forever unhooked Big Self to smile in the world consciously through every bit of our participation in this life.

From the perspective of the Big Self, there are no distinctions, no boundaries, no resistances, no hooks, and nothing to hook. There is only the release of everything. Even the Path itself is released since it is ultimately a concept of the mind. Where the Path leads, on the other hand, is not illusory; in fact, it is the only "thing" that is real because, paradoxically, it is precisely no-thing at all—and all things at once. It is the totally effulgent Divinity that shows up in the most remarkable and most mundane ways—something teachers can point to, but not anything that any of us can conceive.

Teachers

So why is it that so many seemingly enlightened masters get into so much trouble? If someone Awakens, we might imagine that he or she is beyond all of the bad stuff. Unfortunately, this isn't true. I guess the answers to these and other questions about harmful choices made by teachers depend on what we mean by "enlightened." On the one hand, if particular individuals no longer identify with anything other than the spaciousness of the present moment and they act from this space, then they might be considered enlightened by many people. After all, they can talk the talk and seduce the masses with the beautiful ways in which they reflect the sacred back toward everything and everyone. In order to accomplish this seduction, these "teachers" probably had an experience of a still and silent unity pointing out that there is no self, no body, no time, and no mind, but then they mistakenly chose to reconfigure this new perspective into some method of teaching reflective of a kind of personal attachment. Their insights into the nature of Emptiness may have been profound, but their integration of them into the world of form was only partial. This lack of integration is what gets the teachers, the teaching, and entire communities into trouble, and this problem always comes from a deluded view that sees itself as an embodiment of Truth.

Years before I showed up, a situation like this happened at my home temple. Zentatsu Richard Baker was the charismatic and brilliant heir to Shunryu Suzuki, the founder of San Francisco Zen Center. Under Baker's direction, the Zen Center grew to own properties and businesses throughout the Bay Area. As a center of spiritual activity it thrived as well, offering the first Soto Zen monastic training program outside of Japan beginning in the late 1960s. For all that the Zen Center offered, deep dysfunction began to surface in its leadership. In the early 1980s, Richard Baker was forced to leave his position for several reasons, not the least of which involved sleeping with some of his students. It's taken years to undo the damage that Baker caused. His insights as well as his ability to convey their meaning may have been deep and profound, but his lack of integration led his ego to see itself as Enlightened.

Baker by no means stands alone. Many people from many different spiritual communities have had to live with the collateral damage that their leaders' missteps have caused. Any teacher from any tradition may have a profound teaching to offer, but just because they assume the mantle of teacher doesn't mean that they won't get caught by an inability to integrate the Ultimate with the all-important conventional versions of Truth. This is because teachers can only offer us partial applications of realization if they personalize their understanding of Truth. Once they do this, their teaching is something that is held tightly in their grip.

Just think of all of the books written on the subject of religion. Differing views abound, with many different teachers suggesting that their view is the right one. This isn't true for every one of them, but many teachers of nonattachment are attached to their own view. And as we know, if any realization becomes personal, it becomes one-sided and out of balance. In the natural world, anything that is out of balance and perpetuates itself is called "disease." So an out-of-balance teacher, teaching, or community can get sick pretty quickly if an open environment of questioning isn't integrated into everyone's practice. This open questioning maintains a conscious fusion of form with Formlessness; it also keeps the teacher, the teaching, and the group from getting hooked on anything. This integration of Ultimate Truth with conventional reality becomes critically important to offering and supporting mature expressions of an Enlightened perspective. Once this integration happens, we see that both the Ultimate and the conventional aspects of existence hold equal weight. Without a balanced representation of these two sides of the equation, there is no authentic or wholesome teaching of Awakening that any teacher can reveal.

No matter where we are on the Mountain of Spirit, it is critical for us to use our common sense. Be careful to affiliate only with those practitioners and teachers who inspire confidence and trust. Look at the most senior students of a particular teacher to get an idea as to where the teacher is guiding his or her group, and choose in accordance with all that rings true to your deepest sense of what is good and authentic. And always be aware that attachment, including attachment to nonattachment, is at the root of bad teaching and compromised Awakening. The unintegrated teacher is one that is caught by some personal view of the world or by his or her view of the impersonal Truth. Maybe it's even some combination of the two. Any way we look at it, whenever a teacher is caught, his or her commitment to generous intentionality is compromised and this derails the process of Awakening. No matter where any clinging occurs, even if it is to the enlightened perspective itself, there will be trouble. If, on the other hand, the teacher lets go of all arising perspectives without denying any of them and then meets everything that shows up in Awareness with his or her full grace and unselfish attention, enlightened activity will naturally unfold as the teacher's moment-to-moment response to living.

Confluence

9

*Those who see worldly life as an obstacle to Dharma see no
Dharma in everyday actions; they have not yet discovered that
there are no everyday actions outside of Dharma.*
—*Eihei Dogen*

The purpose of Zen is the perfection of character.
—*Yamada Roshi*

When clarity and commitment create enough cracks in the walls
of ego's defenses, Spirit starts to shine through each of us as
Enlightenment. Our practice becomes a simple, continual,
and intentional study of our own small self, and through this work we
begin to see how trivial the small self's wants and needs actually are.
Knowing this triviality first hand allows us to let go of our attachments
to the entire system that our small self has established over time. In this
Divine disaster, we begin to expand spiritually into an embodiment of
being that is enlightened by all things. This confluence of the manifest
with the Unmanifest, this merging of form and Emptiness, is our True
Nature realizing itself through us as all things. And in this creative
confluence of Spirit in the world, our Original Face wears an infinite
smile.

Why the smile? Because there is a deep acceptance and recognition
of the paradox that we are an Emptiness that lacks nothing. We are
neither One, nor many, nor both of these, but an Awakened space that
extends beyond all labels and boundaries. Yet the One and the many are
not absent. Rather, they are engaged in a constant emergence with each
other as One Big Flow, where dance partnerships of form with Emptiness,
conventional truth with Ultimate Truth, manifest with Unmanifest,

small self with Big Self, begin a process of a conscious co-creation of a beautiful cosmic tango. At this stage of Awakening, our participation in life means that we freely move from the valley of separation that got us to climb up the Path in the first place, to the top of the Mountain of Spirit, where our realization compels us to bring our Knowing of the Infinite back home into the world.

This all-inclusive spiritual homecoming is what shows us how to walk the Path in the world from a grounded and eternally unmoving openness, no matter where or how we might find things. From here, we find ourselves *in* the world without being caught *by* the world. This is Freedom. It arises because we Know that there is nothing for any of us outside our immediate experience of this very Awareness. This mystical insight reminds us again and again that since nothing is outside this Awareness, all things arise within the divinity that is at the core of each of us. In this way, we actually realize that the Universe is within us as much as we are within the Universe. We, fundamentally, are the Universe and exist as nothing other than a conscious, creatively flowing Infinity. Put another way, we are nothing other than the Awareness of the arising creativity within each moment, in all of its timeless, unbounded fullness. The big change in those of us who practice coming home from the mountaintop is that we move through the world, intentionally sourced from the present moment, and are thus no longer only identified with our thoughts, feelings, and time. The thoughts are still there, as are the feelings, along with past and future, and we can still work with them as needed. But after Awakening, we not only have these aspects of mind with which to work, but we also find that there is an infinite potential for conscious creativity in each and every situation. Every person we meet, every circumstance we uncover, every opening we find, is recognized as an invitation to live and love more deeply.

This process never ends. While the journey might have started out as something we wanted personally, the enlightened perspective shows us that there is fundamentally nothing for us to keep for ourselves. All of us are inextricably connected as the One. We are the One and we are the Many, all at the same Now, and yet we are also totally Empty of even these concepts and labels. As we Awaken to this reality, the painful dualism that dominates experience gives way to a brilliant unity that continually shows us that there is nothing lacking, that we are all things, that all things are us, and that there is an imperative that comes with all of this: we must share this Knowing through everything that we do. Awakening for one is Awakening for all. Keeping Awakening personal, as we've discussed, is not Awakening, but rather an egoically driven spiritual indulgence. Greed for personal Awakening will radically diminish our ability to affect any kind of authentic shift in awareness for every being. Every moment, on the other hand, that we choose to let deep, intentional surrender guide our practice of stillness, wisdom, and compassion at the levels of body, mind, and soul moves us past this trap. This freedom lets us to build a new home that shows itself to be nothing less than the majestic and infinite openness that is in every way a coming together, a confluence, of all things through us. Our new home is one that in every way is without walls, flowing open to the whole Universe as the Universe.

One as All and All as One

As man moves towards spiritual freedom, he moves also towards oneness.
—*Aurobindo*

Before a person studies Zen, mountains are mountains and waters are waters; after a first glimpse into the truth of Zen, mountains are no longer mountains and waters are not waters; after enlightenment, mountains are once again mountains and waters once again waters.
—*Zen saying*

Things are not as they appear, nor are they otherwise.
—*The Lankavatara Sutra*

From the enlightened perspective, "coming home" means that we begin to allow the expansive Ultimate Life to burst through the contraction of all of our circumstances. With each step and breath we bring back into the world the realization of fullness that exists beyond time and mind. But again, we don't do it just to benefit ourselves. We do it for the benefit of all beings. If the Realization is authentic, we don't have a choice about any of it. The inevitability of acting for the benefit of all beings occurs because we know that the subject and object dualism that we'd previously thought to be the whole story simply isn't. In other words, the boundary that separates the me in here from the you out there loses its importance. Instead, the me in here offers itself only as all things, eternally and everywhere, in a spacious, fluid, forgiving, Awareness. Everyone we know and love, including ourselves, as well as everyone we might find difficult to tolerate, still exists and is recognizable, but our recognition that they are in no way separate from us begins to resonate and express itself in all that we do. When this Boundlessness brushes up against and then merges with our "boundaries," compassionate activity works to serve everything and everyone.

Acting from this place of deep compassion is nothing other than total forgiveness, and forgiveness is freely letting go of our clinging. We no longer hold onto anything in our past that has generated resistance of any kind. We simply let it all go while at the same time we do not deny any of it. This letting go creates a space for us to see Spirit more clearly in all of its disguises because we no longer are clinging to any fixed position. Nothing is left unforgiven. We are open, and this openness allows for us to directly experience Spirit as ugliness, as beauty, as loss, as gain, as hatred, as love, with nothing held back.

From here we can be freely intimate with every bit of life without flinching. We get bad news, let's say, but instead of being beaten by it, we become close to the experience, letting it open us to what is beyond all contraction. The loss of a loved one or a job, while brutal and painful, no longer limits our deep sense of the Sacred. Similarly, we get great news, and it doesn't pull us away from our conscious dance with the Infinite. In this welcoming relationship with all that life has for us, the whole world of form shows up as variations of Spirit. Spirit, at the same time, is uncovered as form, and each of us is timelessly expressed as the conscious explosion of the Big Bang.

Integrating this Knowing into the world becomes the most beautiful and creative of all forms of expression. We show others and ourselves to be Spirit gracefully meeting itself in an infinitely forgiving and creative presentation of this moment. Everything we are simply and elegantly shimmers and shines as nothing less than the integrated Awakening of all things right Now.

Nondualism

Coming down the Mountain of Spirit we find that the ego has lost its grip on everything, including its own ability to manage itself. Sometimes, it is helpful to recognize this realization as "ego fully seen." In stories like *The Emperor's New Clothes* and *The Wizard of Oz*, both the emperor and the wizard are exposed for what they are. The Nondual traditions all emphasize the value of this exposure. Zen, Dzogchen, Taoism, Sufiism, Advaita Vedanta, Kabbalah and contemplative Christian practices show us that Spirit, Emptiness, Brahman, God, Big Self, Ein Sof, or the All is the condition of any and all states in which we find ourselves. This means that no matter where or how we might find our experience of being a self, we are still continually expressing the fullness of Spirit. We are, in other words, no longer a dualistic expression of "in here" versus "out there," a "me" versus a "you," or an "us" versus a "them." No matter what state we're in, whether it be the bliss of meditation or the pain of watching a loved one suffer, Spirit is expressing itself, and its Peace is offered to us continually as the timeless, singular, nondual flow of everything all at once.

A few years back, some friends experienced a tragic death in their family. The father died unexpectedly, putting major emotional and financial strains on the wife and two college-aged kids. In speaking with one of the kids, I was amazed at his continual peace in the face of the loss. Several weeks after the funeral I asked him how he was doing, and his reply impressed me.

"Mostly I feel terrible," he said. "Dad's loss aches in a way that I couldn't have imagined. But, at the same time, there is still a deep peace underneath it all."

Peace underneath. What a great way to express the experience of the nondual, timeless flow of our lives, no matter what might be happening. Peace, in other words, is neither dependent on nor independent from experience. It is neither this nor that, but instead the quality that lies underneath everything, equally present in our most glorious and our most painful moments. It is never not right here with us, and yet it can be easily veiled from our sight if our circumstances catch us, or, conversely, if we hang onto our circumstances.

Practicing intimately with our lives helps us find our way clear of attachment. But this is something that we need to do continually, time and again, and in the process we especially need to be aware of our tendency to attach to our practice itself. How dangerous, for example, for any of us to fall prey to the idea that from the nondual perspective, there are ultimately no boundaries and therefore all is illusory. We might falsely conclude that, since everything is an illusion, nothing matters. If we attach to this false logic, our practice will lose its balance, and so lose its ability to be a helpful and steadying force in our world. To prevent this from happening, we can remind ourselves of the simple distillation of the vows taken by sincere practitioners of all traditions: "I will not cause harm." This reminder helps us to self-correct whatever is leaning in our nondual spiritual journey, and so helps us to uncover the peace underneath for everyone.

Embodiment

For us to realize that Enlightenment itself is immediately prior to the temporal experience of all things that arise within our awareness is to awaken with all things. In other words, we can look at the spaciousness of the present moment that always exists, before mind gets into its processes of interpretation and evaluation, as the place of infinite availability and total potentiality that we keep discussing. Enlightenment is always here with us, even before any circumstances arise. This is what Shunryu Suzuki means when he says: "Even before we practice it, enlightenment is there." In other words, Enlightenment is immediately prior to cognition, sensation, perception of any kind, birth, death, time itself. But, since enlightenment is never bound by time, it is also with us during and after every one of our experiences. All of our spiritual work, then, is to conflate, integrate, and then embody our contracted experience with this openness. To embody this work is to bring it fully home into this skin we inhabit.

Embodying Enlightenment, then, arises in this body of ours when we participate in the world by not trying to get anything from anything. This may sound difficult, but as long as whatever we do is coming from a place of "not trying to get anything from anything," we are acting from the place of deep, unattached, surrendered stillness. The action that comes from this nonattachment is always and without fail a fully embodied response that is forever appropriate to whatever is arising in the present moment. In other words, it is here, from this unattached stillness, that we have a chance to act from the place that is prior to mind without being mindless; prior to the body without being absent from the body. Instead of being driven by the impulse that comes "after" pure Knowing, we are acting from the pure Knowing itself. This is the conscious coming together of the manifest world of form with the Unmanifest embodiment of Spirit, and it is here that the entire Universe evolves through our choices and actions as the physical form we inhabit.

On the other hand, as long as we are meditating in order to *attain* Awakening, we will be disappointed in our limited ability to walk the talk of an authentic sage. If there is a "you," for instance, who is trying to address the perception of something lacking, we've got egoic craving. Meditation that is only fueled from this place of greed won't hasten Awakening. In fact, it usually leads us on a major detour. But if you're meditation is balanced, grounded, and sourced from an intention to be helpful to all beings, you neither reach nor avoid, and stillness will spontaneously uncover what's always been prior to any perception of lack. Nothing, once again, is missing from this openness. From this openness it becomes readily apparent that there is no one doing the sitting, no one thinking the thoughts, no one feeling the feelings. All of this simply falls away, and what's left is an embodied Big Self, ready to be put forever into the service of every one and every thing.

No Teachers

As we've discussed, no person can enlighten another. Some realized people have a gift for pointing out Truth, but you must realize it for yourself. Whenever we meet another with the fullness of our attention, this allows for one mind to see itself in two beings and for two minds to see themselves as one being. This is a Divine event of Truth. This is the Teaching. It's the student, the teacher, and the teaching, as neither unified nor separate. Metaphorically, this is like a mother hen pecking on the outside of her egg meeting her chick's peck from the inside. Once this happens an opening to an entirely new experience arises for everyone. When that part of any person who is enlightened meets itself in another, we awaken to the Big Self as the Big Self. It's in all ways already here, so in an absolute sense, there are no teachers of Enlightenment. There aren't any students to teach in this sense either. There is nothing that anyone can teach that we don't already Know at our core. When we hear someone say something that resonates inside of us as an echo of Truth, it does so because we have been reminded of something that we've always Known since before time, body, and mind entered into your personal experience. So in addition to embodying trustworthiness, kindness, strength, clarity, and a good sense of humor, a good spiritual teacher is someone that can relentlessly remind you of what you already know to be True.

At the same time, there are plenty of people who see themselves as teachers who prey upon people's willingness to project myth into flesh. By this I mean that there are individuals who can interrupt the direct connection that each being already has with the Infinite. This interruption can create a space in the student that allows for a misalignment of realization as Truth starts to unfold. When this happens, the student thinks that the teacher is the one enlightening them. But Awakening never works like this. When we think it does, this can be the source of lots of damage.

The reaction to this damage, however, can also be seen as troubling in some cases. There are some groups of people practicing together who consciously decide not to have a teacher as a way of avoiding the problems that traditional spiritual power structures can offer. While this isn't as potentially dangerous as having an abusive leader, these groups often will stay stuck in the contracted realm of personal experience and thus never get beyond the natural tendency of clinging to both time and mind. These are often well-meaning practitioners, but there is a continual and deepening confusion in relation to feeling good about your community of friends while at the same time Awakening to Truth. They may or may not happen together, but this misses the point of practice. Once again, spiritual work is not about feeling good, it's about becoming so conscious that we uncover the True Self that is forever past the limited entity that feels. This practice is about intentionally informing the small self with the Big Self and then coming back into the world as the merging of wisdom and compassion for the good of the entire, evolving Universe.

The masks we created prior to our climb that shielded us from seeing the implications of Awakening have fallen off since we've developed enough humility to devote ourselves to living intimately with all things. This intimacy allows for anything and anyone to become our teacher. No matter whom we might meet, if we devote ourselves to meeting them with all of our being, a space is created where the Infinite can shine as that which has always been there in both of us.

Then this same sacred principle applies to any situation. Whatever it is, if we meet it fully, it can't help but reveal what is prior to all experience. This is the teaching—the freely functioning expression of an Infinity that can never be held by anyone. It is the very essence of everyone and everything. Yet we miss it until, with intense devotion, we let the Big Self compassionately chip away at the shell of the small self. When the shell cracks open, the deeper Truth of an increasingly expansive Universe becomes available. It shows itself through us and as us, regardless of our preferred tradition. And it is All right here, right now, in this life, waiting to be uncovered consciously so that it can dance as you, me, and everything else.

The Smile

If humor is totally absent from this practice, then what's any
of this worth?
—*Question from a renegade Zen student*

Okay… who took my robe?
—*Question from the same Zen student some days later*

After engaging in a spiritual practice with some degree of diligence, it is easy to lose sight of the humor that permeates the entire divine mess. Instead of recognizing the blessings of this life and the lightness that can come from seeing it as an endless gift, we can ossify and harden to the offerings of life. Finding the fluidity, or humor, of it all helps us meet the passage of life with an ever-deepening grace, and while this isn't always easy, it is a sacred potential for all of us once we start on this Path.

I remember how uneasy I felt the first few times I sat formally with a meditation community. I was so confused and uncomfortable. First of all, the building itself was so simple and so beautiful that I could feel a surge of inspiration within my chest. This was new since most of my time was spent in my head analyzing, qualifying, quantifying, and compartmentalizing. I was untested in the arena of opening to what was beyond my thoughts. Secondly, the idea of getting beyond my identification with my thinking seemed impossible. Of course none of the straight-faced senior practitioners, dressed in brown and black patchwork robes told me that I was supposed to do anything other than simply "sit up straight and follow the breath." In my spiritual enthusiasm I'd added some mischief to their simple notion of getting past the thoughts in my mind and even the feelings in my body. Of course this wasn't necessarily wrong of me to do, but for a beginning, self-absorbed sitter, making the practice harder than it needed to be gave my ego a role to grab onto in my newfound practice.

In the years that followed, I was taken by how few giggles I heard around the temple. A few people seemed to have decent senses of humor. Most, however, both the priests on the inside and the lay people who came to sit with us on Sundays seemed sad and often angry.

"They're suffering," my teacher would tell me. "They're facing their lives with courage and this kind of work is very, very hard."

This made sense to me. It reminded me again and again that I could be most helpful to the other practitioners by being sensitive to where they were coming from, rather than where I wanted to see them end up. Of course, I wanted to have everyone end up laughing. That was where my ego felt most comfortable. But just because I was craving more smiles and more laughter didn't mean that I needed to push for it. It was my craving after all. My attachment. I could readily see that I needed to let go of my desire to tease and quip so that others could have a better chance at studying their experience. But this was so hard.

It was all I could do to keep from purposefully distorting the liturgy that we recited each morning after our second period of early morning zazen. Those next to me would often look at me askance when they heard the nonsensical words and phrases that I'd substitute for the real stuff. So I lowered my voice. Chanting the names of the Buddhist ancestors, for example, became a time for me to chant the names of anyone that popped into my head. One time, for instance, instead of "Sekito Kisen Daiosho," I said "Clowns really scare me, die Bozo." I have no idea where this came from, but the guy next to me started to crack up. This of course distracted and annoyed many of the pious. The not-so-pious started to laugh, mostly because this guy, who shortly began giggling through tears, collapsed to the floor grabbing his sides. It was beautiful. So pure. So genuine. Chanting the way I wanted to chant allowed me, at this early stage of my climb, to stay in charge of my experience by playing for personal gain. If we don't know what we're saying in many of the chants anyway, who should care? What were they going to do? Kick me out of monk school?

But something else seemed to be going on at the same time. Laughter, in this case, was the result of nonattachment. Annoyance, on the other hand, was the result of attachment, and not one of the priests was laughing. This isn't to negate their experience. The priests were "working very, very hard." But it was still an eye opener for me, and it made me question where their attachments released.

I wasn't surprised when I learned that one of the senior teachers wanted to meet with me the next day. I was a little nervous but I also felt a certain rebellious defiance, similar to the kind I felt in third grade when I threw the cottage cheese in my lunch at a guy who was bullying my friend. I got a black eye out of that valiant food toss, so maybe I feared the same metaphorical fate from this meeting. Regardless, I approached the door of the teacher, knocked, went in and sat down, cross-legged on a cushion placed directly in front of him. He was a fairly small man, but his robes made him look bigger. I remember being taken by all the cloth management endured by the senior priests—robes on top of robes on top of robes. Layers of Dharma adorning the bodies of modern day Buddhas. Maybe they were just wannabe Buddhas—I couldn't yet say.

Anyway, sitting in front of this heap of robes with a head took me by surprise. Whatever righteousness I had walking in to meet with this guy diminished as soon as my butt touched the cushion. It wasn't that I felt scared, it was that I felt seen; all that was secreted away within was now totally exposed. I came to learn that this kind of meeting helped right my steps along the Path in ways that I wouldn't fully understand until months after our encounters. Just sitting in this man's presence over the years seemed to ignite a fire in me that began to burn away all the unnecessary stuff I carried with me in my spiritual journey.

"Tell me about what happened yesterday," he said calmly. "I hear there was a bit of a stir in the zendo during the service."

"I was screwing around," I said. I was amazed at how I felt like a little boy, ashamed at having let my father down. He just sat there smiling while I kept talking.

"It's just that all the ritual seems so superfluous and in every practice center I've ever been to, everyone seems so stiff," I said. "Where are the smiles? Where is the laughter? If humor is totally absent from this practice, then what's any of it worth?"

"Indeed," he smiled. "What is this worth?"

Then he just stared through me for what seemed like a few minutes. I did everything I could just to hold his gaze, but for some unknown reason, tears came and began to blur everything. Literally everything. It was like I became blind to this teacher, blind to myself, blind to my thoughts, and blind to all I'd ever known to be true. In those moments, with those tears, all the stuff that truly did not matter just fell out of me, washed away by those precious tears, and all that was left was a beautiful silence and a smile that I still share with my teacher.

My compulsion to judge the humorless diminished substantially that day. So, too, did my need to goof around with the morning service, even though the impulse still lingers a little. Recently, a youthful and devilish student of mine asked me what would happen if he started singing the Eagles' "Hotel California" at the top of his lungs during our meditation period. I laughed at how much this young man reminded me of someone I keep trying to forget about, and laughed even harder when I imagined how something like this might cause yet another "stir in the zendo." Still I suggested that he study the impulse that was driving this urge in him in order to see if there was any clinging.

"Yeah, I guess I'm pretty uncomfortable with all of the silence," he said. "So I guess I'm avoiding what's uncomfortable. Or I'm clinging to what's comfortable for me. Funny stuff is pretty comfortable."

"And why is that?" I asked, trying to hide my near total agreement.

He got very quiet. I just smiled, feeling increasingly like I was talking to a more youthful version of me. Only the slightest of boundaries between us.

"I don't know," he said. "I just feel so afraid so much of the time. The joking keeps me safe."

"Safe from what?" I asked.

"I guess from where this whole Path that you're always talking about leads, " he said. "But I know that's the whole point. The silence, the structure, and your talks force us to look at our attachments so we can let go of them. And then... BOOM... we're Awake. Right?"

I didn't say a word, I just kept smiling, holding his stare.

"Isn't that the whole deal?" he asked, looking down at his awkwardly crossed legs.

"That's about half the deal," I said.

His brow then wrinkled and he seemed visibly confused.

"After the whole 'boom' thing," I continued, "you must come back down the mountain, integrating everything the summit showed you into the cells of your body. Then you can truly participate in this life as an Awakened being."

"Then you're done?" he asked.

"Then you've started," I said. "It sounds insurmountable to the small self, but if you begin to live a life where Awakening becomes your deepest concern, then Awakening expresses itself through you, for the benefit of everyone."

"Okay," he sighed. "Thanks," he said as he bowed and left the room.

I returned his bow, feeling so hopeful and so lucky to have been able to share that moment and the potential that it offered. May all of this continue, may all beings uncover peace and joy, and may all of us find ourselves Awake in this life.

Acknowledgments

I owe a debt of gratitude to plenty of people. So many, in fact, that I'm sure that I'll forget some important ones. Forgive me in advance for the slip.

To all of my teachers at Green Gulch Farm Zen Center, deep bows to all of you. Reb, you never allowed for attachment, and your commitment to the practice still inspires me. Linda, your kindness and care kept me climbing even when I wanted to turn around. Nancy, you helped me see that the work was not about states, but about enduring traits. Norman, you showed me how to come home "fat and happy," every single day.

Thanks to all of the members of the Infinite Smile Sangha, in person and virtual, who ultimately gave this work substance. Your dedication and commitment to spreading the Dharma continues to inspire.

Thanks to Jim Burress who instigated much of this process for me. Thanks for your encouragement, your friendship, and your infectious laugh.

Thanks to the late, great Paul Winnacker for his first initial read and criticism of this work. Your presence is in these pages, dear friend.

Thanks to my mom and dad for encouraging me to question things. That simple gift served me and others so well. Thanks also to Skip and to Nan who show me daily that divorces can mean that we have even more people to love in this life. Thanks to all of my stepsiblings and their families.

Thanks to my amazing brothers, Mark, Matt, and Mitch, their equally marvelous spouses, Evette, Jessica, and Renica, as well as my precious nieces and nephews. All of you offered me quiet encouragement in getting this stuff down.

Thanks to my editor, Dr. Charles Burack, whose friendship, professionalism, literary eye, and sense of the Divine made this book into something readable.

Thanks to Dan and Lois for your love and for helping out when it was most needed.

Thanks to Pastor Dan Senter, for reminding me, and so many others, that all paths lead to God.

Thanks to Cade for reminding me every single day that an embodiment of all that is Holy is right in front of me all the time.

And lastly, I wish to thank my wife, whose love, encouragement, and compassion made this book, and this life, possible. She protects my solitude and also reminds me of how deeply connected we all are. Her support and care as I wrote, read, and rewrote will remind me forever of how lucky I am to be married to a Buddha.